World Golf Hall of Fame
One World Golf Place
St. Augustine, Florida 32092-2724
904-940-4000
www.worldgolfhalloffame.org

For more information address The American Golfer, Inc.
200 Railroad Avenue, Greenwich, Connecticut 06830.

American Golfer titles may be purchased for business or promotional use for special sales. For information, please write to: Sales Department, The American Golfer, Inc.,
200 Railroad Avenue, Greenwich, Connecticut 06830.



A special thanks to Marie McCann-Barab for her marvelous art direction.

ISBN 1-888531-13-4

Published by:

The American Golfer
200 Railroad Avenue
Greenwich, Connecticut 06830
203-862-9724 (Fax)
http://www.theamericangolfer.com
mdavis@theamericangolfer.com (e-mail)
imd@aol.com (e-mail)

# World Golf Hall of Fame Alphabetical Index of Members

**World Golf Hall of Fame**
One World Golf Place
St. Augustine, Florida 32092-2724
904-940-4000

www.worldgolfhalloffame.org


The World Golf Hall of Fame is open everyday of the year except Thanksgiving and Christmas.

Monday thru Saturday 10am to 6pm
Sunday 12pm to 6pm


Jack Peter, *Chief Operating Officer*
Jim Pierson, *Business and Golf Development*

Mary Altman, *Sr. Director, Marketing and Brand Development*

Helen Atter, *VP. Business & Legal Affairs*

Bruce Lahti, *General Manager, Director of Operations*

Andy Hunold, *Director of Exhibits and Collections*

A special thanks to PGA TOUR Commissioner Timothy W. Finchem, PGA TOUR Executive VP and Co-Chief Operating Officer Charles L. Zink and Vernon Kelly, President, PGA TOUR Golf Course Properties.

---

*Published by:*

**The American Golfer, Inc.**
200 Railroad Avenue
Greenwich, CT 06830

203-862-9720
fax: 203-862-9724
www.theamericangolfer.com

*Publishers of fine books and magazines on golf.*

Martin Davis - *Editor and Publisher*
Marie McCann-Barab - *Art Director*

*Contributing Writers:*
Jaime Diaz
Tim Rosaforte
Adam Schupak

# Table of Contents

17
St ANDREWS

# World Golf Hall of Fame: The New Inductees

The great passion golfers share is most eloquently defined by the great players and individuals whose accomplishments have built the game's rich history and nurtured its traditions.

This year five new names from various corners of the world and eras have earned golf's highest honor – induction into the World Golf Hall of Fame. Some earned the distinction for their skills with their clubs, while others wrote about their efforts and designed the layouts that continue to confound golfers' today. What they share is a love of the game, which each of them found at various stages in their life.

**Willie Park Sr.** was one of the pioneer golfers of the 19th century. Born in Scotland in 1833, he is considered the first of a long line of professionals to rise from the caddy ranks. Park initially had to make due with inferior equipment since money was difficult to come by and clubs and balls were a costly commodity. In little time Park was out-driving and out-putting other caddies with better equipment.

Courtesy of the Royal and Ancient Golf Club of St. Andrews

*Willie Park Sr.*

LPGA

*Ayako Okamoto*

Park is best known as the winner of the inaugural British Open in 1860. He won the tournament four times. In his day, Park made his living primarily from "Challenge Matches" against rivals such as Old Tom Morris, Willie Dunn and Allan Robertson. They were the most popular form of spectator golf in his era and dominated what little there was in the way of golf headlines in the 1850s and 1860s.

**Bernard Darwin** was a Cambridge educated barrister before he turned to writing about the game he loved. Born in 1876 in England, Darwin's grandfather was Charles Darwin, the great naturalist. In that spirit, he evolved golf writing from simply reporting pars and birdies to a far richer form of literary journalism. For his efforts, Darwin is often called the "father of golf writing" as we know it today.

When his hands weren't tapping a typewriter, they were usually gripping a golf club. Darwin was a semifinalist in the 1909 and 1921 British Amateur and served as captain of Britain's first Walker Cup team, winning his singles match.

Like Darwin, **Alister MacKenzie** grew up in England and began in another profession before making a name for himself in golf. A doctor by trade, MacKenzie found his true calling in designing golf courses that require a surgeon's touch around the green. He mastered the art of making a course look natural. His philosophy of fair and strategic golf without disrupting the site remains a model for golf course design to this day.

MacKenzie is credited with designing or re-designing more than 400 courses. His best known works are Augusta National (along with Bobby Jones), The Cypress Point Club, Royal Melbourne, and Pasatiempo Golf Club, where his ashes were spread following his death in 1934. Annually, 10 of his courses are rated in the top 100 in the world by the major golf magazines.

Japan's **Ayako Okamoto** was her country's best softball pitcher and a member of the 1971 national champi-

USGA

*Bernard Darwin*

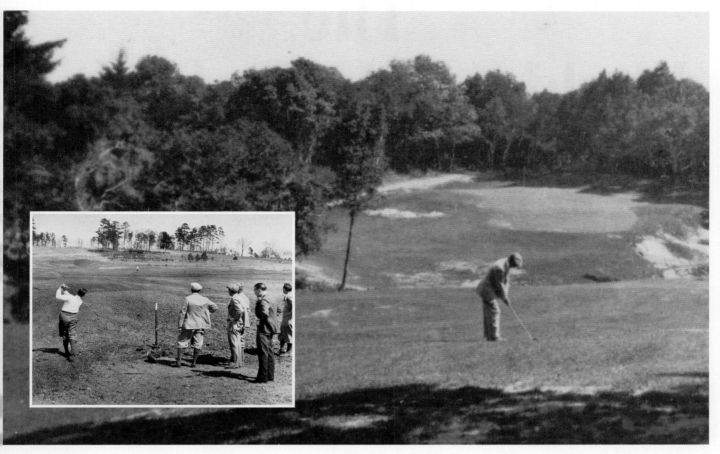

*Alister Mackenzie plays Pasatiempo Golf Club, one of his design masterpieces.* **Inset:** *Bob Jones, MacKenzie's co-designer of Augusta National, hits tee shots on what is now the eighth hole during the initial construction of the course. To Bob's right is Alister MacKenzie and to his right is Hall of Fame member Cliff Roberts.*

onship. She did not take up golf until she was 23 years old. Blessed with amazing hand-eye coordination, she made a seemingly effortless transition to golf and became a champion all over the world. First, she dominated women's golf in Japan, winning 44 times on the LPGA of Japan before setting her sights on competing against the world's best players. Okamoto was the first Japanese player to embrace the American lifestyle. And the first foreign player to win the LPGA Tour money title and Player of the Year honors. She accomplished both feats in 1987. Back in Japan, her celebrity reached new heights and she returned there in 1993 to wind down her career and continue her efforts to grow the game in her homeland.

And then there's **Karrie Webb**, who qualified for the World Golf Hall of Fame at the ripe old age of 25. Australia's most successful female golfer won early and won often. Webb served notice that she might be something special when she won the Women's British Open as a 20-year-old, before she even had earned her LPGA Tour card. The following year she won the LPGA Rookie of the Year Award and topped the money list in 1996. But it was only the beginning. In 1999 and 2000, she dominated women's golf, capturing a total of 13 titles and three of her six major titles. The following year she defended her U.S. Women's Open title and won the LPGA Championship to complete the career grand slam.

At 31, Webb has already won 30 LPGA Tour events and she is still making history. But whatever she accomplishes in the future, it only will add to a grand career; one that will always be linked to the greats of the game now that she and the Class of 2005 have received golf's highest honor.

LPGA

*Karrie Webb*

# The World Golf Hall of Fame

World Golf Hall of Fame

*The World Golf Hall of Fame in St. Augustine, Florida.*

*Each member's image – from Amy Alcott to Babe Zaharias – is captured in hand-crafted bronze reliefs just as they're etched into the very substance of the game.*

The tension of the moment was getting the better of him and Ben Crenshaw could feel himself unraveling. This wasn't The Masters or a crucial putt - this was his Hall of Fame Induction Ceremony speech.

"To be in the Hall of Fame with my heroes – people that I idolized such as Bobby Jones – well, I felt a deep sense of humility that left me speechless," explained Crenshaw.

As his face reddened, Crenshaw tightened every muscle in his body and, by sheer will, forced back the tears. With his composure regained, Crenshaw delivered an eloquent speech that captured the significance of the milestone.

"Joining the World Golf Hall of Fame was like walking up to the 18th hole knowing that I was going to win," he said.

Indeed, membership in the World Golf Hall of Fame is golf's highest honor. Legions of players worldwide who have succumbed to the game's mysterious spell agree. Endlessly fascinating, often exhilarating, unconquerable yet irresistible, golf is more than just a sport, it is a passion. Every golfer's dream is to end up there.

*"Joining the World Golf Hall of Fame was like walking up to the 18th hole knowing that I was going to win," Crenshaw said.*

World Golf Hall of Fame

*Hall of Fame member and Ambassador, Ben Crenshaw*

Located in St. Augustine, FL, a city exuding history, the Hall of Fame immortalizes the most elite golfers and visionaries who have given shape and personality to the sport. With the induction of Bernard Darwin, Alister MacKenzie, Ayako Okamoto, Willie Park Sr., and Karrie Webb in 2005, the Hall of Fame enshrines 109 members. Since opening there in 1998, the Hall of Fame has become the place to celebrate the global game under one roof. And like the game itself, the World Golf Hall of Fame continues to evolve. In 2004, the Hall went through its first significant re-design.

"The success we have seen with Inductee Exhibits, plus the Ben Hogan and Byron Nelson exhibits we unveiled in March 2003 and 2004, respectively, further validated our decision to provide new exhibits on a regular basis about our members and significant stories in golf," said Jack Peter, chief operating officer. "This design transformation provides the flexibility we need with the galleries, while allowing us to further shape and enhance the guest experience throughout the entire museum." The most recent exhibits celebrated the illustrious career of Arnold Palmer and the 75th anniversary of Bobby Jones' Grand Slam.

Museum visitors enter a timeless world that tells the evolution of the game through the stories of its members. In order to do so, the area known as the front nine was re-mapped to better indicate how the Hall of Fame members – from its oldest member, Allan Robertson, to its youngest, Karrie Webb – fit into the history of the game. In particular, the new layout offers a more defined pathway for guests.

The heart and soul of the World Golf Hall of Fame lie within its membership. Shell Hall, named for the Hall of Fame's Founding Corporate Partner, Shell Oil Company, in recognition of its unparalleled commitment to golf, is where the greats of the game are honored. Each member's image – from Amy Alcott to Babe Zaharias – is captured in hand-crafted bronze reliefs just as they're etched into the very substance of the game. The "locker

## SHELL: THE FOUNDING PARTNER

Shell has long been considered a pioneer within its own industry and in golf. Merging the finest players with the finest golf courses, Shell created a unique theater for golf that kicked off the game's explosion in the television age and represents the company's ongoing association with the very best the game has to offer.

Shell's *Wonderful World of Golf* television series was a landmark achievement as the first made-for-TV sports series that debuted in 1961. Several of the memorable matches can be viewed at the World Golf Hall of Fame. The Shell series of more recent vintage featured matches between Arnold Palmer and Jack Nicklaus at the King & Bear course in 2001 and a Gary Player-Lee Trevino duel at the Slammer & Squire course in 1998, both at World Golf Village.

Shell's PGA TOUR event, the Shell Houston Open, has established itself as one of the leading children's charitable fundraising events in all of sports. Since 1992, the tournament has raised more than $28 million for local youth-oriented charities.

Shell serves as the presenting sponsor of *Shell's Science of Golf*, the Hall of Fame's youth educational program that focuses on the scientific principles of golf.

Long recognized for its leadership role in golf and philanthropic endeavors, Shell joins with the World Golf Foundation to bring golf's character-building attributes to the world's youth who may not otherwise have the chance to play the game. As part of its unprecedented 20-year agreement to be the sole Founding Partner of the World Golf Village, Shell will continue its tradition of bringing golf's educational and character-building opportunities to young people through The First Tee program.

room" is where visitors can delve into the lives of Hall of Fame members, examining their personal collections of awards, memorabilia, and personal mementos. A new theater highlights the member's championship moments.

Photo opportunities are available throughout the Hall, including one atop an exact reproduction of the Swilcan Burn Bridge, where a diorama of the Old Course at St Andrews surrounds the guest and serves as the background.

Significant tournament trophies, including men's and women's majors, are displayed in the Hall of Fame Tower.

# Gary Player
## World Golf Hall of Fame
# Global Ambassador

The fourth of Gary Player's ten commandments of life says, "For all we take in life we must pay." In an effort to give back to the game that has been so good to him, Gary Player has taken an active role in supporting the programs of the World Golf Hall of Fame.

The South African was named the Global Ambassador for the World Golf Hall of Fame in November of 2001 and rightfully so. He is arguably the greatest international golfer of all-time. He has traveled more miles than any other sportsman in history.

Awarded the mantle of South Africa's Sportsman of the Century in 2000, Player continues to compete on the Champions Tour and is now in his sixth decade as a professional golfer. When he's not playing golf or consumed with his many golf ventures, Player is probably happiest up on the soapbox extolling the virtues of hard work, education, exercise, and proper nutrition, particularly in the US, a country he truly loves.

World Golf Hall of Fame

*Gary Player*

As Global Ambassador, Gary Player acts as the spokesman for the Hall of Fame on an international level. He attends special events and participates in communications and various marketing programs.

Player was a part of the inaugural class inducted into the World Golf Hall of Fame in 1974.

"To be chosen among the first inductees was one of the greatest honors of my life," Player said.

Player has always been distinguished by character and competitiveness, a doggedness that has transcended his extraordinary game. In addition to being an international ambassador to the game, "The Black Knight" has been an uncommon disciplinarian in taking care of his body and in fighting to the finish – a finish that so often has seen him topple the field. He has won nine professional majors on the PGA TOUR, an equal number on the Champions Tour, and is one of only five players to win golf's modern grand slam.

Perhaps more interesting, however, are the stories that go beyond the artifacts. These can be heard from World Golf Hall of Fame members such as Nancy Lopez, Arnold Palmer, Sam Snead, Tom Watson, and Kathy Whitworth, who provide entertaining and educational commentary via hand-held Acoustiguides. Visitors can also enjoy the "behind the scenes" stories of the Hall and the game during guided tours conducted daily by a dedicated corps of trained volunteers.

Each year new exhibits honoring the class of inductees are unveiled at the Induction Ceremony. These exhibits recognize and honor the significant achievements of the Hall's newest members.

Together, these exhibits exemplify the continuing efforts to keep the Hall of Fame current and vibrant. Several of the Hall's members play an active role in its development. Carol Mann, winner of 38 LPGA Tour titles as well as the 1965 U.S. Women's Open, assists the Hall in exhibit development and member relations. Gary Player, who was named global ambassador in 2001, serves as a spokesman and participates in the induction ceremony. Ben Crenshaw and Arnold Palmer have joined Player as hosts of a series of new public-service announcements for the Hall that air in network golf telecasts.

More than anything, the Hall of Fame is a concept that floods the mind with images while triggering our senses with stories of human passion and dedication as well as weakness and frailty. It is a place where fans can revisit childhood heroes and relive cherished memories; where legends and magical moments can be rediscovered, nourished, and passed on to future generations.

At the World Golf Hall of Fame, golf has a special place where its values, its greatest players and its greatest moments are properly honored, as well as a place where golfers and non-golfers alike can savor this popular pastime in all of its glory.

*The entrance to the Bobby Jones exhibit commemorating the 75th anniversary of the Grand Slam. Right: Peggy and Byron Nelson in the Nelson exhibit.*

World Golf Hall of Fame

# A Place to Create Your Own Hall of Fame Memories

The experience doesn't end once the museum tour is over. The World Golf Village provides visitors with numerous entertainment options.

Golfers can shoot for a hole in one at the 132-yard Challenge Hole, make the rounds on the 18-hole grass putting green course, or watch a giant screen film at the Hall of Fame's IMAX Theater.

The official golf courses of the Hall of Fame, *Slammer & Squire* named for Sam Snead and Gene Sarazen, and the Arnold Palmer-Jack Nicklaus co-designed *King & Bear*, present a legendary playing experience.

At PGA TOUR Golf Academy, a first-class golf facility in the shadow of the World Golf Hall of Fame, students sharpen their skills with instruction from Golf Magazine Top 100 Teacher Scott Sackett.

The Village's two golf-themed dining experiences — Murray Bros. Caddyshack and Fairways Cafe— allow guests to feast on their passion for the game, as well as on great food! Serious shoppers can't pass up the PGA TOUR STOP, a 31,000-square-foot retail golf superstore.

Overnight guest will enjoy above par hospitality at the 300-room Renaissance Resort at World Golf Village.

More than just a golf resort, the Village offers distinctive neighborhoods that blend modern amenities with hometown warmth.

An excursion into nearby historic St. Augustine, America's oldest city, will provide guests an opportunity to savor the charm of Florida's yesteryear and beautiful beaches.

And when it is time to unwind, the PGA TOUR Spa at Laterra is the place to be pampered.

Visitors planning a visit to the Hall of Fame can call 1-800-WGV-GOLF or visit the Hall of Fame's website at www.wgv.com.

# Patty Berg

**No figure in women's golf spanned as many eras or did as much for her sport as Patty Berg.**

Berg was all things to women's golf—a superb player, a great promoter, a wonderful teacher, a charismatic personality. And her gift has been measured over a long period of time. Berg won her first professional event in 1941, in the infancy of women's pro golf, and her last in 1962. But even after cancer surgery in 1971, Berg was still competing at the age of 62 in 1980. Hip replacement surgery later that year finally ended her competitive career.

In all, Berg won 57 professional events, including the first U.S. Women's Open in 1946 (the only time it was played at match play), the Western Open seven times and Titleholders four times. What made these totals even more remarkable is that for the entire prime of her professional career Berg was competing while carrying a full schedule of exhibitions and clinics. She recently estimated that she had given more than 10,000 all over the world.

For Berg, golf was a high calling. One of her rules was: "Don't think you really win until you live up to that high thing within you that makes you do your best, no matter what."

Berg was born Feb. 13, 1918, in Minneapolis, Minn. Her father was a prosperous grain merchant who belonged to the Interlachen C.C. Berg was an all-around athlete as a schoolgirl, competing in speed skating and even playing on a neighborhood football team that included future University of Oklahoma coach Bud Wilkinson. At 13, she turned her focus to golf and never stopped.

After a shaky introduction to amateur golf in the Minneapolis City Championship of 1933, Berg dedicated the next year to her game and won the event in 1934. "That was my proudest victory ever," she said. "After that, I began to dream."

In 1935, the Women's Amateur came to Interlachen, and Berg made it to the final where she was beaten, 3 and 2, by Glenna Collett Vare. She lost the final again in 1937, but won the championship in 1938, a year in which she won 10 of the 13 amateur events she entered.

Berg turned professional in 1940, when there were only a handful of women professionals. Her income was earned doing clinics and exhibitions for Wilson Sporting Goods. For her first victory, the 1941 Women's Western Open, she received a $100 war bond.

Shortly after, Berg was in a car accident that severely injured her left knee. The leg had to be reset twice, but during 18 months away from golf, Berg rehabilitated successfully by working out in the camp of a boxer. After a two-year stint in the Marines, in which she went to cadet school and graduated a second lieutenant, Berg won the first U.S. Women's Open in 1946, defeating Betty Jameson in Spokane, 5 and 4.

In 1948, the LPGA was established, and Berg, along with Babe Didrikson Zaharias, Betty Jameson and Louise Suggs, became the Big Four of the women's game. Berg, who was also the association's first president, won three titles that first year. She was the LPGA's leading money winner in 1954, 1955 and 1957, won the Vare Trophy for lowest scoring average in 1953, 1955 and 1956 and was three times voted outstanding woman athlete of the year by the Associated Press. She is the first woman to win $100,000 in career earnings. In 1963, the USGA honored her with the Bob Jones Award.

Only 5-2 with red hair and a freckled face, Berg was known as a supreme shot maker. Carol Mann called Berg "the most knowledgeable person, man or woman, of different golf shots that I've ever known." According to Mickey Wright, "Patty Berg is the perfect golfer for a woman." The LPGA honored her by establishing the Patty Berg Award in 1978 which is given to the lady golfer who has made the greatest contribution to women's golf during the year.

### THE BERG RECORD

Major Championship Victories .. 16

U.S. Women's Open: 1946

Western Open: 1941, 1943, 1948, 1951, 1955, 1957, 1958

Titleholders: 1937, 1938, 1939, 1948, 1953, 1955, 1957

Women's Amateur: 1938

LPGA Tour Victories ........... 57

Vare Trophy: 1953, 1955, 1956

Leading Money Winner: 1954, 1955, 1957

Bob Jones Award: 1963

W.H.

WORLD GOLF HALL of FAME

# Walter Hagen

**Walter Hagen was golf's greatest showman, a flamboyant, princely romantic who captivated the public and his peers with sheer panache.** He was "Sir Walter," and "The Haig." Such is his legacy as the most colorful character the game has ever seen that it often overshadows what a supreme player he was.

Hagen was the world's first full-time tournament professional. He won so often and in such lavish style that he single-handedly ushered in the era of the playing pro—who through the early century was clearly of a lower station than the game's wealthy amateurs—into the socially exclusive world of golf. As Arnold Palmer, the other great democrat of his sport, once said at a dinner honoring Hagen: "If not for you, Walter, this dinner tonight would be downstairs in the pro shop, not in the ballroom."

Of course, what gave weight to Hagen's persona was his often underrated talent and never overrated champion's heart. Hagen won 11 professional major championships, second only to Jack Nicklaus' total of 18. Between 1914 and 1929, he won the PGA Championship five times (four of them in a row, only the second time that has been accomplished in a major championship); the British Open four times and the U.S. Open twice. He also won the Western Open five times between 1916 and 1931 when it was widely considered a major championship.

Hagen is generally considered the greatest match player of all time. He once won 22 straight 36-hole matches in the PGA and, between the first round in 1921 and the fourth round of 1928, 32 out 33. With a long game often made erratic by the pronounced sway in his swing, but with an incredible ability to scramble and putt, Hagen lived by the principle that "three of those and one of them still count four." After he defeated Bob Jones, 12 and 11, in a 72-hole challenge match in 1926—which temporarily decided which of them was the greatest golfer of the day—even the gentlemanly Jones couldn't contain his frustration. "When a man misses his drive, and then misses his second shot, and then wins the hole with a birdie," said Jones, "it gets my goat."

Hagen had a model attitude during competition, one part bravado and five parts serenity. He understood completely that the only shot that matters is the next one, and wouldn't let a bad one ruffle him. "I expect to make at least seven mistakes a round," he said. "Therefore, when I make a bad shot, it's just one of the seven." He never complained about bad breaks, and, perhaps because of that attitude, always seemed to be getting good ones. "I love to play with Walter," said Jones. "He can come nearer beating luck itself than anybody I know."

It was all a natural extension of his overall philosophy of life. Born in Rochester, N.Y., Dec. 21, 1892, the son of a blacksmith, Hagen came from modest beginnings and entered golf as a caddy, but he resolved to live big. "I never wanted to be a millionaire," he said. "I just wanted to live like one." Although an imposing six feet tall with slick black hair and covered in the finest fabrics, Hagen nonetheless had a kindly face and a twinkle of irony that invited rather than repelled the common man. His gestures were grand, but wonderfully human. When he won the 1922 British Open at Royal St. George's, Hagen's reaction to professionals not being allowed in the clubhouse was to hire an Austro-Daimler limousine, park it directly in front of the clubhouse and change his clothes and take his meals in the car.

Hagen once expressed his creed in these words: "You're only here for a short visit. Don't hurry. Don't worry. And be sure to smell the flowers along the way." When he died in Traverse City, Mich., Oct. 5, 1969, there was no doubt he had lived it.

## THE HAGEN RECORD

Major Championship Victories .... 11
U.S. Open: 1914, 1919
British Open: 1922, 1924, 1928, 1929
PGA: 1921, 1924, 1925, 1926, 1927

PGA TOUR Victories .......... 40

Ryder Cup Teams ............... 6
(7-1-1) .......... 1927, 1929, 1931, 1933, 1935
Captain ......... 1927, 1929, 1931, 1933, 1935, 1937

# Ben Hogan

**It was said Ben Hogan had the secret. He may or may not have—it was not the nature of the man to say.** But if one player deserved to have it—by dint of total dedication and immersion in the game's mystery—it would be Ben Hogan.

Hogan had a code: work, study, endure—that he never betrayed. The way he unwaveringly applied his code to achieving total control of the golf ball engendered a respect that surpasses that of any other player. When he won, it was completely deserved. When he lost, it was poignant because no man ever gave so much. "I always outworked everybody," he said. "Work never bothered me like it bothers some people."

Hogan's record just happened to be something of a byproduct of this higher calling. He won 63 tournaments, his first in 1938 at the Hershey Four Ball (with Vic Ghezzi) and the last the 1959 Colonial. He won nine majors and is one of the only five men to win the Masters, the U.S. Open, the British Open and the PGA at least once. In 1953, he won all three majors he played in, missing the PGA because the dates conflicted with his only journey to the British Open.

Because he was the master of control, the U.S. Open was the canvas upon which Hogan did his best work. He won it four times: 1948, 1950, 1951 and 1953. From 1940 to 1960, excluding the championships of 1949 and 1957, both of which he missed due to injury, Hogan never finished out of the top 10 at any U.S. Open.

Hogan was born Aug. 13, 1912, in Dublin, Texas. His father was a blacksmith who died when Ben was nine. After moving to Fort Worth, Hogan began his life in golf as a caddy, along with Byron Nelson, at the Glen Garden C.C. Hogan joined the professional circuit in 1932, and had very little early success. Small but strong at 5-7, 140 pounds, Hogan was a long hitter who was often undone by a hook. He went broke twice, and when he was on the verge a third time on the eve of 1938 Oakland Open, he thought seriously about giving up. Instead, he shot a final-round 69 to finish second and win $380 to keep going. "I played harder that day than I ever played before or ever will again," he said.

Hogan didn't bloom until he found "a secret"—believed by some to be a weakening of his left hand along with the pronounced clockwise rotation of his left arm on the backswing—that allowed him to play a power fade. After several close calls in major championships, he won his first major at the 1946 PGA. When he won the 1948 PGA Championship in May and the U.S. Open at Riviera three weeks later, Hogan felt he was at his peak.

But on Feb. 2, 1949, a Greyhound bus crossed a center divider and crashed into the car carrying Hogan and his wife, Valerie. Hogan nearly died and suffered permanent leg injuries. Miraculously, Hogan won the 1950 U.S. Open at Merion in an 18-hole playoff with George Fazio and Lloyd Mangrum. "Merion meant the most," he would say later.

Even though Hogan played only a few tournaments a year thereafter, his best golf was ahead. In 1951, he won his first Masters and the U.S. Open at Oakland Hills. In 1953, he had his greatest year, winning his second Masters, his fourth U.S. Open and his only British Open.

He played his last official event in 1971.

## THE HOGAN RECORD

Major Championship Victories .... 9*
- Masters: 1951, 1953
- U.S. Open: 1948, 1950, 1951, 1953
- British Open: 1953
- PGA: 1946, 1948

PGA TOUR Victories .......... 68

Ryder Cup Teams .............. 4
- (3-0-0) ............... 1947, 1951
- Captain .......... 1947, 1949, 1967

PGA Player of the Year: 1948, 1950, 1951, 1953

Vardon Trophy: 1940, 1941, 1948

Leading Money Winner: 1940, 1941, 1942, 1946, 1948

Bob Jones Award: 1976

*Does not include Wartime U.S. Open, 1942

# Robert Tyre Jones Jr.

**More than any player in history, Bobby Jones is the model of the complete golfer.** Supremely gifted, Jones was also a man of vast intelligence and profound character, and he merged all three forces to become not only a singular champion, but a genuine hero. Wrote Herbert Warren Wind, "In the opinion of many people, of all the great athletes, Jones came the closest to being what we called a great man."

As a golfer, Jones was a giant. In the 1920s, he was "an ultra-athlete," according to writer and historian Charles Price, "recognized at being better at his game than any other athlete was at his." While there is no doubt Jones is the finest amateur golfer the game has ever produced, there's a strong argument that he was the greatest golfer, period. Beginning with his victory in the 1923 U.S. Open at Inwood and ending with his U.S. Amateur victory at Merion in 1930, Jones won 13 championships in 20 tries, the most imposing run of major titles the game has ever seen.

His crowning glory was The Grand Slam of 1930, in which he became the only golfer ever to win the U.S. Amateur, British Amateur, British Open and U.S. Open in the same year, indeed, the only golfer to win all four in a career. When he retired at the end of that year at the age of 28, *The New York Times* noted the occasion in an editorial that read, "With dignity, he quit the scene on which he nothing common did, or mean."

Jones was born March 17, 1902, in Atlanta. He was clearly a prodigy, and his first championship was the 1916 U.S. Amateur, where as a 14-year-old he went to the third round.

From the beginning, Jones' swing possessed "a drowsy beauty," in the words of Bernard Darwin. Yet Jones was a passionate man who had to overcome his own frailties of temperament. The strain of competition would cause him to lose as much as 18 pounds in a week. After winning the 1926 U.S. Open, he suddenly broke into tears in his Columbus, Ohio, hotel room, the strain catching up to him. He had to dominate a fiery temper that hindered him as a youth. As talented as he was, he did not win his first championship until 1923, prompting the early part of his career to be labeled "The Seven Lean Years." But Jones had a revelation when he discovered that the key to winning was learning to score well when playing badly. "I think this is what I learned to do best of all," wrote Jones, and "The Seven Fat Years" ensued.

Jones accomplished all this while playing competitive golf no more than three months in a year at any point in his life. The rest of the time was dedicated to academics, and later, the workaday world of the law. He studied mechanical engineering at Georgia Tech, graduating in three years, received a degree in English Literature from Harvard and attended law school at Emory University, withdrawing in his third semester to pass the bar. He would go on to become one of the game's most lucid and enlightening writers.

Besides his record and character, Jones' greatest legacy is Augusta National Golf Club and the Masters Tournament, which he founded in 1934. He played in the tournament several times, never finishing better than 13th. In 1948, he developed syringomyelia, a fluid-filled cavity in his spinal cord causing first pain, then paralysis. Jones never played golf again and was eventually restricted to a wheelchair until his death Dec. 18, 1971.

As Wind wrote, "As a young man he was able to stand up to just about the best that life can offer, which isn't easy, and later he stood up with equal grace to just about the worst."

The USGA's award for distinguished sportsmanship is the Bob Jones Award. "What Jones did was create a model that everyone, consciously or unconsciously, followed," said William Campbell. "It is why we have so many fine people in golf. He showed the world how to do it."

## THE JONES RECORD

Major Championship Victories .... 13
U.S. Amateur: 1924, 1925, 1927, 1928, 1930
British Amateur: 1930
U.S. Open: 1923, 1926, 1929, 1930
British Open: 1926, 1927, 1930

Walker Cup Teams ............... 5
(9-1-0) .......... 1922, 1924, 1926, 1928, 1930
Captain ............... 1928, 1930

Founded Augusta National Golf Club: 1933

Initiated Masters Tournament: 1934

Captain, World Amateur Team Championship: 1958

# Byron Nelson

**Just as there is no argument that perfection in golf is unattainable, no one argues that Byron Nelson has come the closest to attaining it.**

Nelson's streak of 11 victories in a row in 1945 is considered the least attainable record not only in golf, but in sports. His total of 18 victories that year, seven second-place finishes, his 19 consecutive rounds under 70 and his scoring average of 68.33 (and 67.45 in the fourth round) set the standard for the greatest single season in the history of the game.

Nelson is the player most often compared to a machine. In fact, when the USGA developed a mechanical device for testing golf balls and clubs, it named it "Iron Byron." Nelson is also a kind man of quiet dignity for whom the nickname, Lord Byron, fits as well.

"As a competitor, Byron was able to be mean and tough and intimidating—and pleasant," said Ken Venturi, whom Nelson mentored. "You can always argue who was the greatest player, but Byron is the finest gentleman the game has ever known."

In a relatively brief career, Nelson won 52 sanctioned tournaments, including the Masters in 1937 and 1942, the U.S. Open in 1939 and the PGA Championship in 1940 and 1945. In the '40s, he finished in the money 113 straight times. He retired from full-time competition in 1946.

Nelson was born Feb. 4, 1912, outside Waxahachie, Texas, the son of a cotton farmer. He and a boy from the other side of Fort Worth, Ben Hogan, both caddied at the Glen Garden C.C., where young Byron defeated Ben in a playoff for the caddy championship in 1927. Nelson turned pro in 1932.

Tall and rangy at 6-1 with enormous hands, Nelson achieved the pinnacle by developing an action that is considered the basis for the modern golf swing. Coming of age just as the steel shaft was replacing hickory, Nelson learned that using the big muscles in the hips and legs could be a more reliable, powerful and effective way to hit a golf ball than the more wristy method that had been employed in the era of hickory. Nelson was particularly noteworthy for the way his swing was more upright and along the target line, employing a full shoulder turn with restricted wrist cock, and for the way he kept his knees flexed in the downswing.

When Nelson was developing his swing, he would sometimes be stricken with episodes of shanking until he found a forward swing correction. "I actually felt like I moved my head back while my body went forward," he said. "The more I did that, the better I got." Nelson also believed one of the keys to his ability was an uncanny sense for judging distance.

Nelson reached his peak as World War II was ending. In 75 starts from 1944 to the end of 1946, he won 34 times and finished second 16 times. In those three years, he finished out of the top 10 just once, with a tie for 13th at Pensacola in 1946. Arnold Palmer, who grew up with Nelson as his idol, said, "Byron Nelson accomplished things on the pro tour that never have been and never will be approached."

Nelson retired from full-time competition after that 1946 season, settling down at 34 to a Texas ranch whose purchase had been a large part of his motivation when he was winning so often. His last official victory was the 1952 Bing Crosby Pro-Am, and he won the 1955 French Open. Along with his influence on Venturi, Nelson helped many young players with their games, including Tom Watson. Nelson also worked for several years as a television commentator for ABC Sports.

## THE NELSON RECORD

Major Championship Victories ..... 5
- Masters: 1937, 1942
- U.S. Open: 1939
- PGA: 1940, 1945

PGA TOUR Victories ........... 52

Ryder Cup Teams ................ 3
- (3-1-0) ................ 1937, 1947
- Captain ..................... 1965

Vardon Trophy: 1939

Leading Money Winner: 1944, 1945

PGA TOUR Record: 18 wins; 11 consecutive wins in 1945

Bob Jones Award: 1974

# Jack Nicklaus

**By the most objective measure of all—the record—Jack Nicklaus is the greatest player who ever lived.**

There was an immensity to Nicklaus' game. Nicklaus combined tremendous physical ability with boundless mental and psychological resources. At those times when his game was in full song, he would dominate his competition. But Nicklaus' ultimate genius was that when it wasn't, he often found a way to win because he would almost never beat himself. His style was a combination of explosive shotmaking and conservative management that calculated all factors—the course, his opponents and how he was playing. As a golfer, Nicklaus was both Secretariat and Einstein.

Subjective assessments, however, are secondary because Nicklaus' record is a colossus that encapsulates the game. In sheer numbers, it is awesome.

Between 1962 and 1986, Nicklaus won 70 official events on the PGA TOUR, second in total only to Sam Snead. But it is Nicklaus' performance in major championships alone that sets him above all others. He won 20—two U.S. Amateurs, a record six Masters, a record-tying four U.S. Opens, three British Opens and a record-tying five PGAs. He completed three full cycles of the modern Grand Slam, something no other player has ever done more than once. If performance in major championships is the ultimate criterion, then no golfer has ever set himself apart like Nicklaus.

Nicklaus was born Jan. 21, 1940, in Columbus, Ohio. His father, Charlie, was a pharmacist who introduced his son to sports and remained his greatest friend and supporter. While growing up at the Scioto C.C. under the tutelage of Jack Grout, Nicklaus came to idolize Bobby Jones, whose 13 major championships became the reference point for his own career.

As an amateur, Nicklaus was clearly a prodigy. He won the 1956 Ohio State Open at age 16. Three years later, he defeated Charlie Coe, 1 up, in an epic final round in the U.S. Amateur and won it again at Pebble Beach in 1961. In between, he tied for second at the 1960 U.S. Open and shot an astounding 269 at Merion in the World Amateur Team Championship.

By the time Nicklaus came on the pro scene in 1962, he was a stout, crewcut dynamo of 215 pounds who was about to change the game. With a mighty upright swing that allowed him to hit the ball high and generally with a slight fade, Nicklaus became the longest controlled driver in the game's history, as well as the most devastating long-iron player. His technique and strength also allowed him to escape from high grass with more power and control than his rivals. Along with a reliable putting touch that was particularly consistent inside of six feet, Nicklaus' arsenal was designed to conquer the narrow fairways, deep rough and firm, fast greens that characterize major championships. By 1967, he had won seven of them. Between 1970 and 1975, leaner and more fashionably coiffed, he won seven more.

On the PGA TOUR, Nicklaus led the money list eight times, twice while playing only 16 events. Between 1962 and 1979, he finished in the top 10 in 243 of the 357 official events he played in, a rate of 68 percent.

For all his physical gifts, it was Nicklaus' ability to concentrate and gather himself for decisive moments that most separated him. This was never more evident than in his most fulfilling triumph, the 1986 Masters, where, at the age of 46, Nicklaus put together a final-round 65 that included a 30 on the back nine to win by one.

Through it all, Nicklaus completed the ultimate champion's profile by being a gracious loser. He finished second 19 times in majors, but always gave credit to the winner. Win or lose, Jack Nicklaus was the greatest.

## THE NICKLAUS RECORD

Major Championship Victories .... 20
- U.S. Amateur: 1959, 1961
- U.S. Open: 1962, 1967, 1972, 1980
- Masters: 1963, 1965, 1966, 1972, 1975, 1986
- British Open: 1966, 1970, 1978
- PGA: 1963, 1971, 1973, 1975, 1980

Walker Cup Teams ............... 2
- (4-0-0) ................ 1959, 1961

PGA TOUR Victories ...........73

Champions Tour Victories ....... 10

Ryder Cup Teams ................ 8
- (17-8-3) ......... 1969, 1971, 1973, 1975, 1977, 1981
- Captain .............. 1983, 1987

Presidents Cup Captain: 1998, 2003

PGA Player of the Year: 1964, 1965 1967, 1971, 1972, 1973, 1975, 1976

Leading Money Winner: 1964, 1965, 1967, 1971, 1972, 1973, 1975, 1976

Bob Jones Award: 1975

# Francis Ouimet

**They were the shots heard 'round the world, and they, too, started a revolution.**

At the 1913 U.S. Open at The Country Club, Francis Ouimet, a 20-year-old former caddie, didn't just beat British legends Harry Vardon and Ted Ray, he changed the perception of an entire sport. Ouimet's stunning triumph captured the imagination of sports fans across the globe, sweeping away the notion that golf was a stuffy game for the old and rich. Ouimet was American golf's first great hero, and he remains one of the most beloved figures in the sport's history.

Ouimet seemed to step from the pages of a Dickens novel. He had grown up across the street from The Country Club in a working-class home and learned the game with the one old club his older brother, Wilfred, had procured as a caddie. The two boys built three makeshift holes in the family backyard, incorporating a gravel pit, a swamp, a brook and a patch of long, rough grass. Sunken tomato cans were used as cups. At 11, Ouimet began caddying at The Country Club, and by his later teens, he had begun to make a name for himself in tournament competition. After winning the 1913 Massachusetts State Amateur Championship, Ouimet was inspired to enter the National Open.

After three rounds he somehow found himself tied with Vardon, a four-time winner of the British Open, and reigning British Open champion Ray, whose walrus mustache and length off the tee were equally outsized. During the tense final round both Englishmen stumbled home with 79s, and, after a jittery 43 on the front nine, Ouimet joined their playoff by birdieing the 71st hole. The following day, all three men went out in 38, and Ouimet took his first lead when Vardon and Ray three-putted the par-3 10th. By the par-4 17th Ray had given up the fight but Vardon was only one behind when he caught a bunker with his drive and took bogey. Ouimet then drilled a 15-foot birdie putt to put the championship on ice and endear himself to the world, with a little bit of help from his 10-year-old caddie, Eddie Lowery, a pintsized neighborhood kid who added a touch of whimsy to the photographs.

Ouimet proved he was no fluke by winning the 1914 U.S. Amateur, but when he subsequently opened a sporting goods shop he was banned from amateur competition by the USGA, a miscarriage of justice that was later reversed. Ouimet returned to play on the inaugural Walker Cup team in 1922 and the seven that followed, serving as captain in four more thereafter. In 1931, his temples specked with gray, he won another U.S. Amateur at age 38. Ouimet was an important international figure as well. In 1951, he became the first American to captain the Royal and Ancient Golf Club at St. Andrews.

His legacy transcends tournament victories. In 1913 it is estimated only 350,000 Americans played golf. Ten years later, fueled by Ouimet's heroics, that number was up to 2,000,000. So it is that Ouimet is rightfully called the Father of American Golf. In 1963, the U.S. Open was again held at The Country Club to commemorate the 50th anniversary of his victory. Said Ouimet in 1932, "To me, the ground here is hallowed. The grass grows greener, the trees bloom better, there is even warmth to the rocks. Somehow or other the sun seems to shine brighter on The Country Club than any other place that I have ever known." He died in nearby Newton in 1967.

## THE OUIMET RECORD

Major Championship Victories ..... 3
- U.S. Open: 1913
- U.S. Amateur: 1914, 1931

Walker Cup Teams .............. 12
- (9-5-2) .... 1922, 1923, 1924, 1926, 1928, 1930, 1932, 1934
- Non-Playing Captain ... 1936, 1938, 1947, 1949

Bob Jones Award: 1955

# Arnold Palmer

**No figure in the history of golf has injected more excitement into the game over a sustained period than Arnold Palmer.** Palmer's ability to win with boldness and charisma was the single biggest factor in the game's explosive growth after 1960. For people born in the second half of the 20th century, it was as if Arnold Palmer invented golf.

Hyperbole aside, Palmer brought golf to the masses. The open passion with which he played, from his whirlybird followthrough on the tee to his fierce animation on the greens, was different from the cool intensity that the great players before him had cultivated. Palmer lashed at the ball with all his might and charged his putts recklessly. With his thick forearms and wasp waist, he was a sweaty 5'10", 165-pound blue-collar dynamo who joyfully made golf an athletic event—the perfect figure to usher in golf's television era. "Arnold Palmer did not play golf, we thought," wrote Dan Jenkins. "He nailed up beams, reupholstered sofas, repaired air-conditioning units. He was the most immeasurable of all golf champions."

As telegenic as Palmer was, he was most magnetic as the leader of the throng that called themselves Arnie's Army. "I tried to look the whole gallery in the eye," he said. "Some people think of me as just plain lucky, and I can't argue with them," he once said. "I would like to say, however, that a man might be walking around lucky and not know it unless he tries."

Nobody tried like Palmer. He learned to love the game in Latrobe, Pa., where he was born Sept. 10, 1929. His father, Deacon, was the professional at the nine-hole Latrobe C.C., and the Palmers lived on the golf course. Young Arnold dreamed of playing golf for a living, and after he won the U.S. Amateur—the victory that remains his favorite—he began living his dream.

Between 1955 and 1973, Palmer won 62 PGA TOUR events, including seven professional major championships—the Masters in 1958, 1960, 1962 and 1964, the 1960 U.S. Open and the 1961 and 1962 British Opens. His most magical golf was produced in 1960, a year he won eight official events. At the Masters, he birdied the final two holes to edge Ken Venturi by one. Two months later at the U.S. Open at Cherry Hills, he began the final round on Saturday seven strokes and 14 players behind. But he drove the green on the 340-yard first hole, shot 30 on the front nine and finished with a 65 to win by two. The Palmer "charge" was born, and for the next two years he seemed unbeatable down the stretch. The next month, when Palmer made a pilgrimage to St. Andrews for the British Open, his presence singlehandedly elevated the game's oldest championship from disrepair to its rightful place.

With a muscular swing that produced a piercing draw, Palmer was one of the finest drivers of the ball who ever lived and, from a distinctive pigeon-toed stance, a superb putter. He led the PGA TOUR's money list four times, and in 1963 became the first player to win more than $100,000 in a season. He played on six Ryder Cup teams and was the winning captain twice.

Palmer's defeats were as dramatic as his victories. In 1962, he lost the Masters by one stroke when he double-bogeyed the 72nd hole. He lost playoffs in three U.S. Opens, the first to Jack Nicklaus in 1962, the second to Julius Boros in 1963 and the third and most heartbreaking to Billy Casper in 1966, where Palmer had led by seven strokes with nine holes to play in regulation. Palmer's best finish in the PGA Championship was second—three times—which kept him from attaining the career Grand Slam.

But his losses, like everything Palmer did, only served to further endear him to his legions. For more than four decades under the spotlight, Arnold Palmer signed every autograph, shook every hand and, most of all, gave everything to every shot.

## THE PALMER RECORD

Major Championship Victories ..... 8
U.S. Amateur: 1954
Masters: 1958, 1960, 1962, 1964
U.S. Open: 1960
British Open: 1961, 1962
PGA TOUR Victories ........... 62
Champions TOUR Victories ...... 10
Ryder Cup Teams ................ 7
(22-8-2) ......... 1961, 1963, 1965, 1967, 1971, 1973
Captain ............... 1963, 1975
Vardon Trophy: 1961, 1962, 1964, 1967
Leading Money Winner: 1958, 1960, 1962, 1963
PGA Player of the Year: 1960, 1962
Bob Jones Award: 1971

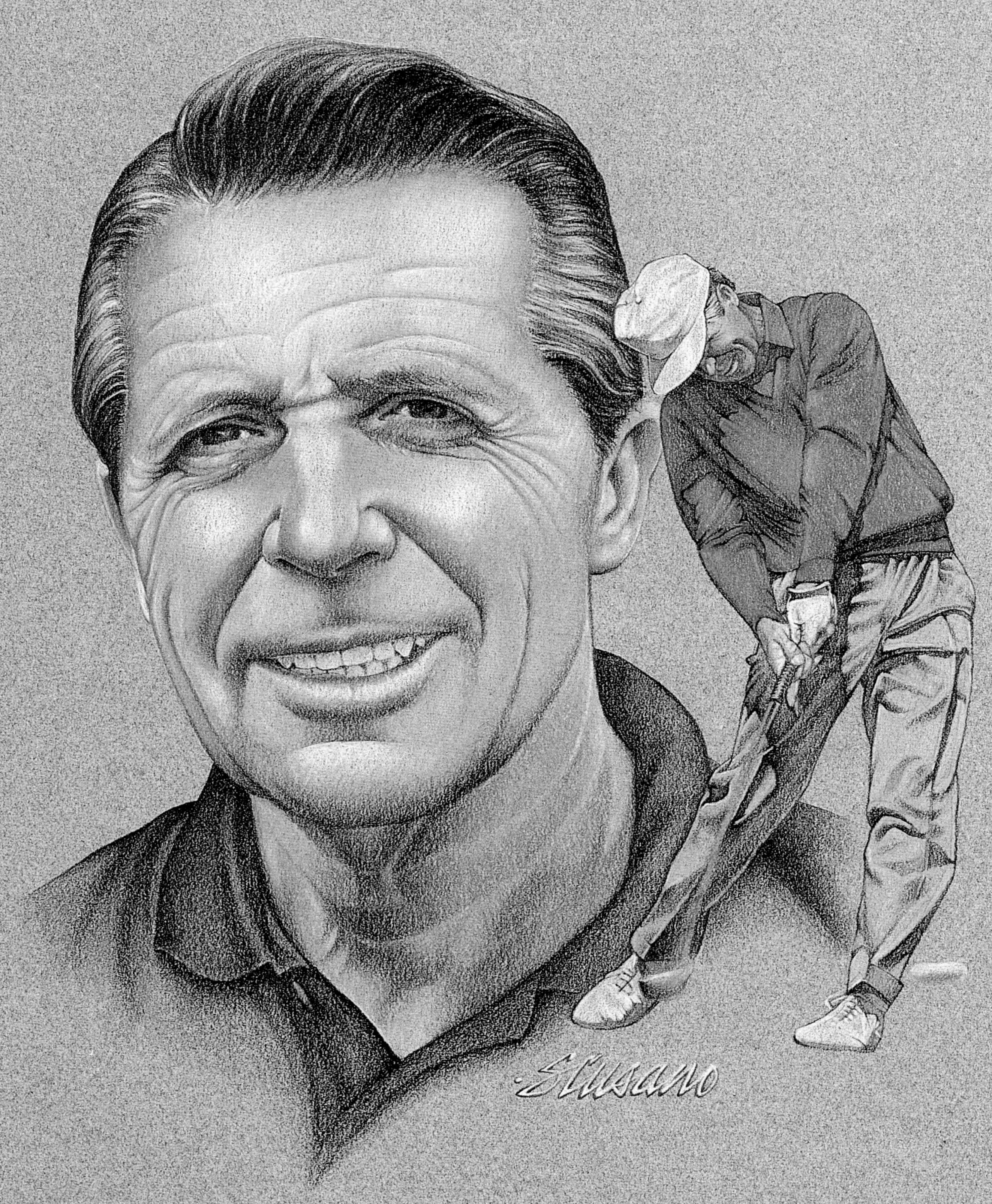

# Gary Player

**When speaking of Gary Player, it's common for observers to say something along the lines of: "He's done more with less than any golfer I've ever seen."**

The less is Player's improbable 5-7, 160 pounds, his unorthodox method and his hailing from a small country in a remote corner of the world. The more includes nine major championships, the modern Grand Slam, 162 tournament victories around the world—including 24 official PGA TOUR victories—and nine Champions Tour majors. Yet Player, in his forthright way, differs with a reductionist view of his career. "I had a great deal of talent," he will say, before adding, "but talent alone will only take you so far."

No, with Player there has always been a palpable sense of something extra. Perhaps no golfer has ever craved victory so much for such a long time. "What I have learned about myself," he wrote in his 1991 autobiography, "is that I am an animal when it comes to achievement and wanting success. There is never enough success for me."

His peers, who included Arnold Palmer and Jack Nicklaus in their primes, knew it. "I don't think Gary was a great driver of the golf ball," said Nicklaus. "I don't think he was a great iron player. He was a good putter, not a great putter. But when he really needed to be, he was a great driver, and a great iron player, and he made the putt when he needed to make it. Gary, as much as anyone I ever saw, has that thing inside him that champions have."

Gary Jim Player was born Nov. 1, 1935, in Johannesburg, South Africa, the third of three children to Harry and Muriel Player. His father was a captain in a gold mine who spent most of his working life 12,000 feet underground. His mother was a well-educated woman who died of cancer when Gary was eight. Player wrote that her loss "has been a means for me, as it were, to settle some unfathomable debt."

He chose to try to pay it back as a golfer, although he didn't take up the game until he was 14. He turned professional in 1953 at age 18 and quickly won several times in Africa, Europe and Australia. In 1957, he came to America, and upon seeing how far the game's best professionals hit the ball, intensified his exercise regimen, weakened his hooker's grip and set about learning how to carry the ball farther. The next year he won the Kentucky Derby Open and was heartened by a second-place finish at the U.S. Open, where his idol, Ben Hogan, locked him with a stare and said, "Son, you are going to be a great player."

From there, Player was off. In his trademark all-black outfits (inspired by his lifelong love of westerns) with body trim and biceps bulging from a weight-lifting program and high-fiber diet that were both 30 years ahead of their time—and with a bunker game that is considered the greatest ever developed—he willed himself to victory. He won the 1959 British Open at Muirfield for his first major, made the 1961 Masters his second and the 1962 PGA at Aronimink his third. At the 1965 U.S. Open at Bellerive, Player defeated Kel Nagle in an 18-hole playoff to complete the modern Grand Slam by age 29.

His other majors included the 1972 PGA Championship, the 1968 and 1974 British Opens, and the 1974 and 1978 Masters. The last is perhaps Player's proudest victory. He began the final round seven strokes out of the lead. But at age 42, he birdied seven of the final 10 to shoot 64 and win by a stroke.

Player is indisputably the greatest international golfer of all time. He estimates he has spent more than three years of his life in airplanes and traveled some 12 million miles. In every year from 1955 to 1982, Player won at least one sanctioned international tournament, a 27-year streak. He won the World Match Play title five times, the Australian Open seven times and the South African Open 13 times. In winning the 1974 Brazilian Open, he shot the only 59 ever in a national open.

## THE PLAYER RECORD

Major Championship Victories ..... 9
- U. S. Open: 1965
- Masters: 1961, 1974, 1978
- British Open: 1959, 1968, 1974
- PGA Championship: 1962, 1972

Total Tournaments Won ........ 162

PGA TOUR Victories ........... 24

Champions Tour Victories ........ 19

Leading Money Winner: 1961

# Gene Sarazen

**As a competitor and innovator, Gene Sarazen spanned golf history like no other great American player.** From pugnacious whiz kid to equipment innovator to mature champion to senior statesman, Sarazen, who died May 13, 1999, remained a presence well into his 90s. When he was not hitting the opening drive at the Masters each year, his ageless wit was a living bridge to the memories of Vardon, Hagen and Jones.

He was born Eugenio Saraceni, the son of an Italian carpenter from Rome, Feb. 27, 1902, in Harrison, N.Y. He dropped out of school in sixth grade and turned pro at 19. It was then that he changed his name to Sarazen because, he once said, "It sounded like a golfer."

At 5-5 and 145 pounds, Sarazen was the shortest of golf's great champions. But he was solidly built and possessed a tremendous competitive heart. In 1922, at the age of 20, he arrived at Skokie C.C. for his first U.S. Open and won, birdieing the final hole and becoming, with a closing 68, the first player to shoot under 70 in the final round to win. Later in the year, he won the PGA Championship at Oakmont. He then challenged Walter Hagen to a 72-hole mano a mano for the "world championship" and beat history's greatest match player. In 1932, he won both the British Open at Sandwich and the U.S. Open at Fresh Meadow, where he played the last 28 holes in 100 strokes, posting a closing round of 66 that would be a record for a winner until 1960.

"When Sarazen saw a chance at the bacon hanging over the last green," wrote his friend, Bob Jones, "he could put as much fire and fury into a finishing round as Jack Dempsey could put into a fight."

In 1935, Sarazen became the first player to win the modern Grand Slam by capturing the Masters. In the final round of that tournament, he hit the most famous shot ever in major championship golf, holing a 4-wood from 235 yards away for a double-eagle 2 on the 15th hole that tied him with Craig Wood, whom he defeated the next day in a playoff. The "shot heard round the world" helped put the Masters on the map.

Altogether, Sarazen won seven major championships among his more than 50 victories around the world and as late as 1940 nearly won his third U.S. Open, losing to Lawson Little in a playoff. He was known for his compact but ferocious swing, the grim delight he seemed to take from competition and his fast play. In 1947, he and George Fazio played a round at Augusta National in one hour and 57 minutes.

But as great as Sarazen's playing record, he did as much for the game with his innovative nature. Taking a tip from Ty Cobb, he developed a weighted practice club in 1929. In 1931, while being taught by Howard Hughes how to fly a plane, Sarazen noticed the tail adjusting downward during takeoff and came upon the idea for the modern sand wedge, which he spent months perfecting. He later called it his biggest contribution to golf. Later, he lobbied unsuccessfully to have the hole enlarged from 4 inches in diameter to eight.

Sarazen was perhaps the greatest early ambassador of golf among American pros, playing exhibitions all over the world. He earned his nickname, "The Squire," after he bought a farm for his family in upstate New York. In the early '60s, he came back into the public eye as the host of *Shell's Wonderful World of Golf*.

In 1973, on the 50th anniversary of his first appearance in the British Open, the 71-year-old Sarazen made a hole-in-one with a punched 5-iron at the short par-3 eighth hole, known as the Postage Stamp, at Troon. In 1992, he was presented the Bob Jones Award from the United States Golf Association.

## THE SARAZEN RECORD

Major Championship Victories ..... 7
- Masters: 1935
- U.S. Open: 1922, 1932
- British Open: 1932
- PGA: 1922, 1923, 1933

PGA TOUR Victories ........... 39

Ryder Cup Teams ................ 6
- (7-2-3) .......... 1927, 1929, 1931, 1933, 1935, 1937

# Sam Snead

**Sam Snead was the greatest athlete among golf's great champions.** The swing he employed to win tournaments over six decades remains the archetype of power and grace, his longevity the benchmark of an incredible talent.

In more than 50 years as an active competitor, Snead won a record 82 official PGA TOUR victories, and he can safely claim more than 140 worldwide. Nicknamed "The Slammer" for the strength of his shots, he won seven major championships.

At a long-limbed 5-10 and 185 pounds, Snead was classically configured and preternaturally gifted. In high school, he could run the 100-yard dash in 10 seconds flat. Into his 70s he could, from a dead standstill, kick the top of a seven-foot doorway. His movements were almost musical, and it was no surprise to anyone that Snead had taught himself to play the banjo and the trumpet by ear. As a boy who preferred to go barefoot, he learned golf in much the same way, and on those rare occasions when his rhythm was off, he could regain it by removing his shoes and socks, as he did for nine holes at the 1942 Masters. Once during the discussion of his swing keys, Snead said simply, "I try to feel oily." On another occasion he said, "When I swing at a golf ball right, my mind is blank and my body is loose as a goose."

Samuel Jackson Snead was born May 27, 1912, in Ashwood, Va., the youngest of five brothers. At the time, his mother, Laura, was 47. Golf first captivated him while watching his older brother, Homer, belt balls across the family's cow and chicken farms, and soon he was fashioning his own clubs out of swamp maple limbs and using balls he had found caddying at the nearby Homestead Hotel Golf Course in Hot Springs. He got his first assistant pro job at 19 at The Homestead, moved to the Greenbrier in 1935 as the playing professional, and in 1936, joined the PGA TOUR.

Immensely long off the tee and a creative shotmaker, Snead took the tour by storm. He won five times in 1937 and seven times in 1938. Under the guidance of promoter Fred Corcoran, who marketed Snead as a hillbilly force of nature out of the Back Creek Mountains of Virginia, he quickly became golf's prime attraction. "Sam Snead," said Gene Sarazen, "is the only person who came into the game possessing every physical attribute—a sound swing, power, a sturdy physique and no bad habits."

The next year, he was even hotter, but suffered a major setback at the U.S. Open at Spring Mill in Philadelphia. Thinking he needed a birdie on the 72nd hole to win, but in reality needing only a par 5, Snead made an 8 to finish fifth. He would go on to finish second in the U.S. Open four times, once when he missed a 30-inch putt on the final green of a playoff with Lew Worsham in 1947.

Still, Snead won three Masters, three PGAs and the British Open in 1946 at St. Andrews. He led the money list three times, won the Vardon Trophy four times, and played on seven Ryder Cup teams. His final major championship victory was perhaps his most memorable. At the 1954 Masters, Snead, tied after 72 holes with Ben Hogan, defeated him in an 18-hole playoff, 70 to 71.

Short putting eventually stopped Snead from winning at his normal pace. Still his achievements in his later years were remarkable. In 1965, Snead, at 52 years and 10 months, became the oldest winner of a PGA TOUR event when he won the Greater Greensboro Open for the eighth time. He was fourth in the PGA Championship at age 60 in 1972, and third in 1974 at age 62. "Desire is the most important thing in sport," he once said. "I have it. Jeez, no one has more than I've got."

## THE SNEAD RECORD

**Major Championship Victories ..... 7**
- Masters: 1949, 1952, 1954
- British Open: 1946
- PGA: 1942, 1949, 1951

**PGA TOUR Victories ........... 82**

**Champions Tour Victories ......... 6**

**Other Significant Victories**
- Greater Greensboro Open: 8 times
- PGA Seniors': 6 times
- World Seniors Championship: 5 times
- Ryder Cup Teams .............. 8
- (10-2-1) ......... 1937, 1947, 1949, 1951, 1953, 1955, 1959
- Captain .......... 1951, 1959, 1969

**Vardon Trophy: 1938, 1949, 1950, 1955**

**Leading Money Winner: 1938, 1949, 1950**

WORLD GOLF HALL of FAME

# Harry Vardon

**Harry Vardon was possessed with a talent and method so singular he was considered a shot-making machine in the improvisational era of hickory and gutta percha.** The winner of the British Open a record six times, he was golf's first superstar.

Vardon was a true original. On his own, he developed the Vardon Grip, in which the little finger of the right hand is rested on top of the index finger of the left hand, the grip used by 90 percent of good players today. Wrote Bernard Darwin of Vardon, "I do not think anyone who saw him play in his prime will disagree as to this, that a greater genius is inconceivable."

Vardon was born May 9, 1870, in Grouville, Jersey, one of the Channel Islands between England and France. The son of a gardener, he was one of six boys and two girls. When the town went about building a golf course, the children built their own, and Vardon taught himself the effortless, upright swing that would serve him the rest of his life.

Still, as a child he played very few actual rounds of golf, never had a lesson and at age 13 became an apprentice gardener. He played in a few tournaments into his late teens and didn't decide to make it a career until he saw that his older brother, Tom, had turned professional and was doing well in tournaments.

But Vardon was made for golf. Although only 5-feet 9-inches and 155 pounds, he had enormous hands that melted perfectly around the club. He also possessed a sweet, peaceful temperament.

Most of all, Vardon had a swing that repeated monotonously. His swing was more upright and his ball flight higher than his contemporaries, giving Vardon's approach shots the advantage of greater carry and softer landing. He took only the thinnest of divots.

Vardon played in knickers (the first professional to do so), fancy-topped stockings, a hard collar and tie and tightly buttoned jacket, but still there was a wonderful freedom to his movement. He allowed his left arm to bend as he reached the top of the backswing, and there was a lack of muscular stress or tension at any part of the swing. "Relaxation," he said, "added to a few necessary fundamental principles, is the basis of this great game."

Vardon won the British Open in 1896, 1898, 1899, 1903, 1911 and, at the age of 44, 1914. He was second on four other occasions.

Golf was never again so easy for Vardon. He felt that fashioning shots to American turf conditions got him into some bad habits, and the wound rubber Haskell ball that came into fashion reduced his shot-making advantage over the field. Finally, after winning the British Open again in 1903, Vardon was diagnosed with tuberculosis. It forced him out of competition and into sanitariums for long spells until 1910.

Heeled but enfeebled, Vardon validated his true greatness after the age of 40, winning the British Open again in 1911 and 1914. The previous year, Vardon had been beaten in a three-way playoff for the U.S. Open at Brookline by Francis Ouimet. In 1920, at the age of 50, he led the U.S. Open by four strokes with only seven holes to play, before bad weather and a shaky putter left him tied for second.

Vardon died March 20, 1937, in London. On both the European and U.S. PGA tours, the Vardon Trophy is awarded annually to the professional with the lowest stroke average.

### THE VARDON RECORD

Major Championship Victories . . . . . 7
U.S. Open: 1900
British Open: 1896, 1898, 1899, 1903, 1911, 1914
Total Tournament Victories . . . . . . 62

A. Ravielli

# Babe Didrikson Zaharias

**Olympic gold medal winner in track and field.** All-American basketball player in college. Champion golfer. If there was a Jim Thorpe among women athletes, it was Mildred "Babe" Didrikson Zaharias. As a professional golfer, she won 31 tournaments, including three U.S. Women's Opens, and helped found the Ladies Professional Golf Association. "Babe changed the game of golf for women," said Patty Berg.

Didrikson didn't even take up golf seriously until she was 21. She was introduced to the game by Grantland Rice in Los Angeles during the 1932 Olympics. Somewhere in between winning gold medals in the javelin and hurdles—she might have won the high jump, too, had she not been disqualified—Didrikson joined Rice and three other sportswriters for a round of golf at Brentwood C.C. According to Rice, the Babe shot 91 that day and regularly hit drives measuring 250 yards.

The following year, while she was touring the country with the House of David baseball team, Didrikson traveled back to Los Angeles and took golf lessons from pro Stan Kertes at Brentwood. Two years later, she won the Texas Women's Amateur Championship with an eagle on the 34th hole. The United States Golf Association ruled the following day that as a professional athlete Didrikson could no longer compete in amateur events.

This led Didrikson to go on exhibition tours and to celebrity pro-ams. In 1938, during a tournament in California, she was paired with a professional wrestler named George Zaharias. They married later that year, and with Zaharias supporting his wife and managing her career, the Babe applied for amateur reinstatement. The USGA granted her wish in 1943, and immediately after World War II Zaharias went on a tear that included the U.S. Women's Amateur in 1946 and the British Women's Amateur in 1947. Published reports had her winning 16 consecutive tournaments, and this led her to turn professional, sign with sports promoter Fred Corcoran and, along with Berg, help form the LPGA Tour.

As a professional, Zaharias was just as dominant, winning 31 of the 128 events in which she played from 1948-1953. Asked what the secret of her success was, Zaharias would usually answer with her favorite expression. "Aw," she'd say, "I just loosen my girdle and take a whack at it."

Zaharias' last seven wins, including the 1954 Women's Open, came after she was diagnosed with cancer and had a colostomy. The Women's Open victory, by 12 strokes over Betty Hicks at Salem (Mass.) C.C., was one of the five victories that year. The pain returned in 1955, and although she won twice that year, it wasn't long before Babe Zaharias was gone. She died Sept. 27, 1956, at the age of 42.

Berg called her "the most physically talented woman I've ever seen," and that statement applied not only to golf, but to the rest of the sports Babe Didrikson Zaharias mastered. These included bowling, tennis and, if card games count, those too. In her autobiography, *This Life I've Led,* Zaharias wrote, "All my life, I've had the urge to do things better than anyone else." She may have been the greatest woman athlete in history.

## THE ZAHARIAS RECORD

Major Championship Victories .... 12
- U.S. Women's Amateur: 1946
- British Women's Amateur: 1947
- Western Open: 1944, 1945, 1947, 1950
- U.S. Women's Open: 1948, 1950, 1954
- Titleholders: 1948, 1950, 1954
- Vare Trophy: 1954

Leading Money Winner: 1948, 1949, 1950, 1951

Bob Jones Award: 1957

Associated Press Woman of the Year: 1931, 1945, 1946, 1947, 1950, 1954

# Betty Jameson

**A pioneer of women's professional golf, Betty Jameson is one of only six women to have won both the U. S. Women's Open and U. S. Women's Amateur championships.**

In her prime, Jameson was a tall, stylish woman who was sometimes referred to as golf's first "glamour girl." She was a founding member of both the Women's Professional Golf Association and the Ladies Professional Golf Association. She was also the first woman to break 300 for a 72-hole event.

Elizabeth Jameson was born May 19, 1919, in Norman, Okla. After her family moved to Dallas, she began playing golf at age 11 and was soon completing as many as 50 holes a day on a nine-hole course.

Her long, graceful swing was much admired. Herbert Warren Wind wrote after watching her that "all you are conscious of is how perfectly the left hand does what the left hand is supposed to do, and, as she moves into the ball, an acceleration which keeps building so smoothly that it is hardly perceptible." According to Lawson Little, Jameson had "the soundest swing, the best pivot and the greatest follow through of the hips of any woman player except Joyce Wethered."

Jameson won the 1932 Texas Publinx at age 13, followed by the state championship. At age 15, she captured the Texas Women's Amateur and went on to win it four years in a row. In 1939, she won the U.S. Amateur at Wee Burn in Connecticut and repeated the next year at Pebble Beach. In 1942, she became the first player to win the Western Open and the Western Amateur in the same year.

Something went out of Jameson when her mother died in 1942. "My mother knew I could be a world beater—that was the old-fashioned term," Jameson told author Liz Kahn in her 1996 book on the LPGA. "I cried a lot at her death, for everyone needs someone in her corner, and my mother was a great motivator. Maybe I didn't have the same stimulus after that."

Because tournament play was virtually suspended during World War II, Jameson held jobs that included a stint on the copy desk of *The Dallas Times Herald.* In 1945, she joined the fledging WPGA and accepted an offer from the Spalding Company to turn professional and perform clinics.

In 1946, the WPGA put on the first U.S. Women's Open in Spokane, in which Jameson was defeated by Patty Berg in the final, 5 and 4, the only time the championship was contested at match play. The next year, at the Starmount Forest Country Club in Greensboro, N.C., Jameson became the first woman to break 300 for 72 holes, her 295 total winning by six strokes. She was runner-up again in 1952.

When the LPGA was started in 1948, Jameson, along with Patty Berg, Louise Suggs and Babe Didrikson Zaharias, made up the tour's "Big Four." However, Jameson wasn't as inspired by the professional game as she had been as an amateur. Among her 10 victories were the 1949 Texas Open, the 1952 World Championship and the 1954 Western Open. Her best year was 1955 when she won four tournaments. Although she played until 1963, she never won again.

"I love my career, though I think it was a little time-wasting," said Jameson, who after retiring from competition taught golf and made a living as a painter. "I didn't dream that without match play the whole essence and drama of golf would disappear. I didn't realize how humdrum it is, playing hole after hole and not daring to take chances."

In 1951, Jameson was named one of the 11 charter members of the LPGA Hall of Fame. It was Jameson who conceived the idea annually honoring the player with the best scoring average on the LPGA Tour and, in 1952, donated the trophy that would become the Vare Trophy in honor of her idol, Glenna Collett Vare.

## THE JAMESON RECORD

Major Championship Victories ..... 5

- U.S. Amateur: 1939, 1940
- U.S. Women's Open: 1947
- Women's Western Open: 1942, 1954

Leading Money Winner: 1947

# Willie Anderson

**Willie Anderson's place in U.S. Open history belongs on the same pantheon as Bobby Jones, Ben Hogan and Jack Nicklaus.** He was the first to win four U.S. Open Championships and the only golfer in history to win three in succession. The sad part of Anderson's biography is that he died at the age of 30 from what has been described as an overindulgent lifestyle. Since his death in 1910, only five golfers—including Hogan (1950, 1951) and Curtis Strange (1988, 1989)—have won two consecutive Opens, and only Hogan has come close to winning four out of five years, as Anderson did in 1901, 1903, 1904 and 1905.

Alex Smith, a Scotsman who finished second to Anderson in two U.S. Opens, believed that "most likely, had he lived longer, Willie would have set a record for Open championships that would never be beaten." From 1897 to 1910, Anderson won the Open four times, finished second once, third once, fourth twice and fifth three times. He also won the Western Open four times, which at the time was considered a major championship.

Reared on the links of North Berwick, Scotland, Anderson was a sturdy man with muscular shoulders, brawny forearms and exceptionally large hands. He played with a flat, full-sweeping action that was characteristic of the Scots and known as the "St. Andrews swing." Despite what many considered to be swing flaws, Anderson was consistently accurate. Gene Sarazen was once practicing bunker shots when another pro casually asked him if Willie Anderson could have gotten out of those bunkers as well as he was doing. "Get out of them?" Sarazen said. "He was never in them!"

Anderson's first U.S. Open victory came at Myopia Hunt Club in 1901. Using a gutta percha ball, he defeated Alec Smith in the first playoff in Open history. Five strokes down with five holes to play, Anderson finished 4-4-4-4-4 to defeat Smith, 85 to 86. It was payback for the 1897 Open, where Smith hit a brassie to eight feet on the closing hole and made the putt to defeat the 17-year-old Anderson. It was also a showcase for Anderson to make a stand for social change. The custom was for the professionals to eat their lunch in the clubhouse kitchen, but Anderson would not stand for that. "Nae, nae, we're nae goin' t' eat in the kitchen," he said, swinging his club and taking a divot out of the club's lawn. A compromise was reached: Myopia erected a tent and the pros ate there.

After finishing fifth in 1902, Anderson went on his historic run. He won at Baltusrol—where he later was host professional—in 1903 in a playoff against Deacon Davey Brown. The next year, Anderson set the Open scoring record by shooting 303 to win by five strokes over Gil Nichollas at Glen View Golf Club. In 1905, Anderson completed his successive hat trick by making up a five-stroke deficit with 36 holes to play at Myopia. His streak ended in 1906 at Onwentsia, where, needing 72 in the final round, he staggered home in 84.

Anderson was modest in nature, never boasting about the level of his play, always letting his game speak for itself. For this he developed a reputation of being dour. "You couldn't tell whether he was winning or losing by looking at him," said Fred McLeod, the U.S. Open champion of 1908.

Unlike J.H. Taylor and Harold Hilton, he never wrote an instructional book, but he taught effectively and many aspiring amateurs worshipped him. He died in 1910, five years after winning his fourth Open. The official cause of his death was arteriosclerosis, a hardening of the arteries.

"How good was Willie Anderson?" wrote Robert Sommers in the *USGA Golf Journal.* "Those who played against him and watched the great players of later years said he was as good as anyone who ever played."

## THE ANDERSON RECORD

Major Championship Victories ..... 4
U.S. Open: 1901, 1903, 1904, 1905
Other Significant Victories
Western Open: 1902, 1904, 1908, 1909

OFFICIAL

WORLD GOLF HALL of FAME

# Fred Corcoran

**You won't find his name in any golf record book, but Fred Corcoran was one of golf's pioneers.** In the years following World War II, Corcoran helped found the Ladies Professional Golf Association, the World Cup and Golf Writers Association of America. His ideas helped spawn the World Golf Hall of Fame, and he was one of the sport's first agents, managing the careers of Babe Zaharias, Tony Lema and Sam Snead. But perhaps the biggest imprint Corcoran left on the game was that, for a decade, he guided tournament golf in this country into its Golden Age.

Part idea man, part hustler, part mover-and-shaker, part publicist, all-around good guy, Corcoran was as much a fixture in golf during his heyday than any of the players. He had a sharp mind, a great sense of timing and all the connections. If golf writers wanted an anecdote, a quote or a stat, they went to Corcoran. If tournaments wanted a player, they went to Corcoran. If players wanted representation, they went to Corcoran. For a while, it seemed like he was the center of golf's universe.

Corcoran was nine when he got his first job in golf, caddying at Belmont C.C. near Boston. He advanced to caddy master at age 12 and kept moving up. As a teenager, he served as Belmont's assistant golf secretary for the Massachusetts Golf Association. It was in this role that Corcoran turned tournament scoring into an art form. By using an elaborate, multicolored crayon system, Corcoran was able to keep spectators and the media up to date on the tournament's progress. The United States Golf Association took notice and made Corcoran the official scorer for its events.

From there, Corcoran went to Pinehurst, where he worked as an assistant golf secretary in the office of Donald Ross, the golf course architect. His career took off in 1936, when the PGA of America hired him to replace Bob Harlow as tournament manager of the professional tour. The only problem the PGA had with Harlow was that he was wearing too many hats. With Corcoran, who was then only 28, the stipulation was that he would concentrate solely on running and promoting the tour. He was paid $5,000 a year, plus $5 a day in expense money.

But Corcoran's timing was always incredible. Shortly after he was hired, a young Virginian named Sam Snead won the Oakland Open and became a hot commodity. Tempted by a series of lucrative exhibitions, Snead was ready to skip the Phoenix Open and collect the guaranteed money. Corcoran went to PGA President George Jacobus, who told Corcoran to sign Snead to a manager's contract and advise him to play Phoenix. For the next 40 years, he handled the career of Snead and others, including baseball's Ted Williams and Stan Musial.

As golf's P.T. Barnum, Corcoran sold golf to America. He raised the men's annual purses from $150,000 to $750,000 within 10 years, then moved on. In 1948, he put together the struggling Women's Professional Golf Association with Wilson Sporting Goods, and this led to the formation of the LPGA. Three years later, Corcoran and John Jay Hopkins put together the International Golf Association, which led to an event called the Canada Cup, which later became the World Cup. His inclusion in the World Golf Hall of Fame needs no further explaining. Fred Corcoran was golf.

## THE CORCORAN RECORD

Official Scorer for 34 USGA Championships

Tournament Manager, PGA: 1936-1947

Manager, Ryder Cup Team: 1937, 1939, 1953

Co-Founder, Golf Writers Association of America: 1946

Founder, LPGA: 1948

LPGA Director: 1949-1961

Promotional Director, PGA: 1952-1975

William D. Richardson Award: 1960

UNITED STATES GOLF

WORLD GOLF HALL of FAME

# Joe Dey

**There has been no golf administrator who had a greater influence on the game of golf than Joseph C. Dey Jr.**

His was a 40-year run that brought about sweeping change and was executed in the most dignified manner. Dey served as Executive Director of the United States Golf Association from 1934–1968, and then as Commissioner of the PGA TOUR from 1969-1974. The following year he was named captain of the Royal and Ancient Golf Club of St. Andrews, Scotland, the game's highest honorary position. It is unlikely that anyone else will ever again hold these three positions.

"Joe was a man of great integrity, one who was respected by players, officials and everyone in the game," said Michael Bonallack, Secretary of the Royal and Ancient Golf Club of St. Andrews. "I found you could learn a lot from Joe—not just about golf, but about life."

Dey was the first to popularize the Rules of Golf. He set about expanding interest in and knowledge of the Rules of Golf by producing a series of 8mm films and publications such as Golf Rules in Pictures, and the wallet-sized card referred to as Golf Rules in Brief. He was known as "Mr. Rules of Golf," but this was just the opening paragraph in his list of accomplishments.

It was Dey, Richard Tufts and Isaac Grainger who brought together the USGA with the R&A, unifying the Rules at a conference in Great Britain in 1951. It was Dey who was entrusted with U.S. Open course set-up decisions. These included the feature of changing reachable par-5s into Herculean par-4s, the implementation of gallery ropes at Baltusrol in 1954 and the use of a more sophisticated scoring system. It was also under Dey's administration that five more USGA Championships, including the Women's Open, were added to the schedule, along with the development of its Green Section, the establishment of a velocity regulation to curb ball distance, the move to "Golf House," the building of a USGA Museum and Library, and the foundation of the World Amateur Council.

It was a surprise when he left the USGA at age 61 to head the newly formed Tournament Players Division of the Professional Golfers Association, but Dey felt he had a unique opportunity to create something beneficial to golf. At the time, the tour was in turmoil, having just broken from the PGA of America after a prolonged dispute. It was a public relations nightmare for the touring professionals, but Dey brought the tour respectability and stability. "Joe was one of the few people that both sides would accept," said Jack Tuthill, the tour's former manager and director of tournament operations.

With just $45,000 to work with, Dey steered the ship through the hard times until Deane Beman could take over in 1974, THE PLAYERS Championship was Dey's idea, as was the formation of a secondary tour, now known as the Nationwide Tour, and the mandate that tournament sponsors employ a USGA agronomist to standardize playing conditions.

Born in Norfolk, Va., Nov. 17, 1907, Dey considered entering the ministry before deciding to make golf administration his career. He always carried two books in the pocket of his blue blazer, the Rules of Golf and the New Testament. He lived by the words of both. "In the world of golf," former USGA President William C. Campbell once said, "Joe Dey was the mightiest oak of all."

## THE DEY RECORD

Executive Director, USGA: 1934-1968

Secretary, World Amateur Golf Council: 1958-1969

William D. Richardson Award: 1961

Commissioner, PGA TOUR: 1969-1974

Captain, Royal and Ancient Golf Club of St. Andrews: 1975

Bob Jones Award: 1977

WGA
1899

# Charles 'Chick' Evans

**Charles "Chick" Evans was the first man to win the U.S. Open and the U.S. Amateur in the same year.** Using seven hickory-shafted clubs, Evans led the 1916 Open at Minikahda from start to finish, shooting a record score of 286 that would stand for 20 years. Ten weeks later, at Merion, he won the U.S. Amateur by beating Bob Gardner, the defending champion, in the final. The only other golfer in history to win these two tournaments in the same year was Bobby Jones, who did it in 1930, the year of his Grand Slam.

Gene Sarazen said, "In his day, Chick Evans was a finer iron-player than any of the professionals." Henry Cotton called Evans "undoubtedly the greatest amateur golfer of his generation." And Jones, after losing to Evans in match play, said, "Chick is one of the gamest and best competitive golfers the world ever saw."

Evans also endured despite an ongoing battle with his putting stroke. He competed in every Amateur from 1907 through 1962, winning again in 1920, defeating Francis Ouimet in the final. He was medalist in 1909, advanced to the second round in 1955 against a field that included 15-year-old Jack Nicklaus, was a finalist on three other occasions and holds the record for most matches won (57).

His overall record was just phenomenal: eight Western Amateurs, a Western Open, a North and South, a French Amateur, and a runner-up finish in the 1914 Open, where he lost by a stroke to Walter Hagen.

Yet Evans never felt that his achievements were given their just due. According to historians, he resented Ouimet and Jerome Travers because they were the first two amateurs to win the Open, and later in his career, he fell into the shadow cast by Jones. It was unfortunate because Evans had a 15-year run in which he was as good as any golfer in the world, professional or amateur.

Evans had some peculiar philosophies. "I made a rule never to swing a golf club except to hit a golf ball," he said, "for I had learned that one could swing beautifully when the ball wasn't there, and poorly when it was." He also had his own theory on practice. "Most people seem to consider playing as practice and that is one of the reasons that they never emerge from the heap," he said. "There is a vast difference between practicing golf shots and playing the game of golf."

Evans' legacy involves more than tournament golf. His name is synonymous with the Western Golf Association, and the institution of the Evans Scholars Foundation. This idea was born after Evans won the Open and the Amateur in 1916. Rather than turn professional, Evans decided to take the $5,000 offered to him for making golf instructional phonograph records and establish a golf scholarship fund for caddies. Through funds generated by the Western Open and private donations, more than 219 scholarships were awarded to caddies in 2003 who met the high academic requirements and had a proven need for financial aid. Since 1930, more than 9,000 Evans Scholars Fund recipients had graduated from colleges.

Evans was himself a caddy at Edgewater Golf Club while growing up on Chicago's North Side, and it was that background which helped mold him into one of the game's most popular players. Eventually, his bitterness toward Ouimet, Travers and Jones subsided, and he developed into the type of golfer who joked with people in the gallery, remembered names and faces, and knew how to smile, win or lose.

## THE EVANS RECORD

Major Championship Victories ..... 3
- U.S. Amateur: 1916, 1920
- U.S. Open: 1916
- (Played in 49 U.S. Amateur Championships, winning 57 matches)

Other Significant Victories
- Western Amateur: 8 times
- North and South Amateur: 1911
- French Amateur: 1911

Walker Cup Teams ............... 3
- (3-2-0) .......... 1922, 1924, 1928

Bob Jones Award: 1960

# Young Tom Morris

**Young Tom Morris followed in his father's footsteps, winning four British Open Championships before his tragic death at the age of 24.** With broad shoulders and hands that were both powerful and deft, he dominated the game in the short time he played it. "He was simply too good for the available competition," wrote Ross Goodner in *Golf's Greatest.* That includes his father, Old Tom, whom he succeeded as Open champion in 1868. The following year, Old Tom finished runner-up to his son. It is the only time in major championship history that a son and his father finished first and second.

Young Tom was a prodigy. At age 13, he won an exhibition match in Perth for a first prize of 15 pounds. At 16, Morris won the Open Professional Tournament at Carnoustie against the best golfers in Scotland. At 17, he became the tournament's youngest winner and began his domination of the British Open, winning three consecutive titles to take permanent possession of the Championship Belt in 1870. That was the year he shot 149 over Prestwick's 12-hole course, a score that was 12 strokes better than the competition and unequalled by the Great Triumverate of James Braid, J.H. Taylor and Harry Vardon while the gutta percha ball was in use. His opening round of 47 that year, one-under 4s, included an eagle 3 at the 578-yard first and has been described as the first great round of golf. H.S.C. Everard speculated, "It was probable that Tommy attained a rare pitch of excellence at as early an age as any golfer on record."

The Open wasn't played in 1871, but Morris made it four in a row in 1872, which is a record. That victory also gained Young Tom Morris the distinction of being the first golfer to win the silver claret jug, the permanent trophy for the Open Championship.

Tall, strong and incredibly handsome, Young Tom was to golf in his era what Arnold Palmer became in the later 1950s. It was said he sometimes inadvertently snapped a shaft in two merely by waggling the clubhead, but he also displayed an uncanny finesse around the greens. "Young Tom Morris brought to the game a flamboyance that it had never known," wrote Charles Price in *The World of Golf.*

Like his father, Tom Morris Jr. was idolized not only for the way he played, but the way he competed. In *St. Andrews: Home of Golf,* Young Tom was described as "endearingly modest." Robert Clark, author of *Golf: A Royal and Ancient Game,* wrote about Morris' "amiable temperament...obliging disposition...gentlemanly appearance...manly bearing," and "undaunted determination." Today, he would be described as having the total package. "Golfers may come and golfers may go, but it is very much open to doubt whether any golfers will be quite the idol of the day as Young Tom was during his brilliant career," wrote Harold Hutchinson in *The Book of Golf and Golfers*.

His life came to an end in 1875. Playing an exhibition match with his father in North Berwick against Willie and Mungo Park, Morris received a telegram that his wife of a year and son had both died during childbirth. It was a mournful party that made the voyage across the Firth of Forth to St. Andrews, and Morris never recovered from the shock of his loss. He died three months later, on Christmas Eve, of what had been described as a broken heart. His memory is perpetuated by a plaque in St. Andrews Cathedral which bears the inscription, "Deeply regretted by numerous friends and all golfers, he thrice in succession won the championship belt and held it without rivalry and yet without envy, his many amiable golfing qualities being no less acknowledged than his golfing achievements."

### THE YOUNG TOM MORRIS RECORD

**Major Championship Victories ..... 4**

**British Open: 1868, 1869, 1870, 1872**

**In his victory in 1868, he was the first to record a hole-in-one in a major championship.**

# J. H. Taylor

**It was the legendary Scotsman, Andrew Kirkaldy, who first saw the greatness in John Henry Taylor.** After losing a challenge match to Taylor in 1891, Kirkaldy went back to St. Andrews and predicted that the young Englishman who just defeated him would win many Open Championships. "You'll see more of Taylor," he said. "And then you'll know why he beat me, and why he will beat all the best of the day."

Kirkaldy proved to be right, of course. Three years after defeating Kirkaldy, he became the first Englishman to win the Open. Taylor captured five British Opens, joining Harry Vardon and James Braid to form the Great Triumvirate.

Taylor's accuracy was legendary. At Sandwich, where he won his first Open by five strokes in 1894, he would have the directional posts removed from the blind holes out of fear that his drives would hit them and carom into bunkers. The following year, he won by four strokes over Sandy Herd at St. Andrews, with Kirkaldy six shots further back in third place.

"The mon's a machine," Kirkaldy said. "He can dae naething wrang."

Vardon and amateur Harold Hilton came along to dominate the Open from 1896-99, but Taylor returned to form in 1900 at St. Andrews. Pulling away from the field after every round, he won by eight strokes over Vardon, with Braid 13 back in third place. Later in the year, he finished second to Vardon in the U.S. Open at Chicago Golf Club.

Taylor won the British Open twice more, both times in convincing manner, in 1909 over Braid at Deal and in 1913 over Ted Ray at Hoylake. The latter tied Taylor with Braid and Vardon with five Open victories and was considered his most satisfying win since it came in horrendous conditions. In heavy wind and rain, Taylor pulled his cap down over his eyes, stuck out his chin, and anchored his large boots to the ground to maximize control over his compact swing. Nineteen years after his first Open victory, Taylor shot 304 to win by eight strokes over Ray, the defending champion.

Taylor took the game seriously, and once wrote: "To try to play golf really well is far from being a joke, and lightheartedness of endeavor is a sure sign of eventual failure." Bernard Darwin, who was a close friend, recalled that nobody, not even Bobby Jones, suffered more over championships than Taylor did. "Like Bobby," said Darwin, "(Taylor) had great control and might appear outwardly cool, but the flames leaped up from within."

Taylor was competitive for many years, finishing fourth at the age of 53 in the 1924 British Open at Hoylake. Most of his later life was dedicated to writing books, making clubs, designing courses and forming the British PGA, the Artisan Golfers Association and the Public Golf Courses Association. As a young boy, he left school early to caddy and work as a gardener's assistant, a mason's laborer and a greenkeeper. But he educated himself by reading Dickens and Boswell and was able to author *Golf, My Life's Work,* without a ghostwriter. He took great pride in having grown up an Englishman, on the links of Westward Ho! rather than the links of St. Andrews or East Lothian in Scotland.

Taylor's final years were spent in his native village of Northam overlooking Westward Ho!, enjoying the view he called "the finest in Christendom." His death in 1963 just short of his 92nd birthday marked the passing of the last of the great golfers from the 19th century.

## THE TAYLOR RECORD

Major Championship Victories ..... 5
- British Open: 1894, 1895, 1900, 1909, 1913

Other Significant Victories
- British Match Play: 1904, 1908
- French Open: 1908, 1909
- German Open: 1912

Ryder Cup (Non-Playing Captain): 1933

FRANK C.
BENSING

# Glenna Collett Vare

**Glenna Collett Vare was known as the female Bobby Jones. She was the greatest female golfer of her day, but equally important as the number of times she won was the way she won.** As Jones once wrote, "Aside from her skill with her clubs, Miss Collett typified all that the word 'sportsmanship' stands for." Renowned as the "Queen of American Golf," Vare won a record six U.S. Women's Amateur Championships, two Canadian Women's Amateurs and a French Women's Amateur in an era when there was no Ladies Professional Golf Association Tour. She did it with style and dignity, raising the awareness of women's golf in this country that didn't know the sport existed. "Glenna was the first woman," said former USGA President Richard Tufts, "to attack the hole rather than just to play to the green."

In 1924, Collett won 59 out of 60 matches, losing only on the 19th hole of the semifinal of the Women's Amateur when Mary K. Browne's ball caromed off hers and into the cup. Joyce Wethered of Great Britain was Collett Vare's only equal, and even she admitted that when Glenna was on her game, nobody could touch her. "If she is finding her true form, then there is little hope, except by miracle, of surviving," Wethered wrote in her book, *Golfing Memories and Methods.* It was Wethered, however, who handed Collett her most disappointing loss, coming back from five down after 11 holes to win the 1929 Ladies' British Amateur Championship. "Her charm to my mind as a golfer and a companion lies in a freedom of spirit which does not make her feel that success is everything in the world," said Wethered.

## THE VARE RECORD

Major Championship victories ..... 6
U.S. Women's Amateur: 1922, 1925, 1928, 1929, 1930, 1935

Other Significant Victories
Canadian Amateur: 1923, 1924
French Amateur: 1925
Eastern Women's Championship: 7 times
North and South Amateur: 6 times

Curtis Cup Teams ................ 6
(4-2-1) .......... 1932, 1934, 1936, 1938, 1948, 1950
Captain ............... 1934, 1936

Bob Jones Award: 1965

What made Collett Vare such a dominant player was the prodigious length she hit the ball. One of her drives was measured at 307 yards, and she used this strength to overpower the competition. She won and qualified with scores that were 10 strokes lower than women had been scoring previous to World War I. Enid Wilson, who played against Collett Vare in the Curtis Cup, marveled how Glenna could hit the ball harder than any woman in America had done before. "Her vigorous game set up an entirely fresh standard for her countrywomen, and the young up-and-coming golfers in the 1930s were inspired by her example," said Wilson.

Born in New Haven, Conn., June 20, 1903, and raised in Providence, R.I., Collett didn't start playing golf until she was 14. Taught by former British Open champion Alex Smith at the Metacomet Club, she won the Amateur for the first time at age 19. Her final U.S. Women's Amateur victory came as Mrs. Edwin H. Vare Jr., when she was a 32-year-old mother of two against 17-year-old Patty Berg. Although the LPGA gives its Vare Trophy to the player with the low stroke average on its tour, most of Vare's victories came in match play. She won the North and South six times, the Eastern Amateur seven times and was 4-2-1 as a player and player-captain in the Curtis Cup, an event she helped originate.

"To make oneself a successful match-player, there are certain qualities to be sought after, certain ideas must be kept in mind, and certain phases of one's attitude towards the game that come in for special notice," Collett Vare once said. "The three I have taken are these: love of combat, serenity of mind and fearlessness."

WORLD GOLF HALL of FAME

# Joyce Wethered

**She combined feminine grace with the type of precision no golfer of her era was able to achieve.** She amazed Henry Cotton with her ball-striking, and Glenna Collett Vare with her tenacity. Joyce Wethered, who later went by the more proper married name of Lady Heathcoat-Armory, was revered as the queen of British amateur golf. Bob Jones considered her to be the best golfer, man or woman, he had seen.

Wethered won the British Women's Amateur Championship four times, the English Ladies' Championship five times in a row, and was a leading force in the founding of the Curtis Cup.

Jones had the opportunity to play with Wethered from the back tees before the British Amateur in 1930. With a breeze blowing off the sea, Wethered did not miss a shot, half heartedly three-putted the 17th from 12 feet after the match was over and went around the Old Course in 75. It was as clean a round of golf as Jones had ever seen.

"I have not played golf with anyone, man or woman, amateur or professional, who made me feel so utterly outclassed," said Jones. "It was not so much the score she made as the way she made it. It was impossible to expect that Miss Wethered would ever miss a shot— and she never did."

Cotton played in an exhibition with Wethered after she married Sir John Heathcoat-Armory in 1937. She hit the ball 240 yards off the tee and could play low-flying shots with the mashie that exhibited brilliant touch. Some felt that at her best Wethered could play No. 4 or No. 5 on the British Walker Cup team, and Cotton agreed. "In my time, no golfer has stood out so far ahead of his or her contemporaries as Lady Heathcoat-Armory," said Cotton. "I do not think a golf ball has ever been hit, except perhaps by Harry Vardon, with such a straight flight by any other person."

Wethered established her reputation in this country by twice thwarting the efforts of Collett in the British Ladies' Amateur. Their first match occurred at Troon in 1925, just after Vare had won her second U.S. Women's Amateur and the French Open Championship. "The match anticipated between her and myself was worked up to such a pitch beforehand that, when the day came, one of two things was almost bound to happen. Either we should rise to the occasion or one of us would fall under the strain of it."

It was Wethered who rose—making four birdies in 15 holes—and Collett who fell, by a score of 4 and 3. Wethered went on to defeat Cecil Leitch in the final for her third British Women's Amateur title. Four years later, Wethered and Collett met again in the final at St. Andrews. Wethered was coming out of a three-year retirement, but Collett was coming off her fourth of five U.S. Women's Amateur titles. With an outward nine of 34, Collett went 5 up. At the 12th, she had a 3-footer to go 6 up and missed. Slowly the holes began to come back, and at the lunch break, Collett was only 2 up. Bernard Darwin wrote that the general impression of the British people was, "It's all right now. You'll see. Joyce will win comfortably."

The 3 and 1 defeat of Collett indicates that Wethered did, indeed, win comfortably. They met again in the inaugural Curtis Cup, with the police clearing the road home for the two heroines, and Wethered returned home to England, where the only competition she played was the Worplesdon mixed foursomes, an event she won eight times with seven different partners.

## THE WETHERED RECORD

Major Championship Victories ..... 4
British Women's Amateur: 1922, 1924, 1925, 1929

Other Significant Victories
English Ladies' Championship: 1920, 1921, 1922, 1923, 1924

Curtis Cup Teams ................ 1
(1-1-0) .................... 1932
Captain: 1932

# Tommy Armour

**Tommy Armour was the third of only nine golfers in history to win the U.S. Open, the British Open and the PGA Championship. The Silver Scot followed Walter Hagen and Jim Barnes, and preceded Gene Sarazen, Ben Hogan, Jack Nicklaus, Gary Player, Lee Trevino and Tiger Woods, finishing his career just a Masters victory short of achieving the career Grand Slam.** While not achieving the ultimate measure of golfing greatness, Armour did, however, win the Western Open, an event then regarded as a major championship, as well as three Canadian Opens and 24 other events in the United States. The Scotsman was considered a closer who played his best golf on the toughest golf courses. Known as an exceptional striker of the ball, and one of the finest wood-club players of all time, Armour played the game with a conservative philosophy: "It is not solely the capacity to make great shots that makes champions, but the essential quality of making very few bad shots."

In 1927, Armour won the first U.S. Open played at Oakmont by finishing with five pars and a birdie, then defeating Harry Cooper in an 18-hole playoff. His next major championship victory came in the 1930 PGA at Fresh Meadow on Long Island. Armour lost five of the first six holes against Johnny Farrell in the quarterfinal, but came back to win, 2 and 1. His opponent in the final was Sarazen, who was playing on his home course. All square going to the 36th hole, Armour won with a par. The following year, he won the first British Open played at Carnoustie, shooting 71 in the final round. It was considered Armour's finest moment, since the victory was recorded close to his birthplace in Edinburgh.

Bernard Darwin was most impressed with Armour's ability to strike a golf ball. "I do not believe that (J.H.) Taylor or (Harry) Vardon at their best ever gave themselves so many possible putts for three with their iron shots as he does," Darwin once wrote. "His style is the perfection of rhythm and beauty."

In *The Story of American Golf*, Herbert Warren Wind described Armour's uncanny ability to finish out a tournament: "Whenever the Silver Scot played himself into a contending position, he always seemed to have that extra something that was the difference between barely losing and barely winning. He was singularly unaffected by the pressure of the last stretch. His hands were hot but his head was cool."

After he retired from competitive golf, Armour became one of the most successful instructors and golf club designers in the world. Based at Winged Foot in the summer and the Boca Raton Hotel in the winter, Armour taught both duffers and the world's best golfers, using the same philosophies and techniques that were part of his best-selling book, *How to Play Your Best Golf All the Time.* Julius Boros called him a genius at teaching you how to play your best golf. Lawson Little claimed that Armour was responsible for whatever success he had in golf.

The great golf writer, Charles Price, described Armour as having "a dash of indifference, a touch of class, (and) a bit of majesty." In *Golf's Greatest*, Ross Goodner wrote that "Nothing was ever small about Tommy Armour's reputation. At one time or another, he was known as the greatest iron player, the greatest raconteur, the greatest drinker and the greatest and most expensive teacher in golf." Some called him dour and temperamental, yet Bobby Cruickshank, claiming to know Armour for 60 years, said, "He was the kindest, best-hearted fellow you ever saw."

Certainly, Tommy Armour was a complex man and misunderstood, but he seemed to like it that way.

## THE ARMOUR RECORD

Major Championship Victories ..... 3
- U.S. Open: 1927
- British Open: 1931
- PGA: 1930

Other Significant Victories
- Canadian Open: 1927, 1930, 1934
- Western Open: 1929

PGA TOUR Victories ........... 25

WORLD GOLF HALL of FAME

# James Braid

**He swung with a divine fury and putted like a demon.** Without him, there would not have been a Great Triumverate. But James Braid's contributions to golf are not just based on his five British Open victories and his place in history next to Harry Vardon and J.H. Taylor. He was a man of great character, who was a friend of princes, peers and commoners. He also left behind one of the world's great golf courses and was a pioneer in elevating the status of professional golfers by helping to form the British PGA.

As a golfer, Braid was considered to be a late bloomer. He did not win his first British Open Championship, in 1901, until Vardon and Taylor had already won three each. But once Braid won his first, there was no stopping him: He captured the Open again in 1905, 1906, 1908 and 1910, thus becoming the first man to raise the old claret jug five times.

The difference between Braid's winning and just finishing among the contenders at the Open was an aluminum-headed putter made by Mills of Sunderland that came into his possession after the 1900 Open at St. Andrews. He had finished sixth in 1896, second in 1897, fifth in 1899 and third in 1900. Once the putts began to fall, Braid began to rise ahead of Vardon and Taylor. In fact, it was Taylor who said, "I have yet to meet the player who could hole the 10-yard putts with greater regularity" than Braid.

And when Braid won, he won by large margins. At Muirfield in 1901, he began with a drive out of bounds at the first hole, but from there on he played superb golf to defeat Vardon by three strokes and Taylor by four. At St. Andrews in 1905, he sailed to a five-stroke victory over Taylor. At Muirfield in 1906, he triumphed by four strokes over Taylor. His greatest performance came at Prestwick in 1908 when he shot the Open record of 291 to win by eight strokes over Tom Ball. That record stood until Bob Jones broke it by six strokes at St. Andrews in 1927. Braid finished runner-up to Taylor in 1909, but came back the next year at St. Andrews to win his fourth Open in six years, this time by four strokes over Alexander Herd.

In 1904, he was also the first player in an Open to break 70, shooting 69 in the third round at Royal St. George's.

Born in Fife, Scotland, in 1870, Braid grew up in humble circumstances. His father worked behind a plow in the farming town about 15 miles south of St. Andrews called Earlsferry, and did not play golf or promote his son's interest in the sport. Braid left school at 13 to become an apprentice joiner, sneaking in rounds of golf on his travels. Three years later he was a scratch player, and at 23 he moved to London and became a clubmaker, working at the Army and Navy Stores for eight pence an hour. His golf came after work and on Sunday. Eight years later, he began his remarkable string of British Open victories.

In his later years, Braid remained competitive. After World War I, he was still good enough to play in the first Britain vs. America matches, and in 1927, at the age of 57, fought his way into the final of the British Match Play Championship. At that point in his life, Braid was playing most of his golf at Walton Heath, where he served as head professional for 45 years. He also enjoyed a successful career as a golf course architect, designing such lasting treasures as Carnoustie and the King's and Queen's courses at Gleneagles. James Braid died in London in 1950.

## THE BRAID RECORD

**Major Tournament Victories ...... 5**

**British Open: 1901, 1905, 1906, 1908, 1910**

**Other Significant Victories**

**British Professional Match Play: 1903, 1905, 1907, 1911**

**French Open: 1910**

WORLD GOLF HALL of FAME

# Old Tom Morris

**Old Tom Morris didn't invent the game of golf, but he is recognized as the sport's founding father.** He played in the first 36 British Opens, winning four times, and sired a son, Tom Morris Jr., who won the world's oldest golf championship four times on his own. But as much as his successes in tournament golf and as a parent are significant, Tom Morris Sr. left behind the legacy of being a champion among men.

The authors of the day came to respect him for the way he handled victory as well as defeat; and there was no greater loss than when Tom Morris Jr., mourning the death of his wife and child, died at the age of 24. Horace Hutchinson wrote about Morris' "unruffled serenity of temper." John L. Low described the way Morris was "always cheerful during a life which met with almost continual disappointments and sorrows." Yet, according to Hutchinson and Low, what separated Old Tom was his humbleness and the way he addressed himself to men of all classes.

In *The Book of Golf and Golfers*, Hutchinson described him as "One of the most remarkable men — best of men and best of golfers — that ever missed a short putt." Hutchison concluded that Morris "has been written of as often as a Prime Minister, he has been photographed as often as professional beauty, and yet he remains, through all the advertisement, exactly the same, simple and kindly."

Born in St. Andrews, Scotland, June 16, 1820, Morris spent 12 years as a golf-ball maker under Allan Robertson before moving to Prestwick, where he became custodian of the newly formed club that, in 1860, gave birth to the British Open. He finished second to Willie Park in the first Open Championship, won the next two, finished second to Park again in 1863, then won again in 1864 and 1867. He had a slow, smooth swing and was fiercely competitive; his only flaw was a difficulty with short putts. In 1862, he didn't miss many, winning the Open by 13 strokes, a record that still stands.

Morris moved back to St. Andrews in 1865 to become greenkeeper for the Royal and Ancient Golf Club. It was a position he held until his retirement in 1904. Today, his portrait hangs in the R&A Clubhouse and the 18th green of the Old Course is named in his memory. He is revered today not only as a golfer, but as a course designer — he had a hand in Prestwick, Royal Dornoch, Muirfield and Carnoustie, among other great Scottish courses — and statesmen. It was the way Old Tom Morris carried himself that defined the sport as a gentleman's game.

"As St. Andrews became increasingly a mecca of golfers, so, too, did the sturdy patriarchal figure and bearing of Old Tom come to symbolize all that was finest in the Scottish character and in the ancient Scottish game," wrote James K. Robertson in *St. Andrews, Home of Golf.* "His kindly, yet capable and gentle nature, enshrined him a good many years before his death as the authentic Grand Old Man of Golf. To generations of people all over the world his name and his picture epitomized the game."

When Morris died, in 1908 at the age of 87, the funeral procession extended the entire length of South Street in St. Andrews, from the port to the cathedral. It was described by Andrew Kirkaldy as "a cloud of people," and as Kirkaldy noted, "There were many wet eyes among us, for Old Tom was beloved by everybody."

## THE MORRIS SR. RECORD

Major Championship Victories ..... 4
British Open: 1861, 1862, 1864, 1867

Greenkeeper at St. Andrews: 1865-1904

Golf course architecture:
He designed or remodeled 75 courses.

# Jerome D. Travers

**Some of the words used to describe Jerry Travers have not been kind—cold, somber, ruthless—yet these were the qualities that made him the most feared golfer of his time.** In a nine-year stretch from 1906-1915, Travers won four U.S. Amateurs, five Metropolitan Amateurs and a U.S. Open. Only Bob Jones won more amateur titles and Travers was one of only five amateurs to win the Open. And his battles with Walter Travis, in the words of Herbert Warren Wind, "formed the crucible in which a talented young golfer was made into the greatest match player of his decade."

Yet, in assessing his career, the words unfulfilled and disappointing have been used, too. The truth is, Jerry Travers never became a true hero of American golf, and his accomplishments are the least remembered among history's greats. Why? For the same reasons that Travers was so successful, and also because his run of greatness concluded so abruptly. Although he lived to 63, Travers' championship career came to an end at age 28. In the midst of his heyday, he twice didn't bother to enter the Amateur. And he never entered the Open again after winning in 1915.

Bizarre? Peculiar? Indeed. Jerry Travers had a reputation for being undisciplined off the golf course and lacking a steadying influence in his life. He also seemed to thrive on being hard to read. "He was anything but an outgoing person," Jess Sweetser recalls. "He was totally lacking in what today is called charisma."

Among his peers, however, Travers earned ultimate, almost intimidating respect. Chick Evans called him "the coldest, hardest golfer I ever knew." Francis Ouimet described him as "the best match player in the country." Alex Smith, the National Open champion who taught Travers, called his student, "the greatest competitor I have ever known."

At only 5-feet-7 and 140 pounds, Travers had to be tough to survive.

One on one, he was so absorbed in his work and the shot at hand that it was impossible to read his emotions. "I could always tell whether a golfer was winning or losing by looking at him," said Smith. "But I never knew how Travers stood."

Neither, sometimes, did Travers. Francis Ouimet recalled the time he beat Travers in the 1914 Amateur, 6 and 5, in the third round: "I waited for Jerry to do the customary handshaking act, but to my surprise he walked to his caddy, selected a driver and hastened to the next tee. The referee then hustled over to Travers and asked him if he intended to play the bye holes. 'Why?' asked Travers. 'Is the match over?' I was somewhat embarrassed as Jerry apologized for his error and his congratulations were as warm as they could possibly be."

What also made Travers so great was his ability to putt the ball. Harold Hilton, who defeated Travers on his way to the Amateur title at Apawamis in 1911, called him, "The greatest putter I ever saw." Travers believed that putting was more a combination of the mental and physical than any stroke in the game, and he worked for hours perfecting his method.

What, then, went wrong? It is theorized that a combination of burnout and lifestyle led to the disappearance of Jerry Travers, and although he returned for exhibitions, and later as a teaching professional, he was clearly not the Jerry Travers who relentlessly once dominated the world of amateur golf.

### THE TRAVERS RECORD

**Major Championship Victories . . . . . 5**
- U.S. Amateur: 1907, 1908, 1912, 1913
- U.S. Open: 1915

**Other Significant Victories**
- New Jersey Amateur: 5 times
- Metropolitan (New York) Amateur: 5 times

# Mickey Wright

**Ben Hogan described her swing as the best he ever saw.** So did Byron Nelson. For 14 years, she dominated women's golf, winning 82 tournaments and carrying the Ladies Professional Golf Association Tour on her shoulders. Mickey Wright was not burdened by potential–potential, in her words, was but a hope to be fulfilled. What made her retire, at age 34, was the burden of being Mickey Wright.

"The pressure was so great," remembers Kathy Whitworth. "Sponsors threatened to cancel their tournaments if she didn't play. And, knowing that if they canceled, the rest of us wouldn't be able to play, Mickey would always play."

The buzzword today is burnout. Wright played 33 tournaments in 1962, another 30 in 1963 and 27 in 1964. She won 10, 13 and 11 tournaments in those years, and as the LPGA's president, it was Wright's duty to promote the tour by doing every conceivable interview and attending every press conference that was scheduled. That just wasn't her. "I'm not real good as far as wanting to be in front of people, glorying in it and loving it," Wright has said. "I think you have to love that to make that kind of pressure tolerable. It finally got to where it wasn't tolerable to me."

It had also reached the point where there wasn't much left to accomplish. Wright won the U.S. Women's Open and the LPGA Championship four times each. She won the Vare Trophy five times, was the leading money winner four times, twice had winning streaks of four straight tournaments and held LPGA records for lowest round (62), lowest nine-hole score (30) and most birdies in a round (nine). At the peak of her career, Herbert Warren Wind described her as "a tall, good-looking girl who struck the ball with the same decisive hand action that the best men players use, she fused her hitting action smoothly with the rest of her swing, which was like Hogan's in that all the unfunctional moves had been pared away, and like Jones' in that its cohesive timing disguised the effort that went into it."

Citing an adverse reaction to sunlight, an aversion to flying and foot problems, Wright cut back her schedule dramatically after the 1969 season to lead a quieter, simpler life, in Port St. Lucie, Fla. Although she came back in 1973 to win the Dinah Shore, Wright knew that she had fulfilled her potential and elected to bow out on her terms. "I maintain that she could have won 100 tournaments if she hadn't quit early," says Whitworth, who won 88.

Born Feb. 14, 1935, in San Diego, Wright began to hit balls with her father at age 4. At the age of 11 she received her first lesson at La Jolla CC, and within a year had broken 100. Three years later, she posted a round of 70 in a local tournament and, in 1952, Wright won the USGA Girls' Junior championship for her first national title.

For a year, Wright studied psychology at Stanford, but she left school after her freshman year to play a full-time schedule. In the summer of 1954, she lost in the final of the U.S. Women's Amateur, finished fourth in the Women's Open to Babe Zaharias and won the World Amateur staged by golf promoter George S. May. Those three tournaments convinced Wright to leave school and turn professional.

"Golf has brought me more rewards, financially and personally, than I ever could have earned had I become the psychology teacher I set out to be," Wright said later in life. "I feel as if I've earned my own version of a master's degree in psychology in study and experience, trial and error, on golf courses throughout the United States. For psychology...is as integral a part of good golf as an efficient swing."

## THE WRIGHT RECORD

Major Championship Victories .... 13
- U.S. Open: 1958, 1959, 1961, 1964
- LPGA: 1958, 1960, 1961, 1963
- Titleholders: 1961, 1962
- Western Open: 1962, 1963, 1966

Other Significant Victories
- U.S. Girls' Junior: 1952
- World Amateur: 1954

LPGA Tour Victories ............ 82

Vare Trophy: 1960, 1961, 1962, 1963, 1964

Leading Money Winner: 1961, 1962, 1963, 1964

Associated Press Female Athlete of the Year: 1963, 1964

# Bobby Locke

**Under the category of great putters in golf history, Arthur D'Arcy (Bobby) Locke is certainly at the top of the list—and there are those in a contingent, led by Gary Player, who would argue that the South African was the best of all time.** Locke won four British Opens in a span of eight years and dominated when he did play the PGA TOUR, earning him the distinction as the first great non-British, non-American golfer. He did it, though, by more than just the flat blade.

Locke was described as having a bizarre personality and an unorthodox style. After World War II, he dressed almost exclusively in grey flannel knickers, white buckskin shoes, linen dress shirts with neckties, and white Hogan caps. He played the ukulele and had a reputation for being one of the game's great partiers. On the golf course, he moved at a maddeningly slow pace. Large gaps would open in front of him, his playing partners would grow red-necked in anger, officials would threaten penalties, but Locke was unyielding. He never lost his temper or expressed annoyance and was described as cool, shrewd and imperturbable. The American pros nicknamed him "Muffin Face" because of his changeless expression.

Visually, Locke's golf swing was no work of art. He learned by reading Bobby Jones' instruction books, adapting a wristy inside-out move that consistently produced a hard right-to-left draw. What was so amazing about Locke's shot pattern was its consistency. He rarely missed a green, and when he did, he had the short game and the disposition to save par. This was an adaptation of Jones' philosophy that the real secret of success in golf was turning three shots into two.

Using an old rusty-headed putter with a hickory shaft, Locke would even hook his putts. He'd address the ball at the toe and stroke out at it, imparting topspin which resulted in true, end-over-end rotation. He believed in dying the ball in the hole, using the front and the two sides of the cup. "Very early in my career I realized that putting was half the game of golf," Locke said. "No matter how well I might play the long shots, if I couldn't putt, I would never win."

In this country, Locke was nearly unbeatable. In one 32-month span, he played in 59 tournaments, winning 11, finishing second 10 times, third eight times and fourth five times. This led to bad blood among the Americans he was beating, and in 1949, after winning his first British Open, Locke remained in Great Britain to play a series of exhibitions and autumn events. This led to the PGA of America barring Locke because he had committed to play in selected tournaments on the United States tour.

Although the ban was lifted, Locke never again felt welcome and played most of his golf in Europe. He won the Open again in 1950, 1952 and in 1957, to break Peter Thomson's streak of three Open Championships in a row. Two years later, he was involved in a bad roadside accident in South Africa, and it undoubtedly meant he would never be the same golfer again. Bobby Locke died in 1987 at the age of 69 in Johannesburg, South Africa.

## THE LOCKE RECORD

Major Championship Victories ..... 4
- British Open: 1949, 1950, 1952, 1957

PGA TOUR Victories ........... 15

European Tour Victories ......... 23

South African Tour Victories ..... 38

Other Significant Victories
- South African Amateur: 1935, 1937
- South African Open: 1935, 1937, 1938, 1939, 1940, 1946, 1950, 1951, 1955
- Irish Open: 1938
- New Zealand Open: 1938
- Dunlop Masters: 1950, 1954
- Egyptian Open: 1954
- Swiss Open: 1954

# John Ball

**John Ball dominated amateur golf in Great Britain the way Bob Jones did in the United States.** He won eight British Amateur championships, a British Open and the hearts and respect of his country. In the words of British golf historian Donald Steele, "No golfer ever came to be more of a legend in his own lifetime." He was the first amateur golfer in England to be named by the Royal Empire as an Immortal.

In 1878, at the age of 17, Ball finished fifth in the British Open at Prestwick. His run of Amateur titles began in 1888 and stretched until 1912, when he was 51 years old. His best year was 1890, when he won both the British Amateur and Open Championships. Jones, who won the Grand Slam in 1930, is the only other golfer in history to win those two tournaments in the same year.

Although he gripped the club tightly in the palms of both hands, Ball's swing was the most graceful and stylish of his era. Bernard Darwin wrote, "I have derived greater aesthetic and emotional pleasure from watching John Ball than from any other spectacle in the game."

Ball learned the game competing against Harold Hilton on the links at Hoylake. In 1876, at the age of 15, he competed in his first British Open and finished sixth at St. Andrews. Nine years later, he competed in his first British Amateur, but it wasn't until 1887 that Ball reached the final and lost to Horace Hutchinson. He won his first Amateur title the next year, defeating J.E. Findlay at Prestwick, 5 and 4.

In 1892, Ball defeated Hilton in the final of the British Amateur at Sandwich, but finished runner-up to Hilton in the Open Championship at Muirfield. He would not get as close again in the Open, but continued to play competitive golf at a high standard into his later years. At age 60 he reached the sixth round of the British Amateur. In 1927, at the age of 66, Ball attempted to win his 100th British Amateur match, but was defeated in the second round and came up one victory shy of the milestone. It wasn't long afterward that Ball retired to a farm in North Wales, where he died in 1940.

Ball was famous for refusing to carry a niblick, which had the loft of a modern day 8- or 9-iron. He scorned the use of that club, describing it as "another bloody spade," and admonished the Rules of Golf Committee of the Royal and Ancient for permitting such horrid-looking contraptions to be allowed in competition. In a bunker, Ball would simply lay open the blade of a mid-iron and float the ball toward the hole with a smooth swing.

It was this stubbornness and dogged determination that made Ball such a lion in match play. Darwin once noted that Ball had "a strong vein of hostility and if he wanted a particular player's blood, he would fight his way through a tournament with the sole object of getting at him." Darwin added, "That was not a personal hostility, but rather a desire to measure himself against a foe really worthy of him."

Words from Ball are hard to find. He was a shy man who went about his business without wasted motion. In his book, *Sixty Years of Golf*, Robert Harris wrote that "John's soft, whispering voice, his stoicism, his pawky jibs at easy rules and innovations, his relentless criticism of moderns with their fuss, and his total outlook on the game, were the very essence of golf."

## THE BALL RECORD

Major Championship Victories . . . . . 9

British Amateur: 1888, 1890, 1892, 1894, 1899, 1907, 1910, 1912

British Open: 1890

# Herb Graffis

**Herb Graffis didn't miss much when he sat down at his typewriter.** He was part of a generation of great golf writers that included Grantland Rice, Bernard Darwin, Ring Lardner, Henry Longhurst, Herbert Warren Wind and Charles Price, yet his greatest contributions to the game came not from what he wrote, but through the conception of his ideas.

Along with his brother, Joe, Graffis founded the *Chicago Golfer* in 1923, *Golfdom* in 1927 and then a national monthly, *Golfing*, in 1933. They founded the National Golf Foundation, the Golf Course Superintendents Association and the Club Managers Association, and published the first U.S. Open program in 1928 at Olympia Fields.

It was Graffis who believed that golf was a business as well as a game. *Golfdom*, for example, was a magazine with a controlled circulation that was sent to the president, green chairman, professional, greenkeeper and course manager at each club. *Golfing* was created, in Graffis' words, "because the manufacturers couldn't afford to spend much on ad space in the (*Saturday Evening*) *Post* or *Colliers*, but they wanted to do something that would get in the hands of a select list of golfers." *Golfing* was published five times a year and sent out free. The Graffis philosophy was that "the most important guy was the one reading it, not the guy who was being written about."

In 1936, the Graffis brothers nearly went bankrupt forming the National Golf Foundation as a means of helping promote the growth of the game. It was the NGF's mission to research and publish authoritative information on the game which could be used by investors developing the game of golf.

Graffis also collaborated with Tommy Armour on three best-selling instruction books: *How to Play Your Best Golf All The Time*, *A Round of Golf With Tommy Armour* and *Tommy Armour's ABCs of Golf*. His opus was a book on the history of the PGA of America, published in 1975.

The PGA made him president of National Golf Day and a member of its Advisory Board and Public Relations Committee. The United States Golf Association asked Graffis to serve on its Green Section and Museum committees.

The Graffis resume also included presidencies of the Chicago Press Club, the Headline Club of Chicago, the Indiana Club of Chicago, the Illinois Senior Golf Association and the Golf Writers Association of America, which he cofounded.

For his contributions to golf, Herb Graffis was voted into the World Golf Hall of Fame under the category of "Distinguished Service." Of this honor, the self-effacing Graffis said, "I was voted in by guys who were kind enough to forget that distinguished service means that you had better damn well do, or go broke."

The tributes poured in when Graffis died in 1989 at the age of 95 in Fort Myers, Fla. "He was a friend to all of us," said Ben Hogan. "All of us will miss him. He sure was good for golf," said Sam Snead. Arnold Palmer, who grew up reading *The Greenskeeper Reporter* with his father in Latrobe, Pa., called Graffis "a humorous man, a great guy, a good friend." *The Fort Myers News Press* called Graffis "a giant in the world of golf, a writer about golf, a larger-than-life man known and admired by the game's royalty, its courtiers and its spear-carriers."

But perhaps it was Dr. Joseph F. Beditz, President and CEO of the NGF, who summed up Herb Graffis best. "Herb Graffis' contributions to golf cannot be measured," said Beditz. "No one who ever met Herb will ever forget him. His writing on golf is legendary; his efforts to promote the game and his love for golf will stand as a testimonial for future generations. Only death has silenced one of the great voices of our game."

## THE GRAFFIS RECORD

Golf Columnist, *Chicago Sun Times*

Founder, National Golf Foundation

Founder, *Golfdom* Magazine: 1919

Founder, *Golfing* Magazine: 1933

Author, *History of the PGA*
and 3 books with Tommy Armour

President and Cofounder, Golf Writers Association of America: 1951- 1952

# Donald Ross

**Mention the name Donald Ross to an educated golfer and it will surely bring good thoughts to mind.** That is because Ross, in the words of Jack Nicklaus, designed golf courses that led to positive thinking. "His stamp as an architect was naturalness," Nicklaus said. He was, and still is, considered the Michelangelo of golf.

The Ross name is on some of this nation's most memorable, and playable, courses. His most famous designs are Pinehurst No. 2, Seminole, Oak Hill and Oakland Hills, but Ross was a man of both quality and quantity. He is credited with 600 designs and redesigns, although some were during his "mail order" era when the demand for his work was so high that he would route courses for property he never saw. Ross would take the topographical maps brought to him, lay out a course on the top, and the club's greenkeeper or engineer would oversee the construction. Ross did oversee work on a good percentage of the courses which bear his name.

Ross was born in Dornoch, Scotland, educated in golf at St. Andrews under Old Tom Morris and brought to this country in 1899 by a Harvard professor, Robert Wilson. Investing his entire life's savings into the trip to America, Ross walked off the boat in Boston with only $2 in his pocket, but a job was waiting for him, thanks to Wilson, at Oakley Country Club in Watertown, Mass. The following summer he was brought to North Carolina by James Tufts, the man who founded Pinehurst, as the club's professional. Although he had no experience as a golf course architect, Ross was commissioned by Tufts to design Pinehurst's first four courses and his career skyrocketed to the point where he became one of golf's cult heroes.

Alternating between Boston in the summer and Pinehurst during the winter, Ross won three North and South Opens, two Massachusetts Opens and finished fifth in the 1903 U.S. Open as well as eighth in the 1910 British Open. It was a notable record, but Ross' younger brother, Alex, was the best player in the family, winning the U.S. Open in 1907 in addition to five North and South Opens and six Massachusetts Open titles.

Ross eventually gave up playing and teaching to concentrate on golf course design. Borrowing from what he learned growing up on the links of Dornoch, Ross made the crowned green his trademark. He was a detail man who took great patience to make sure every slope and break met his approval. All his bunkers looked like they hadn't been built at all, but had been made by the hands of nature. There is a seamless, timeless quality to Donald Ross golf courses that required very little earth-moving to construct.

Pinehurst No. 2 is a perfect example. Water comes into sight on only one hole, and it is not in play. The course is not particularly long, there is little rough, it is almost impossible to lose a golf ball, yet any golfer who goes around close to his or her handicap will have had a good day. Ross spent more time tweaking this layout than any other of his designs, if not for any other reason than Bob Jones selected Alister Mackenzie over him to design Augusta National. He wanted to make No. 2 the No. 1 course in the South, and there are those who believe that Ross succeeded. Having already played host to a PGA Championship, a Ryder Cup and two Tour Championships, Pinehurst No. 2, Ross' masterpiece, returned to glory as the site of the U.S. Open in 1999 and is slated to host the 2005 U.S. Open.

### THE ROSS RECORD

North and South Open: 1903, 1905, 1906

Served as apprentice to Old Tom Morris at St. Andrews in 1899

Designer or redesigner of 600 courses, including Pinehurst No. 2, Seminole, Oakland Hills, Oak Hill, Inverness, Scioto, Skokie, Interlachen.

# Sandra Haynie

**This is the story of a renaissance woman who had two careers on the LPGA Tour — one in which she qualified for the Hall of Fame and one in which she came back to remind everyone just how good she really was.**

From 1962-75, Sandra Haynie won 39 tournaments on the LPGA Tour. Two years later, at the age of 34, she left golf. The reasons? An ulcer, brought on by the pressure of competitions, and a circulation problem in her left hand, caused by years of hitting golf balls — she began competing in amateur tournaments when she was 12 — that resulted in arthritis. "I'd come out to the course," she said, describing those years, "and wish I were someplace else."

So rather than fight, she surrendered and returned home to Dallas to find, in her words, "the peaceful center that I knew was somewhere inside me–or ought to be." During that time, she became mentor to Martina Navratilova, managing the tennis great to her first Wimbledon singles victory in 1978. Known as a cerebral golfer, Haynie taught Navratilova the art of winning and in so doing she became more in control of herself.

Haynie's body recovered, and so did her mind. In 1980, watching Jack Nicklaus win the U. S. Open on television, Haynie wondered what it would feel like to do the same thing. In 1974, she had won the LPGA Championship and the U. S. Women's Open within a few weeks of each other, but she was only 29 at the time and didn't fully appreciate what it meant.

Now at 37, she was having thoughts of staging a comeback. "The only question I had was, 'Do I really want to do this all over again?' " she said in a 1982 interview with *The New York Times*. "All the traveling, all the pressure of tournaments, being involved in the growing of the women's tour? Did I want to go through all that stress again? 'Sandra,' I said to myself, 'Are you that crazy?' And the answer was, 'Absolutely.' "

By 1981, she was playing a full schedule on the LPGA Tour again, and her 40th victory came that year, at the Henredon Classic. In 1982, Haynie closed her career by winning back-to-back tournaments, the Rochester International and the Peter Jackson Classic, which was her fourth career major. She won by making a 10-foot par putt on the 72nd hole to avoid a playoff with Beth Daniel.

Listening to Haynie describe it makes you realize just how strong she was mentally. "I just put my head down and concentrated. I focused on the shot totally," she said. "I thought about my stroke, which had been so good all day. And then I looked at the hole. It looked huge. As soon as I hit the putt, I knew it was good. I didn't even see it go in the hole. I just whooped."

That victory was her last and 42nd. Her knee gave out in 1984, and in 1985 she underwent electrode treatment to deaden the sensitivity in her lower back. She became involved with the National Arthritis Foundation. In 1988, she passed the $1 million mark in career earnings, and at that point, there was nothing left to accomplish. This time she did walk away, but on her terms.

## THE HAYNIE RECORD

Major championship Victories ..... 4
- U. S. Women's Open: 1974
- LPGA: 1965, 1974
- Peter Jackson Classic: 1982

LPGA Tour Victories ............ 42

Player of the Year: 1970

# Carol Mann

**She was literally one of the giants of the game, both on the golf course and for the work she did in the formation of the "modern" Ladies Professional Golf Association.** She was a natural leader, winning a U.S. Women's Open, 38 events and serving as one of the LPGA's most influential presidents. Yes, she was 6-feet-3, and yes, she was self-conscious about her height, but Carol Mann always seemed quite natural in her surroundings, whether it was taking on Kathy Whitworth and Mickey Wright, or selling the ladies' tour to corporate America. There was a time when she was the LPGA's Mann for all seasons.

In 1968, she won 10 times and the Vare Trophy with a then-record 72.04 scoring average. The next year she won eight times and was the LPGA's leading money winner. Starting with the Women's Western Open in 1964 and ending with Lawson's Open in 1975, she towered over everybody in the competition except Whitworth. And then it all became too much for her. Like Whitworth and Sandra Haynie in the late 1970s, she just burned out. "I had made a tremendous effort, and it still wasn't satisfying," Mann told Liz Kahn in her unauthorized history of the LPGA. "I said to my father: 'Daddy, is this all there is to life? Is this all the accomplishment I can expect? Is this the only kick I'm going to have? Do I have to keep doing this?' "

He replied, "No, baby, this isn't all there is."

She read Norman Vincent Peale's *The Power of Positive Thinking* and did self-hypnosis with Bob Hagge. Unlike Whitworth and Haynie, Mann could never resurrect her playing career, in part because she was too busy helping shape and run the ladies' tour.

Mann was the LPGA's president from September 1973 to May 31, 1976. It was during this time that the LPGA hired marketing genius Ray Volpe as its commissioner. Playing competitive golf had become secondary. "I could barely get to the course in time to tee off; there was so much other activity," she remembers. "By June 1976, I went down the tubes. I was depressed thinking that no one on tour would say thank you to me for what I had done. Some would, others never would, and 10 years later, players wouldn't give a damn."

Mann was appreciated; she received the Babe Zaharias Award in 1976 and was looked upon as one of the "100 Heroes of American Golf." She was inducted into the LPGA's Hall of Fame in 1977.

Mann didn't develop a golf swing until she was 13 years old, after the family moved to Chicago and took a membership at Olympia Fields C.C. Commuting to tournaments on trains, Mann won the Western Junior and the Chicago Junior in 1958, and the Chicago Women's Amateur in 1960. "I was awkward, shy, without any poise, and I giggled," Mann said.

Mann overcame her insecurities to enjoy one of the most productive careers in women's golf history. She retired at age 40 and began to branch out in different directions. The Women's Sports Foundation made her a trustee and she served as president from 1985-1990. She also formed Carol Mann Golf Services, the first woman-owned and operated course design and management firm. Based in Houston, she started teaching at The Woodlands C.C. and took an active role in facilitating the relationship between the Hall of Fame and its members.

"I've walked on the moon," she has said. "I enjoy being a person, and getting old and dying are fine. I never think how people will remember Carol Mann. The mark I made is an intimate satisfaction."

## THE MANN RECORD

Major Championship Victories ..... 2
- Western Open: 1964
- U.S. Women's Open: 1965

LPGA Tour Victories ........... 38

Vare Trophy: 1968

LPGA Leading Money Winner: 1969

LPGA President, LPGA: 1973-1976

Babe Zaharias Award: 1976

WON BY
HORACE RAWLINS
JAMES FOULIS
JOE LLOYD
FRED HERD
WILLIE SMITH
ALEX SMITH
WALTER HAGEN
EDWARD RAY
CYRIL WALKER
BILLY BURKE
OLIN DUTRA
SAM PARKS
TONY MANERO
RALPH GULDAHL
LAWSON LITTLE

# Billy Casper

**Because of an ultra-efficient manner of play and a quiet personality that contrasted with his more famous contemporaries, Billy Casper is perhaps the most underrated star in golf history.**

Between 1956 and 1975, Casper won 51 times on the PGA TOUR, a figure surpassed by only Snead, Nicklaus, Palmer, Hogan and Nelson. He won two U.S. Opens and a Masters. He was a member of eight Ryder Cup teams, winning more points, 23.5, than any other American player. He won the Vardon Trophy five times, a record matched only by Lee Trevino. He was the PGA TOUR Player of the Year in 1966 and 1970.

In his prime, however, Casper was overshadowed by Palmer, Nicklaus and Gary Player, who were marketed as The Big Three. But from 1964 to 1970, Casper won 27 U.S. events, eight more than Palmer and Player combined, and four more than Nicklaus. Casper, of course, did not lack for respect among his peers. "Billy was a killer on the golf course," said Dave Marr. "He just gave you this terrible feeling he was never going to make a mistake, and then of course he'd drive that stake through your heart with that putter. It was a very efficient operation." Said Lee Trevino, "When I came up, I focused on Casper. I figured he was twice as good as me, so I watched how he practiced and decided I would practice three times as much as him."

Casper was born June 24, 1931, in San Diego, Calif., where sports quickly became the center of his life. "When I was in first grade, the kids called me Fatso," he remembered. "It hurt, but the way I overcame it was to outrun every kid in the class. So I developed a thick skin, and athletics became my way of performing and being accepted." He caddied at the San Diego C.C. and came out of the same junior golf environment that also produced Gene Littler and Mickey Wright. "I didn't really worry about form, and to be honest, I was too lazy to go out there and hit the ball," Casper said. "I would chip and putt or play sand shots. That was the genesis of my short game."

Among the game's greatest winners, Casper was the greatest putter. He used a pigeon-toed stance and gave the ball a brisk, wristy pop. Casper's self-taught swing was distinctive for the way his right foot would slide through impact. Off the tee, it produced a fade that was always in play and approaches that inevitably finished pin high. Whatever shot Casper was playing it was executed with supreme touch and feel. "Billy has the greatest pair of hands God ever gave a human being," contends Johnny Miller.

He was also a tremendous competitor. The most enduring memory for those who watched and competed against him in his prime is the serene assurance of the supremely confident athlete who knew he would be at his best when it mattered most. The greatest example of this relentless quality was at the 1966 U.S. Open where he made up seven strokes on the final nine to tie Arnold Palmer and then defeated him in a playoff the next day.

But Casper seemed a ghostly figure. At the peak of his powers, Casper got more attention for his allergies, his conversion to Mormonism, his 11 children (six of them adopted) and his offbeat diet of buffalo meat and organically grown vegetables. At first he was hefty and later lost 70 pounds to drop to 170. When he played, it seemed as if he was in a trance. "It came from my feelings for Hogan," said Casper, who indeed experimented with self-hypnosis. "He seemed to be in this sort of hypnotic state, and I wanted to be just as focused." The public would come to know very little of Billy Casper, making him arguably the best modern golfer who never received his due.

## THE CASPER RECORD

Major Championship Victories ..... 3
- Masters: 1970
- U.S. Open: 1959, 1966

PGA TOUR Victories ........... 51

Champions Tour Victories ......... 8

Ryder Cup Teams ................ 9
- (20-10-7) ...1961, 1963, 1965, 1967, 1969, 1971, 1973, 1975
- Captain: .................... 1979

PGA TOUR Player of the Year: 1966, 1970

Vardon Trophy: 1960, 1963, 1965, 1966, 1968

Leading Money Winner: 1966, 1968

Byron Nelson Award: 1966, 1968, 1970

# Harold Hilton

**Harold Hilton's place in golf history was literally etched in stone at Apawamis Country Club in Rye, N.Y.** Playing the 37th hole of the 1911 U.S. Amateur final against Fred Herreshoff, Hilton hit a spoon (3-wood) that was headed into a rock bed right of the first green. As if guided by the hands of fate, the ball ricocheted onto the putting surface, stunning Herreshoff, who half-topped his approach shot and made bogey. With three British Amateur and two British Open victories to his credit, Hilton two-putted for par and at age 42 became the first foreign-born player to win the U.S. Amateur. At Apawamis, they still call it Hilton's Rock.

The shock waves sent off by Hilton's victory were far-reaching. Herbert Warren Wind described it as "the most discussed single shot ever played in an American tournament." In *The Story of American Golf,* Wind wrote, "Americans were not at all pleased over the idea that a foreigner had carried one of our championship cups out of the country, and that men who had never cared about golf before now wanted to know the real inside story." Wind used the press as a touchstone, noting that a New York newspaper which identified the Englishman as "Horace H. Hilton" in a story prior to the Amateur had gotten Hilton's first name right when he won the event.

In Great Britain, Hilton had been famous since well before the turn of the century. In 1892, he won the first Open Championship played over 72 holes. Few amateurs were in the field, and Hilton wasn't sure about traveling from his home at Hoylake to Muirfield, Scotland, until the week of the event. With only one practice round to draw on, Hilton was seven strokes back at the halfway point. He shot 72-74 over the final 36 holes to shoot 305 and win by three strokes. One of the players he defeated was Royal Liverpool clubmate John Ball, who in 1890 had become the first amateur to win the Open Championship.

Five years later, the Open was played at Hoylake for the first time. Hilton and Ball were among the favorites, but the field of 86 golfers included the "Great Triumverate" of Harry Vardon, James Braid and J.H. Taylor. The tournament came down to the final hole. Hilton had posted 314 and was in the clubhouse, playing billiards, awaiting the outcome. When word came that Braid was playing the 18th, Hilton went out to watch. Braid's cleek shot nearly went in the hole, but the Scotsman missed his birdie putt, and Hilton had won his second Open.

Hilton was a wild swinger, who regripped the club at the top of his backswing. Although standing only 5-feet 5-inches, he was a powerful, if unconventional, shotmaker. After losing to him in the 1913 Amateur at St. Andrews, Robert Harris once wrote of Hilton: "His cap used to fall from his head at the end of a full swing, as if jerked off, but this did not indicate that his swing was not pure if apparently unduly forceful. He was a small man of powerful physique; it was exhilarating to watch his perky walk between shots. His assiduity was his greatness."

After retiring from competitive golf, Hilton became a writer of popular books on golf and was editor of several golf magazines. In 1923, just as Bob Jones and Walter Hagen were coming on the scene, he addressed the impending takeover by the American golfer. What Hilton failed to point out was his victory at Apawamis served as their motivation. It helped shape the course of American golf history.

## THE HILTON RECORD

Major Tournament Victories ...... 7

U.S. Amateur: 1911

British Amateur: 1900, 1901, 1911, 1913

British Open: 1892, 1897

# Dorothy Campbell Hurd

**Dorothy Campbell Hurd was the first woman to dominate international golf.** Between 1905 and 1912, she won 10 national championships in America, England, Scotland and Canada. Then, 12 years later, she won the American title once more.

As Dorothy Campbell, and later as Mrs. J.V. Hurd, her count of national amateurs was three U.S., two British, three Scottish and three Canadian. In 1909, she became the first woman to win the U.S. and British Amateurs in the same year.

Dorothy Campbell was born in 1883 in North Berwick, Scotland. The town's famous links, where her paternal grandfather and eight uncles all played, proved her playground. She took her first swing when she was 18 months, and by age five, was playing matches against her older sisters.

Campbell did not evolve into a top player until her later teens, when she changed what had been a half swing into a full one. In 1905, Campbell won her first Scottish Ladies title. Played at the North Berwick links, more than 4,000 people watched her win the final on the 19th hole. She repeated in 1906 and 1908. The next year she entered the U.S. Women's Amateur for the first time and won at the Merion Cricket Club. When she returned to achieve her first victory in the British Women's Amateur Championship at Royal Birkdale, it was an unprecedented double.

In 1910, Campbell moved to Canada and won the country's championship three consecutive years before moving to the United States permanently in 1913. When she won the American title again in 1924, she was 41 years old. She remains the championship's oldest winner, and her 15-year span between victories is also the longest in the event's history.

Hurd advanced women's golf in America by being the first to aim directly at the pin on her approaches instead of just the general vicinity of the green. She had a tremendous short game, which she once said, "is almost second nature to me." A deadly putter, she was even better from just off the green. Her favorite club was a goose-necked mashie she called "Thomas." It was "Thomas" that she gave credit to for her American-British double for in the semifinal at Birkdale she used the club to hole out from a dead stymie at a crucial point in the match. In the final of the 1921 North and South championship at Pinehurst, "Thomas" holed two shots.

After her flurry of national titles, Campbell married and her golf career hit a fallow period. When she lost the final of the 1920 U.S. Amateur to Alexa Stirling, it appeared to be her last hurrah. But in 1923, seeing that many women were out-driving her by using a more modern technique, she concluded that her game needed updating.

She changed her swing from a stiff-wristed, sweeping-type motion that produced a straight but short left-to-right shot to a more athletic action in which hand action played an important part. Working with George Sayers, the pro at Merion who was also from North Berwick, she forced herself to switch from the baseball to the Vardon grip. After 10 months of work, Hurd was literally a new player. At the 1924 U.S. Amateur at Rhode Island C.C., she rolled through the field, ultimately defeating Mary K. Browne, the national lawn tennis champion of 1912 and 1913, 7 and 6, in the final.

Although it was Hurd's last championship, she was far from finished as a golfer. In 1926, she set out to surpass the record for fewest putts in 18 holes, 21, which had been set by Walter J. Travis. At the Augusta C.C., Hurd came to the 18th hole with 19 putts, when she holed out from off the green using "Thomas," her famous mashie.

## THE HURD RECORD

Major Championship Victories ..... 5

- Women's Amateur: 1909, 1910, 1924
- British Women's Amateur: 1909, 1911

Other Significant Victories

- Scottish Ladies: 1905, 1906, 1908
- Canadian Ladies Open: 1910, 1911, 1912
- U.S. Women's Senior: 1938, 1939

HIRSCHFELD

# Bing Crosby

**Throw out Jones and Palmer, and Bing Crosby may be the person most responsible for popularizing the game of golf.** Since 1937 the Crosby Clambake—which now carries the heftier title AT&T Pebble Beach National Pro-Am—has been the game's most glamorous event, a four-day party combining glittering Hollywood stars, sweeping ocean vistas and some surprisingly serious golf. "This little tournament is the best advertisement golf has ever had," Crosby once said, and his words still hold true.

Born Harry Lillis Crosby in 1904 in Tacoma, Wash., Crosby first took up the game at 12 as a caddy, dropped it and started again in 1930 with some fellow cast members in Hollywood during the filming of "The King of Jazz." Although he made his name as a singer, vaudeville performer and silver screen luminary, he would probably prefer to be remembered as a two handicap who competed in both the British and U.S. Amateur championships, a five-time club champion at Lakeside Golf Club in Hollywood, and as one of only a few players to have made a hole-in-one on the 16th at Cypress Point.

He conceived his tournament as a friendly little pro-am for his fellow members at Lakeside Golf Club and any stray touring pros who could use some pocket change. The first edition of the Clambake was played at Rancho Santa Fe C.C., in northern San Diego county, where Crosby was also member. He kicked in $3,000 of his own money for the purse, which led inaugural champion Sam Snead to ask if he might get his $700 in cash instead of a check. Snead's suspicions notwithstanding, the tournament was a rollicking success, thanks to the merry membership of Lakeside, an entertainment industry enclave in North Hollywood. That first tournament set the precedent for all that followed as it was as much about partying as it was about golf.

Of course, the competitors were sodden in more ways that one. The first Clambake was played in such a deluge, an on-course bridge was washed out, and this foul weather would also become a hallmark. "One thing about Crosby weather, there's lots of it," the host once said. Relocating to Monterey Peninsula after World War II only made it worse. In 1962, snow postponed the event for a day, and 34 years later rain wiped it out altogether.

Still, moving up north was the best thing that ever happened to the Clambake. Rotating among Pebble Beach Golf Links, the Cypress Point Club and Spyglass Hill, the tournament finally had golf courses that could match the star power of the golfers. The climactic final round was always played at Pebble, helping to establish the course not only as a major championship venue but also the one track that every duffer dreams of playing.

Crosby died in 1977 of a heart attack while on a golf course in Madrid, having just played 18 holes with Spanish professional Manuel Pinero. His tournament continued to thrive under the watchful eye of his son, Nathaniel, the U.S. Amateur champion in 1981. Among the reasons to tune in every year were to witness Jack Lemmon's increasingly quixotic quest to make the cut and more recently Bill Murray's hilarious antics. Though it no longer carries his name, the Pebble Beach National Pro-Am will always be Bing Crosby's tournament. As he once said, "If I were asked what single thing has given me the most gratification in my long and sometimes pedestrian career, I think I would have to say it is this tournament."

## THE CROSBY RECORD

**Started Bing Crosby Clambake: 1937**

**William D. Richardson Award: 1950**

**Bob Jones Award: 1978**

# Clifford Roberts

**The words used to describe Clifford Roberts were autocratic, mysterious, intimidating and often enigmatic.** He seemed to rule the Masters tournament and Augusta National Golf Club from behind an iron curtain, yet those who knew him respected him and what he did for golf. While Bobby Jones got much of the credit, Cliff Roberts did most of the work.

They were the good cop and the bad cop, the ying and the yang, working together in creating and administrating two of the game's most significant institutions.

Roberts was the perfect complement to Jones, who was loved and revered, and whose influence made the Masters one of golf's major championships. As approachable as Jones was, Roberts was just the opposite. He worked behind the scenes as an administrator, helping to mold the club's conscience and the tournament's reputation as the best-run golf event in the world.

Herbert Warren Wind provided this description of their chemistry when Roberts died in 1977 at age 84 of a self-inflicted gunshot wound: "Jones imparted to the Masters an atmosphere of golf at its best. He was the perfect host since it was a true pleasure for him to greet old and new friends and to see that they were made to feel at home. Roberts, on the other hand, was of an extremely reserved disposition. Spare in build and somewhat stonefaced, he said no more on any subject than he had to."

Roberts was a Wall Street financier who came to enjoy the Augusta spa with friends in the 1920s. It was a time when Jones would travel from Atlanta to play golf, and as Augusta regulars, they formed a bond that would result in the construction of America's most famous golf course and tournament. It was Roberts' idea to form a holding company and sold Jones on the idea of a national membership—no more than 30 people from the Augusta area would be allowed to join the club. The initiation fee was set at $350, with dues at $60 a year. Together, they passed over Donald Ross and decided upon Alister Mackenzie as the course architect. They purchased a 365-acre, pre-Civil War indigo plantation that had been turned into Berckmann's Nursery and made it into a golfing landmark.

When illness struck down Jones, Roberts assumed total responsibility over the club and the tournament. It was the unbending manner in which he refused to grant special favors that made the Masters such an efficient operation. "The standards and quality with which he conducted the Masters are unmatched anywhere," said Jack Nicklaus. "All of us in golf appreciate what he has done for the game."

It didn't matter whether it was a member of the media pressing him for tournament attendance figures or a member of the club pushing him on policy. Roberts, as veteran columnist Tom Callahan once wrote, was something of a stone monument.

One year, a member suggested that a mound be put behind a certain green. "Fine, we'll do that," Roberts reportedly said. Several months later the member received a bill for the entire cost of the improvement. Asked in later years if that ever happened, Roberts replied firmly, "I don't remember it."

Roberts instituted such innovations as gallery roping, pairings sheets, course maps, stadium mounding and an elaborate scoring and leader board operation.

"Although he was a tough man, he was a person who was truly dedicated to golf and the quality and standards of the game," Arnold Palmer said. "And when you got to know him—as I was fortunate enough to be able to do—you found him to be a very nice and warm person. I liked and admired him very much."

## THE ROBERTS RECORD

**Co-Founder, Augusta National Golf Club: 1933**

**Chairman, Masters Tournament**

# Louise Suggs

**"She was bound to be a winner," Ben Hogan once said of Louise Suggs. "And she was."**

No truer words have been spoken in describing the first female inductee into the World Golf Hall of Fame. Suggs won a U.S. Amateur, a British Amateur, two U.S. Women's Opens, an LPGA Championship and a Vare Trophy. In all, she won 50 tournaments, including 13 major championships.

Overshadowed only by the popularity of Babe Zaharias, Suggs won often and in record-setting ways. In the 1949 Women's Open, she set the 72-hole scoring record of 291 and won by 14 strokes over Zaharias, which stood alone as an LPGA record until Cindy Mackey matched the total at the 1986 MasterCard International. Four years later, Suggs broke her own LPGA scoring record by shooting 288 to win the 1953 Tampa Open at Palma Ceia.

In the foreword to Suggs' book, *Par Golf for Women*, Hogan wrote: "If I were to single out one woman in the world today as a model for any other woman aspiring to ideal golf form it would be Miss Suggs. Her swing combines all the desirable elements of efficiency, timing and coordination. It appears to be completely effortless. Yes, despite her slight build, she is consistently as long off the tee and through the fairway as any of her feminine contemporaries in competitive golf. And no one is 'right down the middle' any more than this sweet-swinging Georgia miss."

Born in Atlanta, Suggs had the benefit of growing up in a golf environment (her father, John, a former pitcher with the New York Yankees and Atlanta Crackers, owned and managed a golf course). She won the Georgia State Amateur in 1940 and 1942, the Southern Amateur twice, the Western Amateur twice and the North and South three times. She won the Titleholders, which was then considered a major championship, as an amateur in 1946 and followed that with the U.S. and British Amateurs in 1947 and 1948, respectively.

With nothing left to accomplish on the amateur level, Suggs turned pro and made her first victory the record-setting performance over Zaharias in the Women's Open. It was an especially sweet victory for Suggs, who resented the tremendous publicity given to Babe. It was because of Babe, however, that sponsors became interested in ladies golf, and with the help of golf promoter Fred Corcoran, Suggs, Zaharias, Patty Berg, Marilynn Smith and Betty Jameson helped found the LPGA in 1950. Berg was the first president and she was succeeded by Suggs from 1955-1957.

Sadly, Suggs' career came to an end over a matter of principle. In 1962, she was fined $25 for failing to play in an event in Milwaukee that she signed up for. Feeling wronged, she never played a full schedule again. "She was at the height of her career and in her prime when she quit," said Betsy Rawls, who was president of the LPGA at the time. "It was hard for me to understand that kind of thinking. I would have paid for her myself, although the money was nothing to Louise. I forever regretted it for her, and I thought it was one of the saddest things in the LPGA history."

## THE SUGGS RECORD

Major Championship Victories .... 13
- U.S. Women's Amateur: 1947
- British Women's Amateur: 1948
- U.S. Women's Open: 1949, 1952
- Women's Western Open: 1946, 1947, 1949, 1953
- LPGA: 1957
- Titleholders: 1946, 1954, 1956, 1959

LPGA Tour Victories ............ 50

Curtis Cup Teams ............... 1
(0-1-1) ..................... 1948

Vare Trophy: 1957

Leading Money Winner: 1953, 1960

LPGA President: 3 times

# Walter Travis

**There has not been a golfer who played so well after starting so late in life as Walter J. Travis.** Here was a man who didn't hit his first golf ball until he was 35, yet one month later he won his first tournament and two years later he reached the semifinals of the U.S. Amateur. Within four years of picking up a club for the first time, Travis won the first of three National Amateurs. He also was the first American citizen to win the British Amateur and ended his career, at age 53, by winning the prestigious Metropolitan Amateur in New York.

Weighing no more than 140 pounds with small hands and slender wrists, Travis relied on cunning and his short game to excel at match play. He made up for a lack in size by simply outputting and outworking everybody. In his autobiography, first printed in *The American Golfer*, which he founded in 1908, Travis explained how he became a "golf fiend."

"I am not aware of every having possessed any physical advantages that enabled me to climb the ladder as I did in such a comparatively short space of time," Travis wrote. "What success I managed to achieve was primarily due to an intense love of the game, a devotion which made practice not a drudgery but a pleasure. 'Genius,' I think it was Carlyle, who said, 'is the capacity of taking infinite pains.' I practiced at every opportunity."

Born in Australia, Travis came to the United States and made a substantial income in the hardware business. He played cricket and lawn tennis as a young man, without much success, and became hooked on golf after a visit to England in 1896. His most cherished trophy was the pewter tankard won in the first handicap competition at the Oakland Golf Club of Bayside, L.I. His first U.S. Amateur victory came in 1900 at Garden City Golf Club on Long Island, and his name was engraved on the Havemeyer Trophy again in 1901 and 1903.

In 1902, he set a U.S. Open record by shooting 75-74—149 for the final two rounds. The second-place finish to Laurie Auchterlonie was the highest by an amateur in the Open, and rather than collect the $100 prize, Travis asked the USGA to reserve $75 for a trophy. The remaining $25 was given to his playing companion, Alex Smith, whom Travis thought displayed "thoroughly sportsmanlike spirit throughout."

Two years later, Travis traveled to Royal St. George's at Sandwich, England, for the British Amateur. On his way to the final, he defeated two of Britain's best golfers in Harold Hilton and Horace Hutchinson. The final was a relative breeze, as he defeated Ted Blackwell to win the famous cup. It was not until 1926 that another American would come along and win the British Amateur, and those who tried included Jones, Chick Evans, Jerry Travers and Francis Ouimet.

Travis thrived in match play because he was mentally stronger than most of his opponents. "Always be on the aggressive," Travis wrote in *The American Golfer*. "Act as if you are quite sure of yourself and never give an opponent the psychological advantage of imagining you are the least afraid of him. Many a man is beaten before he starts by admitting to himself the other's fancied superiority and unconsciously conveying it in his general bearing. It only gives the opponent that slight encouragement which enables him to pull out a winner in a tight match."

In his later years, Travis hung out on the practice green at Garden City G.C., challenging the members to a putting contest. The stakes were usually a cigar, and it was rare when Travis had to buy. He died in 1927 at age 65 without any regrets. "Full as my cup has been," he said, "I shall never cease to regret the many prior years which were wasted."

## THE TRAVIS RECORD

Major Championship Victories . . . . . 4
- U.S. Amateur: 1900, 1901, 1903
- British Amateur: 1904

Founder, *The American Golfer* Magazine . . . . . . . . . . . . 1908

Mail

# Lawson Little

**In the long history of golf there have been three instances of sustained brilliance. Two are immediately obvious—Bobby Jones' Grand Slam and Ben Hogan's magical 1953 campaign.** Although it is rarely remembered, Lawson Little may have topped them both.

In 1934 and 1935 Little became the first golfer to sweep the British and American Amateur Championships in consecutive years, two "Little Slams" as the pundits of the day referred to them. During his phenomenal run, Little won 32 consecutive matches on both sides of the Atlantic with an overpowering game built on booming drives and brooding intensity. It is a testament to Little's awesome dominance that he followed with a professional career that included seven victories and a U.S. Open title, and it was considered a failure. Wrote Charles Price, "Lawson Little was the greatest match player in the history of golf."

Born in Newport, R. I., in 1910 and raised in Northern California, Little burst onto the scene at Pebble Beach in the 1929 U. S. Amateur when he defeated Johnny Goodman the day after Goodman had electrified the golf world by beating the unbeatable Bobby Jones. Five years later, at the British Amateur at Prestwick, the 24-year-old with the senatorial mane of dark, wavy hair realized that potential. He barely broke a sweat in winning his seven consecutive matches, and in the final he gave Scot James Wallace a spanking of legendary proportions. Little shot an unofficial 66 in the morning, five better than the course record, and was 12 up by lunchtime. In the afternoon he birdied three of the first five holes and put Wallace out of his misery, 14 and 13. In the 23 holes Little had a dozen 3s on his card.

Nicknamed "Cannonball" and often described as "bullnecked and barrel-chested," the 200-pound Little generated tremendous power despite standing only 5'9". He liked to play the ball far back off his right leg and hit an exaggerated hook. At the 1934 U.S. Amateur at The Country Club, Little again overpowered the field, taking six 18-hole matches and a pair at 36 holes including the final in which Spec Goldman succumbed, 8 and 7. Harold Hilton and Bobby Jones were (and are) the only other golfers to hold the British and American amateur titles simultaneously.

For all his strength, Little had an expert short game. He used a variety of clubs from around the green, and in fact often carried as many as seven wedges among his 26 clubs, an excess which in 1938 prompted the USGA to institute the 14-club limit.

As Little's reputation as a merciless competitor continued to mushroom, so did the estimation that he was a surly and unlikable champion. Having grown up the son of a colonel in the Army Medical Corps, bouncing from base to base across the United States and China, Little was admittedly withdrawn, but he attributed his on-course demeanor to an unparalleled concentration.

"The man who doesn't plan out every shot to the very top of his capacity for thought can't attain championship form," he said. Little also believed, "Winners hit their bad shots best."

In the spring of 1935, Little went to St. Anne's to defend his British Amateur title, and he was lucky not to lose his first match. Despite a shaky 80 he stole the match on the 18th green, and from there he took the title without incident. Little's inexorable march into the record books was completed at the Cleveland Country Club.

Little turned pro shortly thereafter, and his mediocre record was often attributed to a lack of desire that came from being among the first pros with significant endorsement money. When he defeated Gene Sarazen in a playoff to win the 1940 U.S. Open, it was a reminder of what his talents once were. With the advent of World War II, Little lost direction as the major championships were cancelled and he became more interested in the stock market than in competitive golf. "He never practiced," said Jack Burke Jr. "Little either had it that week or he didn't. But when he did have it, it was lights out."

## THE LITTLE RECORD

Major Championship Victories ..... 5
- U.S. Amateur: 1934, 1935
- British Amateur: 1934, 1935
- U.S. Open: 1940

PGA TOUR Victories ........ 8

Other Significant Victories
- Canadian Open: 1936
- Los Angeles Open: 1940
- Texas Open: 1941

Walker Cup Teams .............. 1
- (2-0-0) ...................... 1934

# Henry Cotton

**"Maestro."**

There was a style and substance about Henry Cotton that made him not only unique, but a British national hero. He was much more than just a three-time British Open champion. He also championed the cause of British golf professionals seeking a higher ground in their country's society and became a patriarch of the European Golf Tour. Described as witty, handsome, intelligent, urbane and a non-conformist, Cotton authored 10 books, designed golf courses and was the most respected and prolific British instructor of his era. His philosophy was simple: "To be a champion, you must act like one."

Cotton was born Jan. 26, 1907, at Holmes Chapel in Cheshire, England. He left private school at age 16 in a dispute with his cricket coach and set out to learn the trade of golf on his own terms. This meant dressing smartly but shunning the traditional jacket and tie, and behaving properly, but never subserviently. Encouraged by Harry Vardon, James Braid and J. H. Taylor, Cotton took his first head professional job three years later, but soon moved to the Waterloo Club in Brussels, where he was treated as an equal.

Cotton's devotion to practice was almost maniacal for he believed the only secrets to becoming a champion golfer were hard work and strong hands. For hours upon hours, Cotton was known to hit balls from thick rough until his hands blistered and bled. It was an obsession that paid off in the 1934 Open at Royal St. George's. With opening rounds of 67-65—132, Cotton set two scoring records and opened a lead that was insurmountable. Even with a 79 in the final round, Cotton was able to win by five strokes and end a run of overseas victors that had lasted since Arthur Havers' triumph in 1923.

Cotton's second British Open triumph came three years later at Carnoustie, where his final round of 71, shot in a downpour, was considered every bit as good as his record 65. That gave Cotton a two-stroke victory against a field that included every member of a United States Ryder Cup team captained by Walter Hagen which included Gene Sarazen, Byron Nelson, Sam Snead, Ralph Guldahl, Denny Shute and Henry Picard.

It was his third Open Championship at Muirfield in 1948 that completed Cotton's transformation from the anti-establishment rebel to a national sporting legend and celebrity. Now 41 and robbed of his prime by World War II, Cotton shot a course-record 66 in the second round that was witnessed by King George VI. It was the only time a reigning monarch had been present at the Open.

In addition to those popular victories, Cotton also won three British Match Play Championships and 11 national championships on the continent of Europe. He played for his country in three Ryder Cup matches and twice captained the British team, but most of his time after the 1948 British Open at Muirfield was dedicated to instruction, designing golf courses and giving back to the game that had given so much to him. Whether it was giving no-cost instruction to junior golfers through the Golf Foundation, or doing exhibitions to raise money for the Red Cross, Henry Cotton was as hard-working and devoted as he had been about learning how to swing a golf club. For this, he was honored with a Knighthood, and on New Year's Day of 1988, just one week after his death, Henry Cotton MBE officially became Sir Henry Cotton, Knight Commander of the Most Honourable Order of St. Michael and St. George.

## THE COTTON RECORD

Major Championship Victories ..... 3
British Open: 1934, 1937, 1948

European Tour Victories: 30

Other Significant Victories
British Professional Match Play: 1932, 1940, 1946
Belgian Open: 1930, 1934, 1938
Italian Open: 1936
German Open: 1937, 1939
French Open: 1946, 1947

Ryder Cup Teams ................ 4
(2-4-0) .......... 1929, 1937, 1947
Captain .............. 1947, 1953

# Lee Trevino

**All golfers are self made, but the man who made the most out of what he started with has to be Lee Trevino.**

Trevino rose from a three-room shack with no plumbing in east Dallas to become arguably the most consistent shotmaker the game has ever seen. Through an agile mind, a tremendous work ethic and a sense of moment that belongs to the natural performer, Trevino carved a way to the top that is unlike any other in golf history.

Starting as a caddy and coming up through the ranks of driving ranges, military golf and hustling, Trevino first burst into big-time professional golf full blown. He was a squat 5-foot-7, 180-pound ball of fire whose rapid wit made players and galleries laugh, but whose game commanded their respect. In June 1968, the still unknown 28-year-old won the U.S. Open at Oak Hill with a record-tying score of 69-68-69-69—275.

Three years later, Trevino won his second U.S. Open, this time at Merion in a classic 18-hole playoff with Jack Nicklaus. Within 20 days he added the Canadian Open and the British Open at Royal Birkdale, completing an unprecedented international sweep. The next year he won the British Open again, this time at Muirfield. His final two major championships would come in the PGA, first at Tanglewood in 1974, and finally at Shoal Creek in 1984.

Trevino was born on Dec. 1, 1939, in Garland, Texas. Reared by his mother and maternal grandfather, a gravedigger, he never knew his father. As a boy, Trevino was in the cotton fields working by the time he was five. "I thought hard work was just how life was," he said. His family's home was 100 yards from the seventh fairway of the Dallas Athletic Club, and by the time Trevino was eight, he was caddying. "That's where I learned my killer instinct, playing games with the caddies and betting everything I had earned that day," he wrote. He quit school in eighth grade to work at a driving range, where he would hit hundreds of balls a day.

The first complete round he ever played was at age 15 when he shot a 77 at a junior tournament. At 17, he joined the Marines and further honed his game. When he got out, he played in money games around Dallas and El Paso, one of which included his hitting the ball around a par-3 course with a Dr. Pepper bottle. "You don't know what pressure is until you play for five bucks with only two in your pocket," he said.

A turning point in his career came when he played at Shady Oaks in Fort Worth and saw Ben Hogan on the practice range. From that day on, Trevino honed a fade that would make him one of the most accurate players the game has ever seen. Sometimes he would yell, "Don't move, hole!" when he'd hit an iron at the pin.

Trevino did it with a strong grip, stood with his body aligned well left of his target and essentially shoved the ball outward with a strong blocking action of his left side. British writer Leonard Crawley called it "an agrarian method," but perhaps no one has ever hit the ball as consistently solid. Trevino said, "Who knows, maybe my method is best." On and around the greens, Trevino was both deft and opportunistic.

Although he was an instant success when he joined the tour, Trevino suffered plenty more hard times. In 1975, he was nearly killed when he was hit by lightning during play at the Western Open and suffered severe back problems. He also lost two fortunes due to bad investments.

But Trevino called on the resiliency born of his beginnings. In 1980, he had one of his best years, winning the Vardon Trophy for the fifth time. His PGA victory at Shoal Creek was his crowning achievement. In all, he won 29 times on the regular tour. Later, he would equal that total on the Champions Tour.

"I've always had a tremendous amount of confidence in Lee Trevino," he said. "But I've always paid the price."

## THE TREVINO RECORD

Major Championship Victories ..... 6
- U. S. Open: 1968, 1971
- British Open: 1971, 1972
- PGA Championship: 1974, 1984

PGA TOUR Victories ........... 29

Champions Tour Victories ....... 29

Ryder Cup Teams ................. 7
- (17-7-6) .........1969, 1971, 1973, 1975, 1979, 1981
- (Non-Playing Captain) ....... 1985
- Vardon Trophy: 1970, 1971, 1972, 1974, 1980

# Ralph Guldahl

**Ralph Guldahl stands alone in golf history as the best player ever to suddenly and completely lose his game.** Guldahl was born the same year as Ben Hogan, Sam Snead and Byron Nelson, and he shot to the top more quickly than any of them. In fact, during a dazzling stretch from 1936 to 1939, Guldahl was the brightest star in golf, winning two U.S. Opens, a Masters and three straight Western Opens. And then, mysteriously, he never won again.

Born in 1911 in Dallas, Texas, the precocious Guldahl joined the pro golf tour in the early 1930s, winning the 1932 Phoenix Open. In the final round of the 1933 U.S. Open at the North Shore G.C. outside Chicago, the tall 20-year-old picked up nine strokes in 11 holes on Johnny Goodman, and on the 72nd holed needed only a four-footer to force a playoff. He missed it and essentially gave up competition for nearly three years.

Guldahl went home to Dallas and became a used-car salesman until he was asked to lay out a nine-hole course in Kilgore, Texas. The project inspired Guldahl to take up the game again. He began practicing and, on the advice of doctors caring for his sickly son, moved his family to the California desert. In 1936, a rededicated Guldahl finished eighth in the U.S. Open and a few weeks later won his first Western Open.

The 1937 season was his best. Guldahl won the Western Open again, as well as the U.S. Open at Oakland Hills, where he closed with 69 for a total of 281 that stood as the championship record until 1948. He would have had three major titles but for an incredible reversal at the Masters. Guldahl was four strokes up with only seven to play, but he hit into the water on both the 12th and 13th holes to score a 5 and 6. On the same holes, Byron Nelson scored a 2 and a 3 to blow past Guldahl and win by two.

He finished second in the Masters again in 1938, but eased the sting of that disappointment by becoming the only golfer to win both the Western and the U.S. Open in consecutive years. The latter victory was achieved by six strokes at Cherry Hills in Denver, where Guldahl became the last U.S. Open champion to win the title wearing a necktie. Finally, in 1939, Guldahl got his green jacket in the most stirring performance of his career. With Snead in the clubhouse with a record score of 280, Guldahl fired a 33 on Augusta National's back nine, highlighted by a 3-wood second to the par-5 13th that finished six feet from the hole and led to an eagle. That scoring record stood until Ben Hogan shattered it in 1953.

Guldahl in his prime was a golfer with an impressive arsenal. Though his fast and quirky swing produced only marginal power, Guldahl was straight and uncanny in controlling the distance of his approaches. "When Ralph was at his peak," said Snead, "his clubhead came back on the line and went through on the line as near perfect as anyone I've ever seen." He was a deadly lag putter, and perhaps most importantly, had an imperturbable manner. Guldahl moved through his rounds slowly and devoid of emotion, his only distinguishing on course gesture a habit of taking out a comb and running it through his thick black hair. "If Guldahl gave someone a blood transfusion, the patient would freeze to death," said Snead.

But Guldahl admitted that "behind my so called poker face, I'm burning up." Somehow, beginning in the 1940 season, he went from being the man to beat to a beaten man. Whether it was due to the rigors of competition, lack of desire or the vagaries of his swing remains a mystery. One theory maintains that Guldahl lost his game after working on a golf instruction book, which forced him to think about swing mechanics for the first time in his life. Guldahl left the tour in 1942 and, except for a brief return in 1949, never played it again. But there was no denying Guldahl's brilliance—while it lasted.

## THE GULDAHL RECORD

**Major Championship Victories ..... 3**
**Masters: 1939**
**U.S. Open: 1937, 1938**
**Other Significant Victories**
**Western Open: 1937, 1938, 1939**
**PGA TOUR Victories ........... 16**
**Ryder Cup Team ................. 1**
**(2-0-0) ..................... 1937**

# Julius Boros

**If any one player personifies the combination of effortless ease, flawless technique and hidden competitive fire, it was Julius Boros.**

Everything about the phlegmatic former accountant conveyed relaxation and imperturbability. But when an opportunity to win a championship was on the line, few converted as efficiently or as briskly as Boros.

Boros never took a practice swing, and didn't tarry on the greens. "Julius wasn't the kind of man who bent over too much," said Dave Marr with his trademark pith. "He was slowest and fastest," wrote *Golf Digest* editor Jerry Tarde. "Slowest walking to the ball and fastest once he got to it."

Although he did not turn professional until the age of 29, and despite suffering from physical maladies all his life, Boros put together a career that was remarkable for its consistency, longevity and brilliance. He won 18 times between 1952 and 1968, including three major championships. He was PGA Player of the Year in 1952 and 1963, led the money list in 1952 and 1955 and played on four Ryder Cup teams.

His first victory was the 1952 U.S. Open, which he won by four at Northwood C.C. in Dallas. He won the championship again in 1963 at Brookline, birdieing two of the last three holes to get into a playoff with Arnold Palmer and Jackie Cupit, and defeating them with a flawless 70 in the playoff. It made him, at 43, the oldest winner of the championship since Ted Ray. Then, in 1968, Boros won the PGA Championship in San Antonio by again defeating Palmer down the stretch and, at 48, became the oldest ever winner of a major.

Besides majors, Boros had a way of winning big-money events. He won the World Championship of Golf in 1952 and 1955 when the first prize was an astronomical $50,000. His last victory was the 1968 Westchester Classic, which then had the biggest first prize in golf at $50,000. In 1975, the 55-year-old Boros came within a whisker of becoming the oldest winner ever of a PGA TOUR event, losing a sudden-death playoff to Gene Littler at Westchester. Asked when he was going to retire, Boros answered, "Retire to what? I'm already a golfer and a fisherman. I have nothing to retire to."

The son of Hungarian immigrants, Boros was born March 3, 1920, in Fairfield, Conn. A big man at 6 feet and considerably more than 200 pounds, he had a nonchalant bearing that earned him the nickname "Moose." He learned to take things even easier after discovering during his military stint that he had a bad heart. Despite his apparent imperturbability, he admitted, "I was as apprehensive as the next guy in a tight situation. It felt like razor blades in my stomach."

The biggest reason Boros was able to last so long was that his technique was so free of strain and technically correct. Boros' motto was "swing easy, hit hard," and he could produce plenty of power. Yet the overall effect was one of grace and control, fairways and greens. "Julius Boros is all hands and wrists, like a man dusting the furniture," said 1964 British Open champion Tony Lema. His iron shots in particular landed with unique softness, as if by a parachute. He was also the master of the sand wedge, particularly out of deep rough around the green, his soft, slow swing feathering the ball with uncanny touch.

It all reflected itself in his success at the championship that is most about control, the U.S. Open. Boros finished in the top five of the U.S. Open nine times between 1951 and 1965. And as late as 1973, he was tied for the lead after 62 holes before finishing tied for seventh.

Boros won the 1977 PGA Seniors' Championship and played a key role in the launch of the Champions Tour by making the final birdie putt on the sixth extra hole of sudden death that gave partner Roberto De Vicenzo and him victory over Tommy Bolt and Art Wall in the 1979 Legends of Golf. Boros died on a golf course near his home in Florida May 28, 1994. His son, Guy, won the 1996 Greater Vancouver Open, making the Boroses one of only three father-son tandems to have won on the PGA TOUR.

## THE BOROS RECORD

Major Championship Victories ..... 3
U.S. Open: 1952, 1963
PGA: 1968
Other Significant Victories
PGA Seniors': 1971, 1977
PGA TOUR Victories ........... 18
Ryder Cup Teams ................ 4
(9-3-4) ..... 1959, 1963, 1965, 1967
Leading Money Winner: 1952, 1955
PGA Player of the Year: 1952, 1963

# Kathy Whitworth

**It is one of the most famous records in golf: 88 victories over a span of 23 years, an average of 3.8 victories per season starting with the Kelly Girl Open in 1962 and ending with the United Virginia Bank Classic in 1985.** In those three decades, Kathrynne Ann Whitworth surpassed the victory totals of Mickey Wright (82) and Sam Snead (82) to lodge herself atop the category of Most Tournament Victories By a Professional, Man or Woman.

Whitworth did this with what she considered average talent. "I never had a golf swing," she said. But she did have staying power. From 1963-1973 she was leading money winner eight times, second on the money list twice and third once. In that span, she won the Vare Trophy and Player of the Year honors seven times each.

With all that success, it still took her until 1981 to become the first woman in golf to earn $1 million. Fifteen years later, Karrie Webb became the first woman to accomplish that feat in one year, and she did so with four victories and 12 top-five finishes. Whitworth had eight victories in 1963, eight victories in 1965 and 11 victories in 1968, and in none of those years did she make more than $50,000.

Whitworth passed the seven-figure threshold at the U.S. Women's Open, the one major championship that eluded her. "I would have swapped being the first to make a million for winning the Open, but it was a consolation which took some of the sting out of not winning."

Born in Monahans, Texas, Whitworth grew up in Jal, N.M., where her father owned a hardware store. She got her first set of clubs from her grandmother and started playing golf at 15. Two years later Whitworth won the first of two consecutive New Mexico State Amateur titles.

Her start on the LPGA Tour was less than auspicious. She played 26 events as a rookie and made less than $1,300. After playing so poorly, Whitworth considered quitting, but a visit to Harvey Penick convinced her to keep going. Self-conscious and shy, Whitworth was adopted by Wright, Betsy Rawls, Gloria Armstrong and Jackie Pung. She soon gained confidence in herself and her ability.

"When I won eight tournaments in 1963, I was living on a high," Whitworth said. "I got in a winning syndrome. I played really well and it came easily. You don't think you're that great, but you're in the groove with good concentration. Nothing bothers you."

Whitworth qualified for the LPGA Hall of Fame in 1975, but the stress of playing at such a high level for so long eventually took its toll. She described the 1974 and 1975 seasons as "traumatic," and in the late 1970s, her game deteriorated. Only the pursuit of the $1 million barrier and the records of Wright and Snead kept her going.

Victory No. 82 came in the 1981 Kemper Open. She passed Wright the next year with a victory at the Lady Michelob. She won once in 1983, when she made a 40-foot putt on the 72nd hole of the Kemper Open. With one last push, she won three times in 1984 and again the following season. At that point, she assumed responsibility as the LPGA's vice president and ultimately its president.

"I don't think about the legacy of 88 tournaments–I did it because I wanted to win, not to set a record or a goal that no one else could surpass," she said. "I'm not some great oddity. I was just fortunate to be so successful. What I did in being a better player does not make me a better person. When I'm asked how I would like to be remembered, I feel that if people remember me at all, it will be good enough."

## THE WHITWORTH RECORD

Major Championship Victories ..... 6
LPGA: 1967, 1971, 1975
Titleholders: 1965, 1966

Women's Western Open: 1967

LPGA Tour Victories ............ 88

Player of the Year: 1966, 1967, 1968, 1969, 1971, 1972, 1973

Vare Trophy: 1965, 1966, 1967, 1969, 1970, 1971, 1972

Leading Money Winner: 1965, 1966, 1967, 1968, 1970, 1971, 1972, 1973

Richardson Award: 1985

Foster
Brooks
Pro
Celebrity
Bob Hope
U.S.A.

# Bob Hope

**Bob Hope is not the greatest golfer who has ever played the game, but he might be the most enthusiastic. Since the 1920s he has been one of the sport's great ambassadors.** As he traversed the globe entertaining both black-tie audiences and battalions of scruffy soldiers, Hope made a second career of teeing it up with Presidents, Princes and the King—in fact he teamed with Arnold Palmer to win the pro-am portion of the Palm Springs Desert Classic in 1962. Three years later Hope took the reigns of that tournament and it has borne his name ever since. As the host of this sprawling party Hope has been a constant reminder that golf is meant to be enjoyed, his own glib observations notwithstanding.

"It's wonderful how you can start out with three strangers in the morning, play 18 holes and by the time the day is over you have three solid enemies," Hope once said.

Of course, he has made few enemies on the golf course, in no small part because of his contagious zest for the game. Even though his mansion in Studio City, Calif., was only eight blocks from Lakeside Country Club–which was also home to another of golf's patron saints, Bing Crosby–Hope installed his own kidney-shaped green guarded by a pair of bunkers, with three different sets of tees. Back in the old days it was common for houseguests to repair to the back terrace for cocktails and wedges (another set of tees was 140 yards out and mandated a carry over the swimming pool).

Hope was welcome in almost any foursome. He was a frequent foil for President Eisenhower and a close friend of Ben Hogan, and they supplied many of the countless anecdotes in his ode to the game, *Confessions of a Hooker*. Though he has always liked to poor-mouth his abilities, Hope could actually play a little. He was a four handicap "for about 20 minutes" in his youth, and even teed it up at the 1951 British Amateur at Royal Porthcawl.

If the Bob Hope Desert Classic lacked the celestial field of the Crosby Clambake, it more than made up for it with perfect weather and the enveloping presence of Hope, a peerless master of ceremonies. Along with his sometimes caddie Phyllis Diller, who usually toted Band-Aids and a hip flask to mitigate any potential disaster, Hope oversaw a pro-am that was at least as much about the ams as the pros. Played on four courses over five days to accommodate the biggest possible field, the Hope Classic remains a tribute to all golfers, from the sublime to the ridiculous. Until recently Hope, who turned 100 on May 29 and died shortly thereafter, still swatted the ceremonial first ball. This ardor brings to mind a story Jack Benny used to love to tell.

He encountered Hope one afternoon limping off a course in Palm Springs, moaning about how badly he was playing. Benny went through a whole litany of excuses on Hope's behalf, concluding that with his busy schedule he couldn't possibly play enough golf to keep his game in shape.

"You damn fool," Hope snarled, "I play every day."

## THE HOPE RECORD

**Started the Bob Hope Chrysler Classic:**
1965

A. Ravielli

# Jimmy Demaret

**The impact Jimmy Demaret had on the game of golf was measured by more than his three Masters victories, his impeccable Ryder Cup record and his 44 tournament victories around the world.** Jimmy Demaret was golf's first show biz star. He was the reason, some said, that Bing Crosby invented the pro-am. He could sing, he could tell jokes, and for a while, it wasn't a party or a golf tournament unless Demaret was on the premises. He could outdress, outquip and outplay just about everybody in an era that included Ben Hogan, Sam Snead and Byron Nelson.

In the same sentence, Grantland Rice called him the "singing Texan." Jackie Burke Jr. once said that Jimmy Demaret "was a jet-setter before there were jets." Herbert Warren Wind referred to him as "The Wardrobe" for fashion statements that singlehandedly put golf clothing on the cutting edge of garish. According to Dan Jenkins, Demaret wore lavender, gold, pink, orange, red and aqua slacks, and yellow, emerald, maroon, plaid, checked, striped and polka-dot sport coats. He gave shoe factories a swatch from his pants and had matching saddle oxfords made. As Demaret said, "If you're going to be in the limelight, you might as well dress like it."

He was a master of one liners. After a bumpy flight to Japan to play in the World Cup, Demaret got off the plane and said, "Hey, Lindbergh got eight days of confetti for less than this." When it snowed at Pebble Beach in the 1962 Crosby, Demaret piped, "Geez, I know I was drinking last night but how did I get to Squaw Valley?" And it was Demaret who first said, "Golf and sex are about the only things you can enjoy without being good at them." Bob Hope once called him the funniest amateur comedian in the world.

Demaret was one of the great professional golfers. A stoutly built man with thick arms, he used an elegant wristy swing that shot out low fades with minimal effort. "He was the most underrated golfer in history," said Hogan. "This man played shots I hadn't dreamed of. I learned them. But it was Jimmy who showed them to me first. He was the best wind player I've ever seen in my life."

Born in Houston in 1910, the fifth of nine children, Demaret grew up caddying on sand greens and playing barefoot until he was 15. His father was a carpenter-painter—the source, Demaret said of his lifelong passion for mixing and matching bright colors. At age 17, he was hired by Jackie Burke Sr. as an assistant pro at River Oaks in Houston. His first job was to babysit the toddler who would one day be his partner in forming Champions Golf Club, Jackie Burke Jr. After a brief stint on the pro circuit, Demaret alternated between competitive golf and night club singing before playing the tour full time in 1938. In 1940 he won six consecutive tournaments including the Masters. He won six more and the Masters again in 1947, his best year, when he also led the money list and won the Vardon Trophy. In 1950, he won his third Masters and at the presentation grabbed the microphone and began singing, "Do You Know How Lucky You Are."

In all, Demaret won 31 official events between 1938 and 1957, a year in which he won three events at age 47. He was one of the best players never to have won the U.S. Open, finishing two strokes back in 1946 and 1948, and only a stroke out of a playoff in 1957. In three Ryder Cups between 1947 and 1951, his record was 5-0. Along with Gene Sarazen, he was the host on one of the first television golf shows, *"Shell's Wonderful World of Golf."*

Demaret admitted he would have won more tournaments if he hadn't been so busy enjoying himself. When he died in 1983, golf lost more than just another great champion. It lost a great deal of its charm. "He loves golf," Henry Cotton once said of Demaret, "but no more than a good time."

## THE DEMARET RECORD

Major Championship Victories ..... 3
Masters: 1940, 1947, 1950

PGA TOUR Victories ........... 31

Ryder Cup Teams ................ 3
(5-0-0) .......... 1947, 1949, 1951

Leading Money Winner: 1947

Co-Founder of Champions Golf Club

# JoAnne Carner

**First she was known as "The Great Gundy."** Then "Big Momma."

She loved match play, showboating to the galleries, riding motorcycles and partying in the clubhouse with members after her rounds. As JoAnne Gunderson, and later JoAnne Carner, she dominated women's golf—and nobody had more fun dominating than she did. There was a little Babe Ruth in her, a little Babe Zaharias, a little Walter Hagen and a little Shelly Winters, too. It made for some package.

"The ground shakes when she hits it," Sandra Palmer once said, and with that statement the LPGA had a different type of folk hero to package with the glamour of Jan Stephenson and the youthful innocence of Nancy Lopez. While the youngsters were selling the LPGA Tour, Carner was going back to her Gulfstream motor home, where her husband, Don, had prepared dinner and found a stream where the fish were just waiting to take their lures. "I play better golf living in our trailer," Carner said, and for a long while, nobody played it better.

As an amateur golfer, Gunderson was the historic equal of Zaharias and Glenna Collett Vare. Born in Kirkland, Wash., she came out of the Pacific Northwest and won the U.S. Girls' Junior title in 1956. One month later, she lost in the final of the Women's Amateur to Marlene Stewart to begin a 13-year run where she either won the national title or finished second seven times. Four of her five championship finals were blowout victories, but in 1966, it took Carner 41 holes to defeat the then-married Marlene Stewart Streit. It was the longest final match in U.S. Women's Amateur history.

## THE CARNER RECORD

Major Championship Victories ..... 7
- U.S. Women's Open: 1971, 1976
- Women's Amateur: 1957, 1960, 1962, 1966, 1968

Other Significant Victories
- U.S. Girls' Junior: 1956

Curtis Cup Teams ................ 4
- (6-3-1) ..... 1958, 1960, 1962, 1964

LPGA Rookie of the Year: 1970

LPGA Tour Victories ............ 42

Vare Trophy: 1974, 1975, 1981, 1982, 1983

Leading Money Winner: 1974, 1982, 1983

Player of the Year: 1974, 1981, 1982

Bob Jones Award: 1981

Only Vare, with six, has more U.S. Women's Amateur titles. Carner won her first at age 18 and her last at age 29. It wasn't until after winning the Burdine's Invitational as an amateur in 1969 that Carner finally turned professional. She was also undefeated in Curtis Cup singles (4-0-1). "That first U.S. Amateur victory was a huge thrill," Carner has said. "I really loved playing head-to-head, and I enjoyed all my battles in the Curtis Cup matches."

Realizing there was nothing left to accomplish as an amateur, she turned professional and in just 12 seasons won 35 events to qualify for the LPGA Hall of Fame. "Some people are afraid to win, others are afraid to lose," Carner has said. "I think winning is a lot more fun."

Carner's second victory as a professional came in the 1971 U.S. Women's Open, making her the only golfer in history to win the U.S. Girls' Junior, the U.S. Women's Amateur and the U.S. Women's Open titles. She won the Women's Open again in 1976 and 42 LPGA titles in a 14-year period from 1970 to 1984. Three times she was Player of the Year, five times the Vare Trophy winner and all the time the clubhouse leader in body language, crowd interaction and exhortations.

Win or lose, "Big Momma" was quite a show. "Concentration and getting involved with the shot are important, but if I get too serious I can't play," Carner said. "I relieve the pressure by light chatter with the gallery, although I never get into conversation. I enjoy being able to show more emotion as a professional. I get so enthused with golf that if the ball is going for the pin or in the cup, I am the first one to yell."

# Cary Middlecoff

**Cary Middlecoff is often remembered for his glacial pace of play, his occasionally volcanic temper and his nickname, Doc, which he earned for being a qualified dentist.** What he should be remembered as is one of the few players ever to master the game young and then never loose his grip on it.

Middlecoff won his third tournament as a pro, in 1947, and at least one more in every year until his retirement in 1961. When he hung up his spikes his 40 career victories were eighth on the PGA TOUR's all-time list, and he had also bagged a U. S. Open and two Masters titles. Middlecoff won the Memphis city championship and Tennessee state amateur while still a teenager, took one collegiate tournament by 29 strokes while at the University of Mississippi and later became the first amateur to win the North and South Open, in 1945, while playing in the final group with Ben Hogan and Gene Sarazen.

"I'd give the world to have a swing like that," Bobby Jones once said, all the more remarkable considering Middlecoff never took a lesson.

Middlecoff was born in Halls, Tenn., and earned the nickname "The Ghost" as a boy because he was always haunting the town's country clubs, looking for tips on his game. He was a big kid (eventually growing to 6'2") who was more interested in knocking the stuffing out of the ball than perfecting any technique. Later in life he would use his tremendous length off the tee to overpower golf courses and opponents alike.

Middlecoff had nearly given up golf for dentistry when World War II convinced him otherwise. After serving 18 months of active duty and filling some 7,000 teeth, he decided to give the pro tour a whirl with the caveat that if he wasn't successful within two years he would go back to drilling teeth instead of 2-irons. At the Charlotte Open in his rookie year, Middlecoff tied the course record in the final round and took home the $2,000 winner's check. He never looked back.

Two years later, he won his first major, the 1949 U.S. Open at Medinah. The most dominant performance of Middlecoff's career came at the 1955 Masters, which he won by a then-record seven strokes, stoked by an 86-foot putt for eagle on the 13th during the third round. When he held off Ben Hogan and Julius Boros at the next year's U.S. Open at Oak Hill, Middlecoff established himself as one of the premier golfers of the 1950s.

At the 1957 U.S. Open, Middlecoff shot back-to-back 68s to make up eight strokes and force a playoff with Dick Mayer, but it was memorable for other reasons. Mayer showed up for the playoff with a camping stool, an unsubtle comment on Middlecoff's slow play, which came from an unnatural fastidiousness about his alignment. Indeed, according to writer Dan Jenkins, Middlecoff's fellow pros used to joke that he had given up dentistry because no patient could hold his mouth open that long. How much Mayer's stunt perturbed Middlecoff is unknown, but he shot a woeful 79 to lose the Open by seven strokes.

Middlecoff was deliberate in other ways. At the top of his languid backswing he came to a visible stop. Middlecoff was a pithy commentator on the game and worked for several years as a television analyst. Among his more memorable phrases were, "Nobody wins the Open. It wins you," and "Anyone who hasn't been nervous, or hasn't choked somewhere down the line, is an idiot." Middlecoff's theories on the golf swing, collected in a book appropriately entitled *The Golf Swing*, are considered among the most accessible ever written. Which is not surprising, considering the game always came so easy to him.

## THE MIDDLECOFF RECORD

Major Championship Victories ..... 3
- U.S. Open: 1949, 1956
- Masters: 1955

Other Significant Victories
- North and South Open: 1945

PGA TOUR Victories ........... 40

Vardon Trophy: 1956

Ryder Cup Teams ............... 3
- (2-3-1) ....... 1953, 1955, 1959

# Robert Trent Jones

**Robert Trent Jones did not invent golf course architecture, it only seems that way.**

In a career that spanned nearly 70 years, Jones built or rebuilt some 400 courses in 45 states in the U.S. and 35 countries worldwide, with more than three dozen of them having played host to national or international championships. Still, the numbers tell only part of the story.

Jones made an art form of heroic architecture, institutionalizing the risk-reward shot in modern courses. With his oft-quoted philosophy to make every hole a hard par but an easy bogey, he also had a profound impact on tournament golf. Jones built or remodeled some of the most muscular courses the pros have ever faced, including Firestone, Hazeltine, Spyglass Hill, Baltusrol and Oak Hill. In his early years Jones' designs often engendered criticism as too severe, and the complaints reached a crescendo when he remodeled Oakland Hills for the 1951 U.S. Open. When a victorious Ben Hogan boasted of having brought that "monster to its knees" and Herbert Warren Wind followed with a laudatory—and widely read—article in *The New Yorker*, Jones was introduced to a mass audience and the cult of the golf course architect was born.

Jones was born in Ince, England, in 1906, and he emigrated with his parents to Rochester, N.Y., three years later. He was a scratch golfer by his early teens but an ulcer sidelined him from tournament competition. A high school dropout, Jones was working as a draftsman for a railroad company when Donald Ross came to Rochester to build Oak Hill. Jones was fascinated with what he saw, and in short order, he parlayed some golf connections into a special entry to Cornell University. There he designed his own course of studies to prepare for a career in golf course architecture, and although his special status precluded a degree, he learned his lessons well enough that in 1930 he formed a partnership with Canadian architect Stanley Thompson.

Jones' first masterwork came in 1948 when he collaborated with Bobby Jones on Peachtree Golf Club in Atlanta (to avoid confusion, Jones adopted the name Trent, from the river in England, and it stuck). Peachtree had all the design features that would become Trent Jones hallmarks: enormous, subtly-contoured greens that offered a host of pin positions, expansive tees that permitted numerous setups, unobtrusive hazards and a fanatical devotion to preserving the land's natural beauty. Among the many architects to be influenced by these design features are Jones' two sons, Robert Jr. and Rees, both prominent architects in their own right.

Of course, it's impossible to duplicate the real thing, in part because Trent Jones brought an unmistakable showmanship to his craft. This was never more evident than in the wake of his remodeling of Baltusrol's Lower Course in 1952, when a particularly outspoken member criticized the newly-designed fourth hole, a 194-yard par-3 over water. Eager to rebuff the sniping, Jones grabbed a spoon and heroically marched his critic and a few bystanders to the tee. He took a swing and the ball took one hop and dived into the hole.

"Gentlemen," said Jones, "I think the hole is eminently fair."

Jones, who spent his final years confined to a wheelchair, held sway in 2000 at 93. After having one stroke, he awakened in his hospital bed to see his two sons at his bedside. "What are you doing here?" he questioned. "You had a little setback," he was told. "You had a stroke." "Do I have to count it?" he asked.

## THE JONES RECORD

**Trent Jones has designed 216 courses in the United States and 45 overseas. He has also remodeled 150 courses around the world.**

**79 Major Championships have been played on his courses.**

# Betsy Rawls

**There is not a more respected woman in the game of golf than Betsy Rawls.** Her 55 career victories rank behind only Kathy Whitworth, Mickey Wright and Patty Berg, and she shares the record with Wright for the most U.S. Women's Opens with four. But as much as what she did on the course, Rawls was admired for her excellence at every level of the game.

The USGA could not have honored a more deserving person than Rawls when it presented her the Bob Jones Award for distinguished service in 1996. "Betsy has always been committed to work and dedicated to the game," said Wright. "I can think of only two women who have achieved as much, not only as players but for their lifetime contributions, and that's Betsy and Patty Berg."

Rawls did not swing a club until she was 17. Four years later, she won the 1949 Texas Amateur and, in 1950, she finished second behind Babe Zaharias in the Women's Open. After graduating Phi Beta Kappa from the University of Texas, she turned professional in 1951 and made the Open her first victory. She led the LPGA in earnings in 1952, won her second Women's Open in 1953 and her third in 1957. Her biggest year was 1959, when she won 10 times, including the LPGA Championship and the Western Open, and the Vare Trophy. Her biggest thrill was winning the LPGA Championship in 1969 because she had reached a point where she wasn't sure if she could win again.

"I thought I was going to be a winner, and as I went along, winning became easier and easier," Rawls has said. "It was something I expected to do. I always played well under pressure because it didn't bother me, which is why I won so many tournaments. I don't take much credit for it, but I could perform under tense situations. It was my physical makeup to allow that to happen."

When Rawls joined the tour, there were about 20 players and 20 tournaments. She served under Zaharias as the LPGA secretary and headed the tournament committee that set up the course, gave rulings, made pairings, kept statistics and did the bookkeeping. The rest of the year was spent barnstorming for Wilson Sporting Goods with Patty Berg. They would do upwards of 120 clinics a year, traveling the country in a car.

When she retired from tournament golf in 1975, Rawls became a tournament director for the LPGA and later took over as executive director of the McDonald's LPGA Championship. She has also served on the USGA's rules committee and the LPGA Tournament Sponsors Association. In 1980, she became the first woman to officiate at the men's U.S. Open.

"Anybody who can make a living in golf is lucky," Rawls said. "Then to receive all the benefits accorded to me in the process...well, it makes me feel fortunate. It's more than I could possibly deserve."

## THE RAWLS RECORD

Major Championship Victories ..... 8
- U.S. Women's Open: 1951, 1953, 1957, 1960
- Women's Western Open: 1952, 1959
- LPGA: 1959, 1969

LPGA Tour Victories ............ 55

Vare Trophy: 1959

Leading Money Winner: 1952, 1959

Bob Jones Award: 1996

Tournament director for the LPGA Championship.

First woman to serve on the Rules Committee for the U. S. Open (men's).

# Tom Watson

**Of all the players who challenged Jack Nicklaus' supremacy, Tom Watson carved out the greatest legacy.**

Watson has won 39 events on the PGA TOUR, including two Masters and a U.S. Open and a remarkable five British Opens.

Beginning in 1977, Watson won six PGA TOUR Player of the Year awards, and he led the money list five times. Yet it was his head-to-head victories against Nicklaus, 10 years his senior, that cemented him as a player for the ages.

The first came at the 1977 Masters where Watson countered Nicklaus' fourth-round charge with four birdies on the closing six holes to win by two. Four months later in the British Open at Turnberry, the two engaged in the most intense and highest caliber sustained battle in the history of major championship golf. Tied after 36 holes, they were paired together in the final two rounds. Nicklaus shot 65-66, only to be beaten by Watson's 65-65.

Then in 1982, Nicklaus, gunning for a record fifth U.S. Open, held the lead down the stretch at Pebble Beach. Again Watson counterattacked, finally pitching in for a birdie from deep rough off the 17th hole to produce one of the most dramatic shots ever seen. When he also birdied the 72nd hole, he had won by two strokes and earned his only U.S. Open title.

Watson was born Sept. 4, 1949, in Kansas City, Mo. An all-around athlete growing up, the fresh-faced but fiercely competitive Watson was nicknamed "Huckleberry Dillinger." After a good but not spectacular junior career, Watson attended Stanford, where he graduated with a degree in psychology and showed occasional but not sustained brilliance as a golfer.

But once Watson joined the PGA TOUR, he showed a determination to excel that soon set him apart. "Tom would never tolerate a weakness," said Lanny Wadkins. "He'd go to the practice tee and beat at it until the darn thing went away."

Still, Watson had trouble winning early in his career. At the 1974 U.S. Open at Winged Foot, he took a one-stroke lead into the final round, only to shoot a 79 that dropped him to fifth. He also led after 36 holes the next year at Medinah but again finished weakly. Watson once said, "I learned how to win by losing and not liking it." And he also learned from Byron Nelson, who later became his teacher and mentor.

At the British Open at Carnoustie, Watson holed a 20-footer for birdie on the 72nd hole to get into a playoff with Jack Newton and prevailed by one stroke in the 18-hole playoff. It would start a pattern of success in the oldest major that best reflected Watson's indefatigable character as a player. Watson won the claret jug four more times, in 1977, 1980, 1982 and 1983. "Tom takes a deep-rooted pleasure at the prospect of the challenge," said his friend and former USGA president Frank "Sandy" Tatum. "What evolves is the focusing of an unusual intelligence on what he is setting out to do."

Although Watson was a long hitter who had frequent streaks of superb ball striking and birdie runs, he was even better as a scrambler who could manufacture good scores with what became know as "Watson pars." During his reign as the best player in the game, Watson was a fearless putter who frequently ran birdie chances well by the hole, but seemingly never missed the comebacker.

After his glory years ended with his last money title in 1984, Watson's putting declined and he won only three times since.

## THE WATSON RECORD

Major Championship Victories ..... 8
- Masters: 1977, 1981
- U.S. Open: 1982
- British Open: 1975, 1977, 1980, 1982, 1983

PGA TOUR Victories ........... 39

Champions Tour Victories ......... 5

Ryder Cup Teams ................ 5
- (10-4-1) .... 1977, 1981, 1983, 1989
- Captain ..................... 1993

Vardon Trophy: 1977, 1978, 1979

Leading Money Winner: 1977, 1978, 1979, 1980, 1984

Bob Jones Award: 1987

# Peter Thomson

**Peter Thomson was the thinking man's golfer.** His clean, brisk game was based on cold logic and a gift for reducing things to their simplest essentials. His style was free of the extraneous, so that the path he would take to victory seemed a remarkably straight line.

Between 1954 and 1965, the Australian won the British Open five times. He and Young Tom Morris were among only four men to win it three times consecutively. He won 26 times in Europe, 19 times in Australia and New Zealand and 11 more times in Asia and Japan. He played only a few seasons in America, garnering one victory in the U.S., the 1956 Texas Open, where he closed with a 63 and defeated Cary Middlecoff and Gene Littler in a playoff.

Thomson was best on fast-running courses where judging the bounce and run of the ball was more important than long hitting. Mostly for that reason, he did not excel when playing on the well-watered and longer courses in the United States. Other than his victory in Texas, Thomson's best showing in a U.S. event was a fourth place in the 1956 U.S. Open and a fifth in the 1957 Masters. He never played in the PGA Championship.

That apparent void in his record is the reason Thomson's victory in the 1965 British Open at Birkdale is considered his finest hour. By that year, most of America's prominent professionals were competing in the oldest championship, and Thomson beat them all handily.

But even without that victory, Thomson's championship mettle is beyond reproach. With his confident gait and serene smile, he had the self-possessed aura of a winner. "I never saw a golfer who seemed so assured of his destiny," wrote Pat Ward-Thomas. "There is about him the unmistakable air of success."

Thomson was born Aug. 23, 1929, in Melbourne, Australia. As a boy, his first strokes were made on the sly at a nine-hole club named Royal Park. When the members saw his talent, he was given playing privileges, and by age 15 was the club champion. After a two-year apprenticeship as an assistant pro along Melbourne's famed sandbelt, Thomson turned professional and quickly dominated Australian golf. "I sensed he had that inevitable something when I first set eyes on him," said the great Australian pro, Norman von Nida. As a young professional, he was profoundly influenced by friendships with Bobby Locke, Ben Hogan and Sam Snead.

Thomson was gifted with a true affinity for being in the thick of the tense closing moments of a championship. "That was the real thrill of it for me," he said in his biography. "I've seen a lot of people find themselves in that situation, and I suspect that very few of them like it, but I really enjoyed it."

By temperament and design, Thomson indeed seemed pressure-proof. His grip was light, his manner at address brisk and his motion through the ball graceful and devoid of much physical effort. He was a reliable and occasionally brilliant putter. "There were no frills," said von Nida, "so virtually nothing could go wrong."

Above all, Thomson had a head for the game. "The most important facets of golf are careful planning, calm and clear thinking and the ordinary logic of common sense," he once wrote. It was the same cool detachment with which he separated his competitive self from the rest of his life. He was truly a balanced man in a world that usually requires obsessive and narrow dedication. Thomson enjoyed reading, the opera and painting. He ran for elected office in Australia in 1982, narrowly losing. After his competitive rounds, when he was abroad, he often wrote cogent dispatches and columns for the *Melbourne Herald*. Later in his career, he designed golf courses, especially in Asia, where he was also instrumental in establishing professional tours. His diverse interests were a big reason why he chose not to uproot himself for America like other Australian golfers.

Thomson did give the Champions Tour a brief try and the results were outstanding. In 1985, he won nine tournaments, a record he shares with Hale Irwin.

## THE THOMSON RECORD

| | |
|---|---|
| Major Championship Victories | 5 |
| British Open: 1954, 1955, 1956, 1958, 1965 | |
| Total Tournaments Won | 57 |
| PGA TOUR Victories | 6 |
| European Tour Victories | 26 |
| Australasia Tour Victories | 19 |
| Champions Tour Victories | 11 |

# Bob Harlow

**Visionary. Trailblazer. Father of the PGA TOUR.** This was Bob Harlow, the man who packaged and promoted golf in this country into an entertainment business. What were innovations for Harlow are institutions today, ideas such as a year-round schedule, the concept of a volunteer system and the PGA's Merchandise Show. "He was the one who really put it in some kind of order, setting up the basic framework that exists today," said golf writer Al Barkow. He did this right after the Depression, selling golf not only as a sport, but as a product. He was the game's first mover and shaker.

Harlow's background was newspapers, but he loved the theatre and reading *Variety*, the show business bible. As a youth, he had been a performer, and he married a woman who was a concert singer. His first connection to golf was through the management of Walter Hagen, but that was a no-brainer. Hagen was a showman, and Harlow wrote most of his material. It was a great marriage.

Hagen was the box office, but it took more than a marquee for Harlow to sell the sport in America. Being the son of a minister certainly helped. Sitting through those Sunday services taught Harlow how to proselytize and raise money. He would go into towns and cities and convince the local Chambers of Commerce and the community leaders that playing host to golf tournaments was the way to go. He would get businesses, country clubs, radio stations and newspapers behind the event, and then he would go on to the next town or city, doing the same deal all over. The PGA of America hired him for $100 a week to do this job, but there were spinoffs that Harlow could cash in on. As the manager for Hagen, Paul Runyan, Horton Smith and Ed Dudley, Harlow practically controlled the show, so he would book these marathon exhibition swings where his players would play against each other, five to six times a week, for more than a month. They would do this traveling through the American heartland, states like Missouri, Illinois, Oklahoma, Texas, Kansas, Nebraska, Colorado, Utah and Idaho.

In November 1930, Harlow proposed the idea of a year-around tournament circuit. He introduced the concept of public relations and published the first media guide called the Tournament Players Record Book. In it, he wrote: "Entertaining of newspapermen is recommended."

Harlow was a master of "spin." During the Depression, he announced that there would be "fewer and better tournaments" for the 1934-1935 season. Purses dropped as low as $1,500, but Harlow kept the tour afloat. "The Tournament Bureau of the PGA is working for a number of worthwhile purposes," Harlow wrote. "First to keep the game of golf before the sports-loving public so that enthusiasm may be maintained in a game which is getting plenty of competition from other sports. The second is to provide a great deal of competition for our professionals so that they can maintain a high standard of play and that new players may be developed."

The PGA eventually felt that Harlow had too many irons in the fire and elected to replace him in 1936 with Fred Corcoran. At age 57, he went on to form the weekly magazine, *Golf World*. The idea, in the words of golf writer Charles Price, was "put the whole community of golf on a party line." Moving to Pinehurst, N.C., he became publicity director for America's golf capital and publisher, writer and photographer for *Golf World*.

There were never enough jobs for Bob Harlow, and it can be said he did them all very well.

## THE HARLOW RECORD

Business Manager, Walter Hagen: 1921-1929

Tournaments Manager, PGA: 1930-1935

Founder, *Golf World* magazine: 1947

The SILVER PAGES
aureus

# Raymond Floyd

**Raymond Floyd carried an aura as a competitor and a winner that drew fear from his rivals whenever his name went on a leader board, which it did during four different decades.**

In notching 22 PGA TOUR victories, including four major championships from 1963 to 1992, Floyd distinguished himself as a player without a discernible weakness and whose strengths were a superb short game and an obvious mental toughness. The latter was manifested in his distinctive stare, the look of complete concentration that invariably took over his features when he was in contention for a title. "I've seen Raymond win without it, but I've never seen him lose with it," said his wife, Maria, the person Floyd maintains has been the key figure in his long career.

When Floyd's game was on, he was capable of some of the hottest 72-hole forays ever seen. In 1976, he won the Masters by eight strokes with a then-record-tying score of 271, using a 5-wood to consistently hit the par-5s in two and playing them in 16 under par for the week. At the 1982 PGA Championship at Southern Hills, Floyd was again on fire, opening with a record 63 and going wire-to-wire again to win by three.

Along with his explosiveness, Floyd had longevity. He and Sam Snead are the only players ever to win official events in four different decades. In 1992, he became the first player to win on the PGA TOUR and Champions Tour in the same year.

Floyd was born Sept. 4, 1942, in Fort Bragg, N.C. His father was a golf professional in the military managing a driving range and later a golf course at Fort Bragg. At 17, Floyd won the National Jaycees, but almost became a professional baseball player before turning down an offer to pitch in the Cleveland Indians farm system.

He joined the tour in 1963 and won in his 11th start at the St. Petersburg Open. Floyd was obviously talented, a long hitter with a gifted short game, but he won only once more in the next six years. By his own admission, the young Floyd was as interested in having a good time away from the golf course as getting the most from his game on it.

But in 1969, he set a goal to win $100,000, win a major championship and make the Ryder Cup team. He did all three while taking the 1969 PGA Championship. Still, Floyd did not become a truly dedicated player until his marriage to Maria Fraietta in 1973. "She got me to respect my ability," said Floyd. "I decided to find out how good I could be, and it made a huge difference." Beginning in 1975, Floyd averaged a victory a year for the next 17 years. In 1983, he won the Vardon Trophy.

Floyd's crowning achievement was winning the 1986 U.S. Open at Shinnecock Hills. Floyd had never played particularly well at the Open, posting only two top-10 finishes in his previous 18 tries. But the spacious feel of Shinnecock brought out his best. He played controlled golf, put together a flawless back nine on Sunday and won by two strokes.

The only major Floyd never won was the British Open, where he tied for second at St. Andrews in 1978 and was joint third in 1981.

Floyd was one of the first players to combine tremendous power with a soft touch, making him an important player in the evolution of the modern game. Floyd's short game is considered exemplary, and he is often acknowledged as one of the greatest chippers the game has ever seen.

## THE FLOYD RECORD

Major Championship Victories ..... 4
- Masters: 1976
- U.S. Open: 1986
- PGA: 1969, 1982

PGA TOUR Victories ........... 22

Champions Tour Victories ....... 14

Ryder Cup Teams ................ 9
(12-16-2) .. 1969, 1975, 1977, 1981, 1983, 1985, 1991, 1993

Captain ...................... 1989

Vardon Trophy: 1983

IZOD
CLUB

# Nancy Lopez

**The year was 1978, and the Ladies Professional Golf Association was suffering an identity crisis.** From Roswell, N.M., came an unidentified flying star, a Mexican-American girl whose father owned an auto-body shop. She won the state amateur when she was 12, two U.S. Girls' Junior titles, an NCAA title, and, in 1975, she finished second in the U.S. Women's Open. If this wasn't the savior, then only God knows who was.

Her name was Nancy Lopez, and it wasn't long before everybody just called her Nancy. She won five consecutive tournaments in 1978, and everybody sort of hitched a ride on her skirt tails: the press, the fans, the sponsors, even the rest of the women playing the sport. These were magical times for women's golf, and nobody seemed to want to get in her way.

She won nine times that year, including the LPGA Championship, eight times in 1979 and she was the nicest person in the world. "After my first year I thought, 'I could be a flash in the pan,' and I was also determined to prove I was not," Lopez has said. "I was determined not to fall on my face, though it is easy enough to choke yourself to death trying to win."

Looking back on these years Jaime Diaz wrote in *Sports Illustrated* that Lopez had burst on the scene with as much charisma as anyone since Babe Didrikson Zaharias.

Not even Zaharias had become a legend so fast. She was all of 21 years old, and the veterans marveled not only at her golfing ability, but her poise and maturity.

"Never in my life have I seen such control from someone so young," said Mickey Wright.

"They've got the wrong person playing Wonder Woman," said Judy Rankin.

"We're all trying to steal Nancy's birth-control pills, but so far we've been unsuccessful," said JoAnne Carner.

After marrying baseball star Ray Knight, she struggled balancing her career with motherhood. By the time she was 30, Nancy Lopez still had won enough tournaments (35) to qualify for the LPGA Hall of Fame. At that point, she was Player of the Year three times, Vare Trophy winner three times and her stroke average in 1985 of 70.73 was then an LPGA record.

Lopez had the ability to close. She was the youngest qualifier for the LPGA Hall of Fame and had to wait six months to be inducted as the rules for admission required that a player be on tour for 10 years. "I feel honored to be with the other women in the Hall of Fame," Lopez said. "I have always respected them and what they have done for women's golf. I look at each player, and some are already legends while others will become legends as time goes by. I feel I'm great now, being in the Hall of Fame, having accomplished what I've done and being with the greatest golfers. I feel great that I can say I'm one of them."

Lopez won her 48th tournament in 1997, and at the age of 40, finished second for the fourth time in the U.S. Women's Open. She shot four rounds in the 60s–the first woman to do so–but lost by a stroke to Alison Nicholas.

"I'd love to have won the Open," Lopez once said. "But I've had enough good things in life that I won't be shattered because I don't."

In 2002 at age 45, with an accumulation of aches, pains and family commitments, Lopez announced that the 25th year of her storied career would be her last playing a full-time schedule. "I am not walking away from golf," she said. "I am at the beginning of a brand new chapter in my golf career."

## THE LOPEZ RECORD

Major Championship Victories ..... 3
LPGA: 1978, 1985, 1989

LPGA Tour Victories ............ 48

Curtis Cup Teams ................ 1
(2-0-0) ..................... 1976

Vare Trophy: 1978, 1979, 1985

Leading Money Winner: 1978, 1979, 1985

Bob Jones Award: 1998

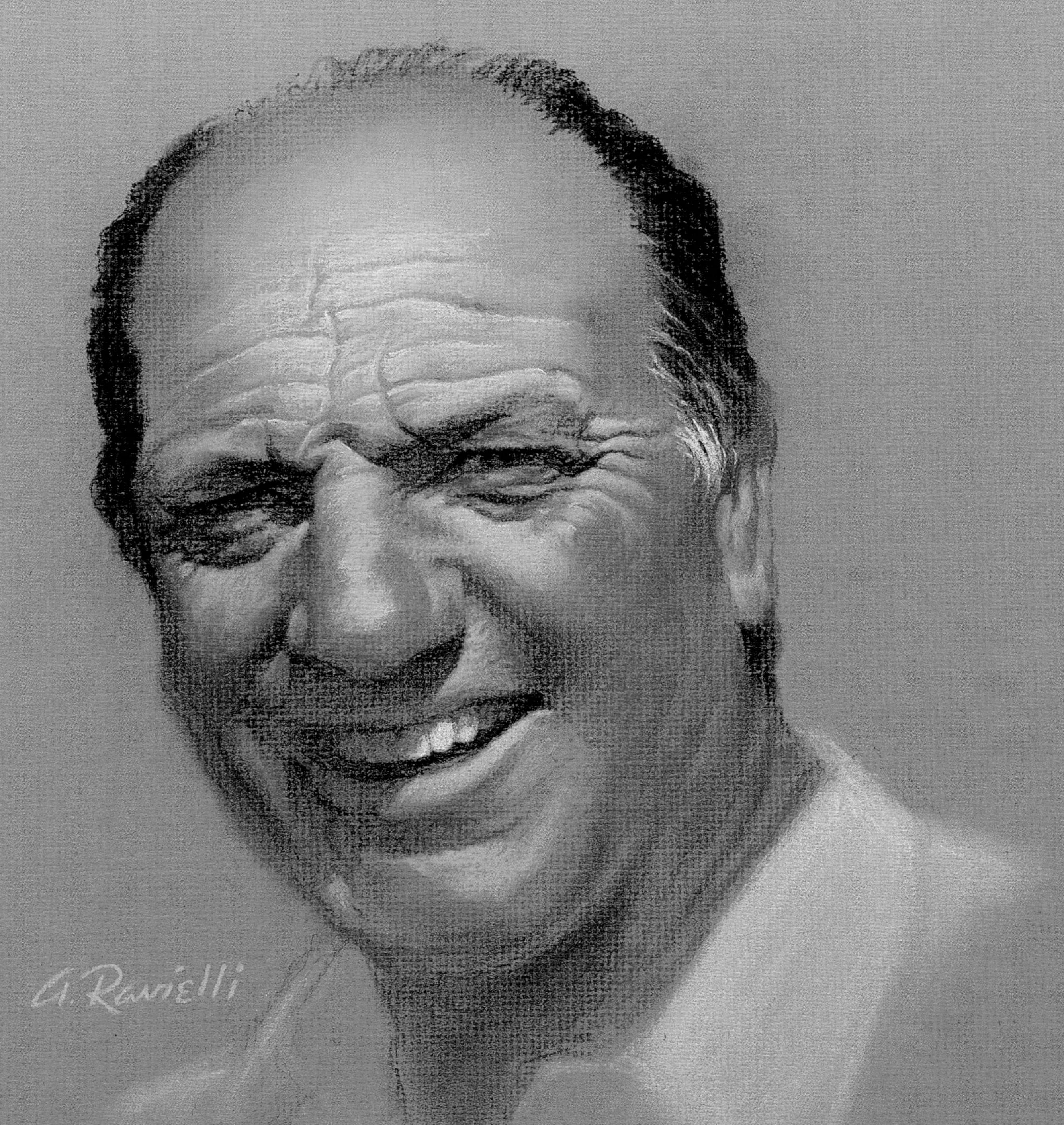
A. Ravielli

# Roberto DeVicenzo

**The world will always remember Roberto De Vicenzo for what he lost, not for what he won—for that careless mistake he made at the 1968 Masters, signing an incorrect scorecard that had him making a par and not a birdie on the 17th hole that Sunday afternoon—and, thus, his uttering of the immortal golf quote, "What a stupid I am."**

Yet there is so much more to De Vicenzo's career and the contributions he made to golf around the world than what occurred in the scorer's tent at Augusta National that should not overshadow the man's legacy. Roberto De Vicenzo won more than 230 golf tournaments, including the 1967 British Open at Hoylake, where he held off the Sunday charges of Jack Nicklaus and Gary Player to become, at 44, the oldest winner of the world's oldest golf championship.

Facing success and catastrophe and treating those twin imposters the same inspired British golf writer Peter Dobereiner to use the Rudyard Kipling quote when giving De Vicenzo his due. In Dobereiner's words, "By that standard, De Vicenzo is a giant of a man because he faced the greatest triumph and the most devastating disaster which the game of golf can provide." The United States Golf Association and the Golf Writers Association of America agreed, presenting De Vicenzo with the Bob Jones and William Richardson Awards, respectively, in 1970.

All the trophies he captured didn't mean as much to De Vicenzo as the friends he made traveling the globe. He won national opens in Belgium, Brazil, Chile, Colombia, Holland, France, Germany, Jamaica, Mexico, Panama, Peru, Spain, Uruguay and Argentina, a country he represented 17 times in the World Cup. Essayist Jack Whitaker once said that if golf were war, Roberto would have conquered more countries than Alexander the Great. But golf was not war to De Vicenzo. And that is what made him so loved.

Born in Buenos Aires April 14, 1923, De Vicenzo learned the game as a caddy's assistant. He turned professional at age 15 and won his first of nine Argentine Open titles six years later. Three-time British Open champion Henry Cotton once said there were very few professionals in the business who would not take the play through the green of Argentine golfing master Roberto De Vicenzo, and his game never left him. At 51 he won the PGA Seniors' Championship and in 1980, at age 57, the inaugural U.S. Senior Open.

He believed in hard practice, routinely hitting 400 balls a day and maintaining a slow pace. "If you hurry," he would say, "then nothing seems to go right." He'd visualize a shot, pick a club and hit. His method was simple to watch, and it held up under pressure.

It did that final round at the Masters in 1968. What's lost behind that staggering mistake made by fellow competitor Tommy Aaron and signed for by De Vicenzo is that Roberto shot what has been called one of the greatest rounds in major championship history. He took only 65 strokes around Augusta National that day, including a bogey at the 18th, on his 45th birthday. His 31 on the front side started with an eagle 2 at the first and tied the course record. It should have been good enough to tie Bob Goalby and set up a playoff which, had he won, would have given Roberto De Vicenzo both the British Open and Masters titles at the same time.

## THE DE VICENZO RECORD

Total Worldwide Victories ...... 240
  Major Championship Victories ... 1
  British Open: 1967
PGA TOUR Victories ............ 5
Other Significant Victories
  PGA Seniors': 1974
  U.S. Senior Open: 1980
Champions Tour Victories ......... 2
Represented Argentina in World Cup 17 times
Bob Jones Award: 1970
William Richardson Award: 1970

# Jim Barnes

**Known as "Long Jim" because of his 6-feet 4-inches in height, lanky build and long hitting, Barnes won four major championships in an era best known for the exploits of Walter Hagen and Gene Sarazen.**

The tallest of the champions for the first half of the century, Jim Barnes won the first PGA Championship ever played, in 1916, and won the next one, played in 1919. He won the 1921 U.S. Open at the Columbia C.C. by nine strokes and the 1925 British Open at Prestwick, when he came from five strokes behind after Macdonald Smith faltered with a final-round 82. He is one of only eight golfers to have won those three. He also won the Western Open three times, which in his day, was considered an elite championship. He never played in the Masters, which began in 1934. On the U.S. tour, he is credited with 21 career victories and 14 seconds.

In his U.S. Open victory, Barnes opened with a 69 to take a three-stroke lead and was never challenged. When Barnes won, he was given the trophy by President Warren Harding, making him the only player in history to receive the U.S. Open trophy from the President of the United States.

Barnes was runner-up in the PGA to Walter Hagen in 1921 and 1924. He was also second in the 1922 British Open. He won the North and South Open in 1916, his first victory, and again in 1919. In 1916, he also won a PGA Stroke Play Championship played after the match-play event, but it was never counted as official.

His last victory came in the 1939 New Jersey Open when he was 52 years old.

Sarazen, who feuded with Barnes because of what he considered the older man's brusque manner, nevertheless rated him the finest 5-iron player he had ever seen. In 1940, Barnes was made one of the 12 original inductees into the PGA Hall of Fame.

Barnes was born in Lelant, England, in 1887. At age 15, he was made an assistant pro. He emigrated to San Francisco in 1906, but never became an American citizen, remaining an intensely patriotic Cornishman. Still, he remained attached to his native country, playing in the British Open regularly and finishing in the top eight seven times between 1920 and 1928. In 1919, Barnes produced a book, *Picture Analysis of Golf Strokes*, which became one of the most widely read instructionals of the day. It featured full photographs of Barnes' strong, compact swing at key points. The book revolutionized printed golf instruction.

"His finish was a model for a tall man who is inclined to spring up too soon after the ball is hit," wrote Bernard Darwin. "Everything he did was pleasant to watch."

Barnes had an angular, serious face that was topped by a thatch of unruly hair that gave him "an aspect which, to the stranger, suggested the Wild West," according to Darwin. He was an intense, quiet competitor who often kept a sprig of clover or grass clamped tightly between his teeth. All his career, he was one of the few players who wore trousers instead of knickers, an "old school" conceit.

Barnes was a man of few words, but he possessed important wisdom, which he imparted when he felt the subject was worthy. He once told the young Jones, "Bobby, you can't always be playing well when it counts. You'll never win golf tournaments until you learn how to score well when you're playing badly." The statement made a profound impact on Jones, who later wrote, "This is perhaps what I learned to do best of all."

Barnes died in 1966.

## THE BARNES RECORD

Major Championship Victories ..... 4
- U.S. Open: 1921
- British Open: 1925
- PGA: 1916, 1919

Other Significant Victories
- North and South Open: 1916, 1919
- Western Open: 1914, 1917, 1919

PGA TOUR Victories ........... 21

# William C. Campbell

**The era is sadly over when some of America's best golfers played the game as amateurs, and it was often what these men and women stood for that was as important as the trophies they won.** Born in West Virginia, educated at Princeton, Bill Campbell never had the desire to chase the buck. After college and the service, he stayed at home, opened an insurance business, served in the legislature and played golf because he loved playing golf. He played it at the highest level and became one of the game's most distinguished statesmen.

Only Chick Evans (49) played in the U.S. Amateur more times than Campbell (37), and not even Evans played in 33 consecutively, as Campbell did from 1941-1977. That he finally won it in 1964, at the age of 41, is a testament to the doggedness of his pursuit. He won it just after Jack Nicklaus and Deane Beman turned pro, and just before names such as Bob Murphy, Bruce Fleisher, Steve Melnyk, Lanny Wadkins, Craig Stadler and Jerry Pate came along to snatch the title in the midst of their college careers. The next day he was back in his office.

"We hadn't reached the point yet where the better amateurs would routinely turn pro," Campbell said. "We weren't into the college golf syndrome where it was a scholarship leading to the tour. It was just the beginning of that. We had quite a number of people like myself who were fair players, who wanted to play competitive golf but had no intention of being professional golfers. The amateur game was pretty lively without being dominated by college golf. It was a fun thing. You'd run into the same people year after year. You grew older as they did. Over that period of the late '40s to the late '60s, I had the pleasure of being a part of that."

It once was written in *Golf Journal* that Bill Campbell was a professional at being an amateur golfer, and that sums it up. He is a man who will go to extremes in order not to take advantage of an opponent, but the gentlemen golfer is also the personification of determination. In the 1947 U.S. Amateur at Pebble Beach, he hit his first two drives out of bounds, but chipped in to halve the hole and went on to win the match.

Campbell won 15 West Virginia State Amateur titles, three West Virginia State Opens, the North and South Amateur four times and was undefeated in Walker Cup singles competition, holding a 7-0-1 record in the eight matches he played between 1951 and 1975. That also gives Campbell a unique record: Most Years Between U.S. Walker Cup Selections (24).

Campbell also served as U.S. Golf Association president in 1982-1983 and was the third American nominated to be captain of the Royal and Ancient Golf Club of St. Andrews, Scotland. When he accepted the position, Campbell wanted to reaffirm the manners that go with golf and remind everyone that it is a game of relationships and of dignity and of self-respect.

"It is an honorable game, an honorable institution, if you will, so that people shouldn't need policemen to keep them straight," Campbell said. "That goes with being a golfer."

## THE CAMPBELL RECORD

Major Championship Victories ..... 1
- U.S. Amateur: 1964
- (Played in 37 Amateurs, including a record 33 straight from 1941 to 1977.)

Walker Cup Teams .............. 8
- (11-4-3) ... 1951, 1953, 1955, 1957, 1965, 1967, 1971, 1975
- Captain .................... 1955

Other Significant Victories
- North and South Amateur: 1950, 1953, 1957, 1967
- West Virginia State Amateur: 15 times
- Mexican Amateur: 1956
- U.S. Senior Amateur: 1979, 1980

Bob Jones Award: 1956

President, USGA: 1982, 1983

# Paul Runyan

**No player in the history of golf was a more feared little man than Paul Runyan.** His career was the fulfillment of his goal to be the best truly light-hitting player who ever lived.

Slight at 5-7, 125 pounds, Runyan could produce little power with a swing that featured a pronounced sway—in tournaments where his drives were measured, he barely averaged 230 yards off the tee. But Runyan was deadly straight, a tremendously accurate fairway-wood player and reliable with the irons. Around and on the greens he was an absolute a genius. Throw in killer instinct and Depression-bred toughness and you get the golfer known as "Little Poison."

"Don't let the bad shots get to you," said Runyan. "Don't let yourself become angry. The true scramblers are thick-skinned. And they always beat the whiners."

Between 1930 and 1941, Runyan won 29 times on the PGA Tour. In 1933, he racked up nine victories and, in 1934, he won six more and captured the money title the first year such records were kept with a total of $6,767.

He also won the 1934 PGA, beating Craig Wood on the 38th hole. Four years later at Shawnee-on-Delaware, Pa., he won the PGA again, defeating Sam Snead in the final, 8 and 7, in what has become golf history's definitive David vs. Goliath story. Although Snead was out-driving him by 45 yards and more, Runyan kept hitting his fairway-wood approaches inside of the stronger man. On the par 5s, where Snead figured to have a decided advantage, Runyan zeroed in from inside 100 yards to birdie six of the seven that were played. "This isn't golf, it's magic," said Snead at one point during the match. Later he would write, "I don't suppose anyone ever got more out of their golf game than Paul Runyan. He could get the ball up and down from a manhole."

During that 1938 PGA, Runyan was 24 under par for the 196 holes he played, including 64 consecutive holes without going over par. He felt he was at his best in match play, in large part because his style of play wore down opponents psychologically, and because of his own nature. "You are in for the fight of your life," he said. "It is just instinctive that I fight."

Runyan was born July 12, 1908, in Hot Springs, Ark. His father was a farmer who assigned his son plenty of chores, but the young Runyan soon gravitated to the town golf club across the road, where he discovered he could make more money caddying and working for the pro. He also became consumed with the new game.

"I had to work for it," he said. "I was not a natural. All the kids in the caddy pen beat me, until I just dug it out and became better."

Runyan was made an apprentice at the club and would play four holes on the way to school and five on the way back. He recognized early that he would have to have a good short game to be competitive, and he made it his specialty. Byron Nelson chose Runyan as the finest chipper he ever saw, and his wrist-free stroke is a staple of the short-game method that Runyan later imparted to Gene Littler and Phil Rodgers.

"Through necessity, I began my lifelong devotion to the short game," he wrote, "the searching for shortcuts that would somehow let me compete, and hopefully excel, in a world of stronger players." Runyan ultimately came to regard his short game as an offensive weapon for defeating the course and demoralizing an opponent.

Runyan was tenacious, cocky and indomitable. As late as 1951, he was one shot from the lead in the U.S. Open at Oakland Hills after three rounds before finishing tied for sixth. He won the U.S. PGA Seniors' in 1961 and 1962. Runyan, who was equally renowned as an instructor, passed away at age 93 on March 17, 2002.

"I've taken some pleasure out of being the little guy who has beaten the big fellows," he said. "I would like to be remembered as the best of the truly light hitters." He is.

## THE RUNYAN RECORD

Major Championship Victories ..... 2
PGA: 1934, 1938
Other Significant Victories
PGA Seniors': 1961, 1962
PGA TOUR Victories ........... 29
Ryder Cup Teams ................ 2
(2-2-0) ................ 1933, 1935
Leading Money Winner: 1934

WORLD GOLF HALL of FAME

# Gene Littler

**Great swings last, and if longevity was the only measure, Gene Littler would have to be considered among the giants of the game.** As it was, he won 29 PGA TOUR tournaments including a U.S. Open, was a stalwart in the Ryder Cup across two decades and was a dominant force in the early years of the Champions Tour. But unquestionably Littler's sustained excellence is what made his career so noteworthy. Only once during the quarter century from 1954 to 1979 did he finish out of the top 60 on the money list, and that was in 1972, when he was sidelined by surgery to remove a cancerous lymph node. Littler bounced back from that to win three tournaments and finish fifth on the money list in 1975 at the age of 45 and two years later he won again at 47.

Imagine how good Littler's career could have been if he was more passionate about golf. He was often criticized for wanting to spend more time at home in sunny Rancho Santa Fe, Calif., among his vintage car collection than grinding it out on the golf circuit. What allowed Littler to coast was one of the finest natural swings the game has ever known. Gene Sarazen called it "a perfect swing like Sam Snead's—only better," and also talked of Littler's "remarkable physical equipment. He has a pair of wrists like wagon tongues and hands like hams." Littler himself had little explanation for the beauty and simplicity of his swing. "I just put the ball down and hit," he once said. Economy, softspokeness and dry wit were part of his makeup. He once said, "I drew a big gallery today. I was paired with Palmer." Former tennis champion Ted Schroeder, father of golfer John Schroeder, summed up his friend thusly: "He gave me a typical Littler conversation. Three yeps, two nopes and two nods."

Littler was born in San Diego in 1930 and first attracted national notice 23 years later, when he sank an 18-foot birdie putt on the 18th green at the Oklahoma C.C. to win the U.S. Amateur, 1 up, over Dale Morey. Four months later Littler won the San Diego Open as an amateur, and two days after that, he turned pro. The following year he won four times, earning the nickname "Gene the Machine" for his remarkably consistent ball-striking. Often overlooked was his outstanding short game.

Littler's tendency to fiddle with his near-perfect swing led to a pronounced slump (by his lofty standards) in 1957 and 1958, but after changing his grip on the advice of Paul Runyan, he quickly found his old form. In 1961, he won his only professional major, the U.S. Open at Oakland Hills. He closed with a 68 to hold off Bob Goalby and Doug Sanders by one stroke. He came close in two other majors. The closest he came was the 1970 Masters, when he shot a steady 69-70-70-70 to tie Billy Casper, but was outgunned, 74 to 69, by his boyhood friend and rival in the playoff that followed. In the 1977 PGA Championship at Pebble Beach, Littler led from the first round, but closed with a 76 and was tied by Lanny Watkins, who won on the third extra hole the first time a major championship was ever decided in sudden death. Littler also played on seven U.S. Ryder Cup teams, compiling a superb 14-5-8 record.

In 1980, Littler became eligible for the Champions Tour and proceeded to win three of his first five tournaments. Littler's play surprised no one because after 30 years "Gene the Machine" winning golf tournaments had come to be expected.

## THE LITTLER RECORD

Major Championship Victories ..... 2
U.S. Amateur: 1953
U.S. Open: 1961

PGA Tour Victories ............. 29

Champions Tour Victories ......... 8

Other Senior Victories ............ 9

Walker Cup Teams ............... 1
(2-0-0) ..................... 1953

Ryder Cup Teams ................ 7
(14-5-8) ......... 1961, 1963, 1965, 1967, 1969, 1971, 1975

Bob Jones Award: 1973

Ben Hogan Award: 1973

WORLD GOLF HALL of FAME

# Horton Smith

**Horton Smith was one of golf's first boy wonders.** In 1929, at the age of 21, he played a PGA TOUR then in its infancy and won eight of 22 events as well as finishing second six times.

Smith and Paul Runyan were the tour's top players during the Depression years. In all, Smith won 32 events and finished second 37 times. A tall, stylish man, he was a smooth swinger with a superb putting touch. Byron Nelson rated Smith the finest putter and chipper of his era, and long after he won his final tournament in 1941, Smith was much sought after by other players for putting advice.

Although Smith was never again quite as good as he had been in 1929, his greatest fame will always come from being the first winner of the Masters, then known as the Augusta National Invitational. In the fourth round, Craig Wood posted 285 early, so Smith knew he needed a 72 or better. After making a 20-foot birdie putt on the 17th hole, he knocked in a four-foot downhiller on the final green to win.

Smith won the event again in 1936. Two strokes behind Harry Cooper with five holes to go, he holed a 45-foot chip on the 68th, an eight-footer on the 69th, and a 16-footer on the 71st drenched by torrential rain. That year he also led the tour's money list with $7,662.

Smith was born in Springfield, Mo., on May 22, 1908, and took up golf when he was 12. He grew to 6-1 1/2 and 163 pounds, and honed his game as an assistant pro at the Springfield C.C. When he joined the tour he earned the nickname the Missouri Rover by tirelessly travelling the country by car, train and even boat to get to tournaments.

Indeed, one year Smith suffered a fractured wrist when he hit it against a metal sign while stretching his arm out of a car driven by Joe Kirkwood.

Smith is believed to be the first professional to use a sand wedge in competition, a 23-ounce model invented by Texas cotton farmer Edward Kerr McClain. Smith used it in 1930 before it was banned for having a concave face. Smith also gave one to Bobby Jones, who used it to make a crucial birdie in the final round of the British Open at Hoylake on his way to the Grand Slam. Earlier in the year, Smith had won the Savannah Open to become the last man to defeat Jones in competition before his retirement.

According to Herbert Warren Wind, Smith was a student of the game who could be "overlogical, studious, finicky," and probably experimented with his swing too much. Fairly early in his career, Smith's swing lost its compact groove but soon became "the simplified and correct thing it had been."

Smith didn't smoke or drink. He was one of the rare professionals of his day who had attended college, the State Teacher's College in Springfield. Later, showing organizational and public relations talent, Smith became chairman of the the tour's competition committee and eventually president of the PGA from 1952 to 1954.

Smith was chosen for five Ryder Cup teams and was never beaten. During his run of victories in 1929, he shot an all-time tour low 72-hole score of 245 at the par-64, 4,700-yard Catalina CC in California in 1928. He had scores of 63, 58, 61 and 63. He finished third at the U.S. Open in 1930 and 1940, and in the 1930 British Open. He died in 1963.

## THE SMITH RECORD

Major Championship Victories ..... 2
Masters: 1934, 1936

PGA TOUR Victories ........... 32

Other Significant Victories
French Open: 1928
Florida Open: 1929
North and South Open: 1929, 1937

Ryder Cup Teams ................ 5
(3-0-1) .......... 1929, 1931, 1933, 1935, 1937

Leading Money Winner: 1929, 1936

President, PGA: 1952, 1953, 1954

# Pat Bradley

**There has not been a more consistent performer or dedicated individual in Ladies Professional Golf Association history than Pat Bradley.** This is a woman who made it on course management, patience and dogged determination, who experienced the highest of highs and the lowest of lows, and then came back to become the 12th woman enshrined in the LPGA Hall of Fame. "Commitment was the key," Bradley said. "You can have success, failure, setback and defeat, and rise above it."

During her prime, Bradley competed in 627 tournaments, posting 312 top-10 finishes, with 208 of those in the top five. She became the first woman golfer to surpass the $2 million (1986), $3 million (1990) and $4 million (1991) marks in career earnings and was the first woman to win all four of the modern major golf championships. In 1986, she won the Nabisco Dinah Shore, the LPGA Championship, the du Maurier and finished fifth at the U.S. Women's Open, three strokes out of the Jane Geddes-Sally Little playoff.

That was the year that defined Bradley's career. "I have been a very consistent and very good player, but I really believe that in 1986 I was tapped to be a little bit more distinguished than the other players," Bradley said. "I think somewhere, someone up above picked me to have a year that will go down in golfing history and will make me just a little more special than other people. I honestly wish everyone could experience what I did in that dream-come-true year. I was invincible."

After every one of her victories, it became a tradition for Bradley's mother to stand on the porch of their home in Westford, Mass., and ring a Swiss cow bell. Kathleen Bradley rang it and rang it, starting in 1975 when her daughter won the Colgate Far East Open, and ending in 1991 when Pat won for the 30th time to qualify for the LPGA Hall of Fame. The bell was retired and is part of an exhibit at the World Golf Hall of Fame in St. Augustine, Fla.

Qualifying for the Hall was a goal of Bradley's father, Richard, who died in 1988. That was the same year that Pat was diagnosed with Graves Disease and had plummeted to 109th on the money list with barely more than $15,000 in earnings. "I had a fear of failing him," Bradley said. "For many years I felt in my heart I was Hall of Fame material, but not in my mind. I was not completing the mission."

Bradley rebounded from the emotional loss of her father and the overactive thyroid in 1989, winning the Al Star/Centinela Classic. Three more victories followed in 1990, then three more in 1991 leading up to the MBS LPGA Classic at Los Coyotes C.C. in Buena Park, Calif. Bradley had won the SAFECO Classic the week before in Seattle and was ready to get it over with. She started the final round four strokes back, took the lead on Sunday with a birdie at the 13th hole and won by a stroke. When she was told that she had won, Bradley broke down in the scorer's tent and cried. The mission had been completed.

"I may not be up there attracting publicity or may not be a household name," Bradley has said. "I may be far behind in superstar quality, not as acceptable as some others, but in facts and figures, I'm up there with the greats."

## THE BRADLEY RECORD

Major Championship Victories ..... 6
- U. S. Women's Open: 1981
- LPGA: 1986
- Nabisco Dinah Shore: 1986
- Peter Jackson Classic: 1980
- du Maurier Classic: 1985, 1986

LPGA Tour Victories ............ 31

Rolex Player of the Year: 1986, 1991

Vare Trophy: 1986, 1991

Ben Hogan Award: 1991

Patty Berg Award: 2001

Solheim Cup: 4
- (2-5-1) .......... 1990, 1992, 1996,
- Captain ..................... 2000

WORLD GOLF HALL of FAME

# Hale Irwin

**When it comes to the toughest competitors and most analytical course managers ever to play, Hale Irwin is near the top of the list.**

Irwin's distinction was excelling when the conditions were toughest, and his three victories in the U.S. Open attest to a sharp mind, a solid game and an iron will.

It was never more apparent than at the 1974 U.S. Open, when Irwin persevered to win the so-called "Massacre at Winged Foot" with a score of seven-over-par 287. In perhaps the most difficult conditions an Open has ever been played under, Irwin shot rounds of 73-70-71-73 to win by two strokes.

Five years later at Inverness, on another punishing Open layout, Irwin shot even par to win by two. The scenario was quite different in 1990 at Medinah. Irwin was 45 and had not won on the PGA TOUR in five years. He received a special exemption to get into the championship. Lurking, but never in the thick of it until the final nine holes, Irwin made a 50-foot birdie putt on the final green that tied Mike Donald. The next day he fell behind but drew even when Donald bogeyed the 18th. Then, in the first sudden-death finish ever in the U.S. Open, Irwin birdied the 19th hole to win. Irwin became the oldest winner of the championship.

From 1971 to 1994, Irwin won 20 events on the PGA TOUR, on such difficult courses as Harbour Town—where his first, second and, at age 48, final PGA TOUR victories came—Butler National, Muirfield Village, Riviera and Pebble Beach. He is one of only 35 players in PGA TOUR history with 20 or more victories, but even when he wasn't winning, Irwin was, above all, consistent. His string of 86 consecutive tournaments from 1975 to 1978 without missing a cut is the fourth best in the PGA TOUR history, behind Byron Nelson, Jack Nicklaus and Tiger Woods.

Irwin came close in the other three majors, but never did better than a tie for second in the 1979 British Open. He played on five Ryder Cup teams, compiling a 13-5-2 record. It was Irwin's half with Bernhard Langer in the excruciatingly tense final singles match of the 1991 Ryder Cup that provided the margin of victory for the U.S.

Irwin was born June 3, 1945, in Joplin, Mo. As a boy, he began playing golf in Baxter Springs, Kan., on a 9-hole course with sand greens. He was, and remains, almost completely self taught. Irwin played all sports. At the University of Colorado he was a two-time All-Big Eight defensive back, as well as an academic All-American. As a golfer, he was the 1967 NCAA champion.

"I had to out-try, I had to out-hustle," said Irwin of his efforts in both sports. "When I got onto the tour, I relished the harder courses because I just felt I was going to try harder."

Irwin's game is neat and clean, not long but straight. One of his great strengths is a classically orthodox method due, in part, to an athletically proportioned 6-feet 175-pounds physique, but also in larger measure to Irwin's own studious development of good fundamentals. Says 1964 U.S. Open champion Ken Venturi, "Esthetically and technically, Hale stands at the ball as well as any player I've ever seen."

Just as he excels on difficult golf courses, Irwin excels on difficult shots. Each of his U.S. Open victories is remembered for superb strokes with a 2-iron at vital moments. At Winged Foot, Irwin closed the door on the 72nd hole with a 2-iron to eight feet. At Inverness, he took control of the championship on the 13th hole of the third round with a 2-iron from 225 yards to three feet that led to an eagle. And at Medinah, he hooked a 2-iron around trees to six feet on the 16th hole of the playoff to set up a birdie.

Irwin was captain of the U.S. team in the inaugural Presidents Cup in 1994. He has had spectacular results on the Champions Tour, winning a record 39 times. In 2002 he earned a record $3,028,304 to become the first man to win $3 million in a season.

### THE IRWIN RECORD

| | |
|---|---|
| Major Championship Victories | 3 |
| U.S. Open: 1974, 1979, 1990 | |
| PGA TOUR Victories | 20 |
| Champions Tour Victories | 39 |
| Ryder Cup Teams | 5 |
| (13-5-2) | 1975, 1977, 1979, 1981, 1991 |
| Presidents Cup Teams | 1 |
| (2-1) | 1994 |
| Playing Captain | 1994 |

# Chi Chi Rodriguez

**From the time he first fashioned one from the branch of a guava tree, Chi Chi Rodriguez was a magician with a golf club.** Yet for all his accomplishments as a player, his contributions as an entertainer and a humanitarian are even greater. From the famous sword dance he breaks into when he makes a putt to the success of his youth foundation, Rodriguez has made the world a better place.

Born in Rio Piedras, Puerto Rico, Oct. 23, 1935, Juan Rodriguez was the frailest of six children and nearly died at age four from rickets and tropical sprue. His father worked long hours cutting sugar cane with a machete but never made more that $18 a week, and the young Rodriguez saw in athletics a chance at a better life. As a teenager, he boxed in the streets for sodas and was a pitcher good enough to play alongside Roberto Clemente, Orlando Cepeda and local legend Chi Chi Flores, who became his namesake. A caddie since the age of eight, Rodriguez also had a natural aptitude for belting a golf ball when he had one, a rolled-up tin can when he didn't. After a two-year stint in the Army, he returned to caddie at the Dorado Beach Resort and at age 17 finished second in the Puerto Rican Open. With the help of longtime touring pro Pete Cooper, Rodriguez continued to improve, and in 1960 secured a stake of $12,000 from Laurence Rockefeller, one of the resort's owners. Rodriguez headed for the PGA TOUR, won $450 in his first event and was on his way.

From 1963 to 1979, Rodriguez won eight official events in the U.S., including the 1964 Western Open, and was a member of the 1973 U.S. Ryder Cup team. A natural showman, he quickly became a fan favorite for his habit of covering the hole with his straw hat after making a birdie, or waving his putter like a swordsman after holing a putt of any length–a routine that has grown into one of the game's treasured rituals. His flamboyance initially created a stir among his more reserved peers, but Rodriguez toned down and then defused them with his wit. "I'm a hot dog pro," he said. "That's when someone in the gallery looks at his pairing sheet and says, 'Here comes Joe Baloney, Sam Sausage and Chi Chi Rodriguez. Let's go get a hot dog.' " It was also Rodriguez who invented the line, "Jack Nicklaus has become a legend in his spare time."

As a player, he was unique. Whippet thin at 5-7 and 117 pounds when he joined the tour, Rodriguez coiled and uncoiled as violently as any top player ever has and in his prime drilled out low, hot-running drives that made him pound-for-pound the longest hitter the professional game had ever seen. He excelled in his ability to improvise shots and possessed legendary talent with the wedges, particularly from sand. Rodriguez surely would have won many more tournaments had he been an outstanding putter.

Rodriguez' career underwent a renaissance when he joined the Champions Tour. After winning three times in 1986, he had the greatest season of his career in 1987. He won seven times and set two Champions Tour records that still stand: most consecutive victories, four; and most consecutive birdies, eight. His 22 Champions Tour wins are tied for fifth most all-time.

Rodriguez has helped raise more than $4 million for his youth foundation in Clearwater, Fla., which annually brings 600 children from low income families or broken homes to a 9-hole municipal course to learn responsibility and discipline by working at the various jobs in golf. "A man never stands taller than when he stoops to help a child," Rodriguez says. For living his life accordingly, he received the Bob Jones Award from the USGA in 1989 and was elected to the World Humanitarian Sports Hall of Fame in 1994.

## THE RODRIGUEZ RECORD

PGA TOUR Victories ............ 8

Champions Tour Victories ....... 22

Ryder Cup Teams ................ 1
(0-1-1) ..................... 1973

Bob Jones Award: 1989

Represented Puerto Rico on 12 World Cup Teams

# Richard S. Tufts

**He has been called The Man Who Was Pinehurst.** He served as President of the United States Golf Association, Walker Cup captain and was such a staunch believer in amateurism that he wrote a creed on the subject. This was Richard Tufts, a man who was known in this country quite simply as "Mr. Golf."

While Pinehurst will remain his legacy, it was amateur golf that drove Tufts to be so passionate about the game. "In my mind an amateur is one who competes in a sport for the joy of playing, for the companionship it affords, for health-giving exercise and for relaxation from more serious matters," were the words Tufts wanted left behind. "As part of his light-hearted approach to the game, he accepts cheerfully all adverse breaks, is considerate of his opponent, plays the game fairly and squarely in accordance with the rules, maintains self-control and strives to do his best, not in order to win, but rather as a test of his own skill and ability. These are his only interests, and, in them, material considerations have no part. The returns which amateur sport will bring to those who play it in this spirit are greater than those any money can possibly buy."

Tufts was the grandson of James Walker Tufts, the founder of Pinehurst. He grew up in Massachusetts and was described as a man with a strong Yankee conscience and high personal standards. In 1917, after graduating from Harvard, Tufts went off to serve in World War I. After his tour of duty, he returned to Pinehurst, where his father, Leonard, had been running the resort. Eventually, Richard took over and brought Pinehurst to new heights. He was the leader of an effort that brought the PGA Championship (1936) and Ryder Cup (1951) to Pinehurst, and he ruled over the resort until relatives sold their stock to Diamondhead Corp. and the Tufts family lost controlling interest.

Tufts was many things. He served diligently on every USGA committee imaginable and was part of the delegation, led by Joe Dey, that met in St. Andrews to arrive on a universal code of rules. As time went on, he ascended through the USGA's chain of command, serving as secretary from 1950-1951, vice-president from 1952-1955 and president for two years beginning in 1956.

As a protege of Donald Ross', he built 40 new holes at Pinehurst and revised many more. Ross was the head professional at Pinehurst in 1900, moving South after coming to America from Scotland, where he was given a job at Oakley Country Club in Massachusetts. "There was never anything vulgar about his work," Tufts said of Ross.

Tufts also liked to write and authored *The Scottish Invasion, An Eightsome of Golfing Badgers* and perhaps his best book, *The Principles Behind the Rules of Golf.* "If there is one principle more basic than any of the rest, it must be that you play the course as you find it."

Later, he added: "The second great principle of golf is that you put your own ball in play at the start of the hole and play only your own ball and do not touch it before you lift it from the hole."

To Richard Tufts, this was golf the way golf was meant to be played.

## THE TUFTS RECORD

**USGA President: 1956-1957**

**Walker Cup Captain: 1963**

**Bob Jones Award: 1967**

**Richardson Award: 1951**

# Harry Cooper

**Harry Cooper was one of the finest players and most consistent winners in professional golf in the 1920s and 1930s with but a single void in his career: a major championship—despite several narrow misses.**

Cooper won 31 times on the PGA TOUR between 1925 and 1941, including the Canadian Open and the Los Angeles Open twice each. In 1937, he won eight times, led the money list and won the inaugural Vardon Trophy.

Cooper spent his career around the lead and he racked up 37 runner-up finishes and 25 thirds. The most disappointing seconds were at the 1927 and 1936 U.S. Open and at the 1936 Masters, where he was nipped at the end by the hot putting of Horton Smith. He was also second at Augusta in 1938. He reached the semifinals of the PGA once, losing to Walter Hagen in 1925. He never played in the British Open.

Cooper was born Aug. 4, 1904, in Leatherhead, England, and came to America at age 10. His father, Sid, who had served an apprenticeship under Old Tom Morris at St. Andrews, was the golf professional at Cedar Crest in Dallas. His mother, Alice, also was a fine player who worked in the golf shop and gave lessons.

The young Cooper was a phenom. He won the 1923 Texas PGA at age 18 and repeated the next year. He took his first important title at the 1926 Los Angeles Open. It was there that Damon Runyon dubbed him "Light Horse" for the speed with which he played and the nimble way he carried himself. At the Los Angeles C.C., he and George Von Elm played the last round in 2 hours and 30 minutes. While Cooper floated, his caddy labored with a bag filled with 26 clubs.

Cooper was considered a wonderful swinger of the club. When he was young, he had a long flowing swing, which he described as "about two inches shorter than John Daly's." Shortly after his victory at Los Angeles, he decided he had to make it more compact and competed sparingly for 18 months. When he came back, he had lost some distance but gained accuracy. It gave birth to another nickname, "Pipeline."

Cooper twice came excruciatingly close to winning the U.S. Open. In 1927 at Oakmont, he led after the third round but made three 6s on the final 18, and three-putted the 71st hole from eight feet. Then Tommy Armour holed a 10-footer for birdie on the difficult 18th to tie. In the playoff, Cooper led by two after 11, but he double-bogeyed the 16th and lost the playoff, 76-79. In the 1936 Open at Baltusrol, Cooper led by two through three rounds and finished with a 73 for a record total of 284. While Cooper was being congratulated for his apparent victory, Tony Manero came in with a final-round 67 for 282.

At Augusta in 1936, Cooper led by three after three rounds. However, he got the worst of wind and rain and finished with a 76. Horton Smith was still two strokes behind with five to play, but birdied two of them while Cooper bogeyed the 71st.

After his playing career, Cooper became a distinguished teaching professional passing on his knowledge of the game until shortly before his death in 2000.

Nevertheless, in the era of 1930 to 1945, Cooper was ranked in PGA TOUR statistics as the fourth-best player behind Byron Nelson, Sam Snead and Horton Smith. "First you've got to be good," Cooper once said, "but then you've got to be lucky."

## THE COOPER RECORD

PGA TOUR Victories ........... 31

Vardon Trophy: 1937

Leading Money Winner: 1937

# Patty Sheehan

**It is a tribute of a person's fortitude that she is at her best when life seems at its worst.** That, then, says it all about Patty Sheehan, who has twice answered adversity with achievement, and who has proven that heart and courage mean as much in golf as talent. When you grow up as a downhill skier, you learn how to pick yourself up, and that's what Sheehan has done.

In 1989, Sheehan lost her house, her trophies and nearly all of her life savings in the San Francisco earthquake. She came back the next year to win five tournaments and more than $732,000. Nearly all of that money went to pay bills, but it was the tournament she lost in 1990 that represented as much potential devastation to her career as the earthquake did to her financial security.

The U.S. Women's Open was played at the Atlanta Athletic Club. Sheehan had an 11-stroke lead in the third round and ended up losing it all to Betsy King. As Sheehan later said, "I had owned the Open. It was in my hands. I could break a leg and still shoot well enough to win, but I hadn't been able to do it."

Two years later, Sheehan came to Oakmont C.C. after two consecutive victories. She birdied the 71st and 72nd holes, then went on to defeat Juli Inkster in a playoff. She won the Open again in 1994, but the victory in 1992 at Oakmont was her crowning achievement. "It was such a great comeback from 1990, and emotionally it healed so many wounds," Sheehan told writer Liz Kahn. "It was the most significant win of my career because I overcame so much doubt. It would have been very hard to live the rest of my life without winning an Open. Now I feel I'm on vacation from adversity and that 1992 Open victory made me a different person—much happier and more content. If I never win another tournament, I'm still complete because that was the one I wanted."

Sheehan grew up in Middlebury, Vt., and Lake Tahoe, Nev. Her father, Bobo, was a college ski coach in Vermont and also an Olympic ski coach. As the only girl in the family, Sheehan learned how to compete to survive. She was as good a football player as her three brothers, and at 13, Sheehan was ranked the No. 1 downhill skier for her age in the country. Golf was a secondary sport until Sheehan reached age 18, when her handicap was down to scratch and the University of Nevada-Reno offered her a scholarship.

As an amateur, Sheehan won state titles in Nevada and California, the AIAW National Championship for San Jose State, and was runner-up in the 1979 U.S. Women's Amateur Championship. She was undefeated on the 1980 Curtis Cup team and earned Rookie of the Year honors on the LPGA Tour in 1981.

"I was always very competitive," Sheehan said. "I saw myself as a winner from a very young age. I played with boys all my life, and I seemed to be their equal, if not better. I never thought of myself as anything less than a winner. To be successful, you need drive, determination and a belief in yourself, and some kind of peacefulness about what you're doing."

That attitude resulted in one of the most successful careers in LPGA history. Through the 2003 season, she had won 35 tournaments, including the two Opens, three LPGA Championships and a Dinah Shore. In 1995, she qualified for the Hall of Fame with a win at the SAFECO Classic. "I feel inside I should be there because I stepped up and achieved that level and there's a place for me beside those greats," Sheehan said. "I'm not bragging. I just feel that way."

## THE SHEEHAN RECORD

Major Championship Victories ..... 6
U.S. Women's Open: 1992, 1994
LPGA: 1983, 1984, 1993
Nabisco Dinah Shore: 1996

LPGA Tour Victories ............ 35
LPGA Rookie of the Year: 1981

Vare Trophy: 1984

Solheim Cup ..................... 6
(5-7-1) .......... 1990, 1992, 1994, 1996, 2002, 2003

NABISC
AH SHORE

# Dinah Shore

**Dinah Shore didn't take up the game until the ripe age of 52, and by her own admission she was not a quick study.** "Whenever I break 100 they send up a flare," she once said. And yet Shore was an illuminating presence for women's golf. Since 1972, her eponymous tournament has been one of the LPGA's most visible. Shore's name helped insure network television coverage back when it was a precious commodity, which in turn helped her tournament set the curve for purse increases. Shore had such a lasting effect on the LPGA Tour that in 1994 she was posthumously made the only honorary member of its prestigious Hall of Fame. "This is not an honor given, it's an honor earned," then LPGA Commissioner Charles Mechem said.

Born Frances Rose Shore in Winchester, Tenn., in 1921 (the Dinah came from a New York disc jockey who forgot her name but remembered she sang a song entitled "Dinah"), she began her singing career in Memphis. She gained fame on the radio in the late 1930s in duets with Frank Sinatra and later Eddie Cantor's show. She was one of America's first television stars, first on "The Chevy Show," which ran from 1951 to 1961, and later on the Dinah Shore Show, "Dinah's Place," and "Dinah!" She won 10 Emmy Awards, nine gold records and a Peabody Award.

Shore took a circuitous route to becoming one of the game's matriarchs. She was stricken with polio when she was 18 months old, and in the years that followed she used sports to bury the disease's legacy. "I began to think that it was some dim, dark secret and that if anybody ever found out they would refuse to play with me because I was different," she said. In junior high, Shore played softball, basketball and ran track, and at Vanderbilt University she made the varsity swimming and fencing teams (and, naturally, was part of the drama club, glee club and cheerleading squad). That she didn't play golf was something of an upset because Shore once described her mother as "one of the finest, most enthusiastic golfers in the state of Tennessee. She died when I was young but her encouragement stayed with me."

Once Shore fell for the game, she fell hard. She became the first female member at Los Angeles' tony Hillcrest Country Club, and her home away from home was Mission Hills in Rancho Mirage, where she had a house off the ninth green. She became the first woman to play in PGA TOUR pro-ams at San Diego and Westchester. Her ambition in golf was to shoot 85, after which she said, "I will smile forever."

Shore brought to the women's tour a star quality that was sorely missing. She invited many of the players to appear on her television variety show, and even hooked some up with commercial endorsements. "The tour was still Podunk when we went to Palm Springs, and suddenly we were celebrities," said Jane Blalock, the champion of the inaugural Dinah Shore. "It changed the perception of women's golf." So, too, did the champion's dive into the lake on Mission Hills' 18th, a frolicking tradition Shore and Amy Alcott started.

For all the good times her tournament generated, Shore's legacy is steeped in far more important matters. "I don't like discrimination on the basis of sex," the First Lady of Golf once said. "Ability is the only thing that matters. The tournament we play is awfully powerful proof of that."

## THE SHORE RECORD

**Started Dinah Shore Tournament:**
**1972**

# Betsy King

**It took Betsy King more than seven seasons to win on the LPGA Tour, but her breakthrough led to one of the most phenomenal careers in women's golf history.** In an 11-year span from the 1984 Women's Kemper Open through the 1995 ShopRite LPGA Classic, King won 30 times, including five major championships, to become the 14th member of the LPGA Hall of Fame and the first to cross the $5-million barrier in career earnings. She captured her sixth major in 1997, winning the Nabisco Dinah Shore.

King was born in Reading, Pa., and still maintains a home nearby in the town of Limekiln. She has served as host of the LPGA's Wachovia Betsy King Classic at Berkleigh C.C. in Kutztown, Pa., and has organized the Habitat for Humanity, which has built homes for underprivileged families in Phoenix and Charlotte, N.C. In the off-season, she has traveled to Romania to work with an orphan relief organization and she has been active in the Fellowship of Christian Athletes ministry since 1980.

Her favorite scripture is from 2 Corinthians: "Aim for perfection, listen to my appeal, be of one mind, live in peace. And the God of love and peace will be with you."

It was not easy for King to find peace when she first turned professional. Overshadowed by Nancy Lopez and struggling with the pressure of great expectations—she finished eighth as an amateur in the 1976 U.S. Women's Open—King found salvation in the Bible and the golf instruction of Ed Oldfield. In 1984, she won three times, the LPGA money title and its Player of the Year Award. Her first major championship came in the 1987 Nabisco Dinah Shore and two years later she had what was one of the most lucrative seasons in LPGA history. With six victories, including the U.S. Women's Open, King won $654,132. In those five years, her 20 victories were more than any professional golfer, man or woman, in the world.

Avoiding a letdown, King won her second Dinah and made it back-to-back Opens in 1990. Perhaps her most frustrating year came in 1993 when she won the Vare Trophy, the money title and Player of the Year honors, despite winning only one tournament, the season-ending Toray Japan Queens Cup. With the pressure of the Hall of Fame mounting (her 29 career victories left her one shy of induction), she was second five times that year, including the Dinah Shore and du Maurier, where she held third-round leads.

Shut out in 1994 for the first time in 10 seasons, King came back in 1995 with a final-round 67 at ShopRite to qualify for the LPGA Hall. When she won the Dinah in 1997, it served as testimony of her perseverance. It was her third Dinah Shore, matching Amy Alcott's record, and her sixth major championship, tying her for the seventh on the LPGA's all-time list with Kathy Whitworth and Karrie Webb and two of her more immediate contemporaries, Patty Sheehan and Pat Bradley.

"My faith gives me perspective," King says. "Scripture tells you to forget what is behind and press toward what is ahead, toward the goal to win the prize. The hardest thing is to forget what is behind. I use my faith as my sports psychologist. Why not get it from the guy who knows everything?"

## THE KING RECORD

Major Championship Victories ..... 6
- U. S. Women's Open: 1989, 1990
- LPGA: 1992
- Nabisco Dinah Shore: 1987, 1990, 1997

LPGA Tour Victories ............ 34

Vare Trophy: 1987, 1993

Leading Money Winner: 1984, 1989, 1993

Solheim Cup ..................... 5

(7-6-2) .. 1990, 1992, 1994, 1996, 1998

# Johnny Miller

**In golf's modern era, it's commonly understood that no player has ever achieved the brief but memorable brilliance of Johnny Miller.**

In 1974 and 1975, Miller won 12 tournaments. More important than the number of the victories was the manner in which they were achieved, for during this streak Miller hit the ball consistently closer to the flag than any player in history. At his best, Miller's game was marked by incredibly aggressive and equally accurate iron play.

Miller won five of the first 11 events of 1974 and later three more. The next year, he won four. At Phoenix he shot 260 to win by 14. The next week at Tucson, he closed with a 61 to win by nine.

"It was sort of golfing nirvana," Miller said later. "I'd say my average iron shot for three months in 1975 was within five feet of my line, and I had the means for controlling distance. I could feel the shot so well."

This brilliant stretch was framed by Miller's most important victories. At the 1973 U. S. Open at Oakmont, he was six behind after a third-round 76 when he suddenly caught fire. He birdied the first four holes of the final round and continued to shoot at the flag. He made four more birdies against one bogey for a 63 to win by one. In the 1976 British Open at Royal Birkdale, Miller trailed 19-year-old Seve Ballesteros by two going into the final round but put together a 66 to win by six.

That victory marked the end of Miller's reign at the top of the game as he didn't win another tournament until 1980. Several factors contributed. Miller lacked the insatiable appetite for success that drives the very greatest. Bored with golf, Miller spent a summer working on his ranch and found that his stronger body could not repeat his old swing. Never a brilliant putter, Miller began to suffer from the yips. Finally, Miller's priorities changed the moment he had the first of his six children in 1977.

In all, Miller won 25 times on the PGA TOUR. His final and probably most remarkable victory occurred at Pebble Beach in 1994. Playing on one of his favorite courses, Miller somehow kept making putts—at times closing his eyes during the stroke—and won by a stroke.

Born in San Francisco April 29, 1947, Miller took up golf as a boy under the watchful eye of his father, Larry. "I was very lucky because my father was always positive and never pushed," said Miller. "He always called me Champ." Later, Miller was guided by teacher John Geertson, who shaped Miller's distinctive early wrist-cock takeaway. Miller received playing privileges at the Olympic Club and in 1964 won the U.S. Junior Amateur. As a 19-year-old amateur, he qualified for the 1966 U. S. Open at Olympic and finished eighth.

He attended Brigham Young University and turned professional in 1969, nearly winning the 1971 Masters. After his victory at Oakmont, Miller got his biggest confidence boost by partnering with Jack Nicklaus in the World Cup. "I played every day with Jack for a week, and I started to believe that at the time, I was actually better than him," Miller said. Nicklaus eventually answered Miller's challenge to his station as the game's best by outdueling Tom Weiskopf and Miller down the stretch at the 1975 Masters. "When I got to the mountaintop, I kind of looked at the scenery and wondered, 'Now what?' " Miller once summarized. "When Jack got there, he said, 'Where's the next mountain?' "

Since retiring from regular competition, Miller has become a popular television golf commentator.

### THE MILLER RECORD

Major Championship Victories ..... 2
- U. S. Open: 1973
- British Open: 1976

Other Significant Victories
- U. S. Junior Amateur: 1964

PGA TOUR Victories ........... 25

Ryder Cup Teams ................ 2
(2-2-2) ................ 1975, 1981

Leading Money Winner: 1974

Pringle

# Nick Faldo

**Like Ben Hogan before him, Nick Faldo seeks perfection with such singlemindedness that winning—much like the followthrough of his flawless swing—is a byproduct of a larger goal.**

More than any player of his era, the Englishman has relentlessly pursued golf's holy grail—total control of the golf ball. The swing he has built in that endless chase is one that has not only held up, but excelled in the game's most important moments.

Between 1987 and 1995, Faldo won six major championships—three British Opens and three Masters. Although he has a total of 39 tournament victories around the world, including six events on the PGA TOUR, Faldo's focus has always been on his performance in the Masters, U.S. Open, British Open and PGA Championship. In one stretch between 1988 and 1993, Faldo was never out of the top 20 in a Grand Slam event.

Faldo had relied on dedication, consistency, tempo and one of the strongest competitive minds the game has ever seen. Although he is tall at just over 6-3 and athletically built with wide shoulders, Faldo has never been a particularly powerful player. Consistency, distance control and course management are his strengths. His record makes him arguably the finest player of his height or taller in the history of the game.

Four of his majors were won narrowly in tense battles, either by a single stroke or in a playoff, and often after he had come from behind. At the 1987 British Open, Faldo made 18 pars in the final round and emerged victorious when Paul Azinger bogeyed the final two holes. At the 1989 Masters, he won in sudden death when Scott Hoch missed a 20-inch putt. The next year, Raymond Floyd mishit his approach on the second extra hole to give Faldo victory. In 1992 at Muirfield, Faldo lost a five-stroke lead on Sunday, but rallied with late birdies to win his third British Open by one.

At the 1996 Masters, Faldo started the final day six strokes behind Greg Norman, but put together a flawless 67 to win going away. Faldo's most impressive major victory was the 1990 British Open at St. Andrews. Mastering the Old Course with dazzling iron play, Faldo stood astride the field, shooting 18-under-par 270 to win by five.

Born July 18, 1957, in Welwyn Garden City, England, Faldo was a gifted all-around athlete who had the makings of a first-class cyclist. After his parents bought him a racing cycle when he was 12, the young Faldo horrified them by dismantling the whole machine because he wanted to know how it worked. Years later, he did the same thing with his golf swing. At 14, Faldo took up golf after watching the 1971 Masters on television. An early teacher, Ian Connelly, told him, "The easier you swing, the better you'll hit it," advice which helped shape Faldo's syrupy action.

Faldo won 10 titles in 1975 as an amateur and joined the European Tour the following season. Over the next eight years, he displayed a superb short game and putting stroke in winning several tournaments and establishing his career-long brilliance in the Ryder Cup. But Faldo seemed to fail in the crucible of the major championships, and this did not sit well with his perfectionist nature. At the 1983 British Open at Birkdale, another final-round collapse convinced Faldo that if he was ever going to win majors, he needed to overhaul his swing.

Enlisting swing coach David Leadbetter in 1984, Faldo implored the instructor to "Throw the book at me." For the next three years, he toiled through poor performance as he went through the rigors of a risky mid-career swing change. But the swing that emerged, which emphasized the large muscles of the body in conformance with Leadbetter's overriding tenet that "the dog wags the tail," was more solid, more repeatable and more reliable. Faldo's victory at Muirfield in 1987 was the validation, and the five majors that followed have been the proof.

## THE FALDO RECORD

Major Championship Victories ..... 6
- Masters: 1989, 1990, 1996
- British Open: 1987, 1990, 1992

PGA TOUR Victories ........... 6

European Tour Victories ......... 26

Ryder Cup Teams .............. 11
(23-19-4) ... 1977, 1979, 1981, 1983, 1985, 1987, 1989, 1991, 1993, 1995, 1997

WORLD GOLF HALL of FAME

# Seve Ballesteros

**No golfer has epitomized the spirit of European golf like Severiano Ballesteros.** The native of Spain did for European golf what Arnold Palmer did for golf in America.

Since turning professional in 1975, golf's ultimate competitor has truly represented golf's global appeal by spearheading Europe's rise to Ryder Cup glory.

Ballesteros played on a rare combination of talent and heart. His intensity and style of play have constantly required high-risk recoveries and clutch putting that drew fans into his corner. His gifts of imagination, touch and determination on the course helped Ballesteros win more than 70 professional tournaments, including five majors.

Two decades before Tiger Woods exploded onto the scene as a professional, Seve Ballesteros was golf's teenage prodigy, dazzling the golf world with a runner-up finish at Royal Birkdale as a 19-year-old.

Ballesteros made emotion and a brilliant short game his best allies on the golf course. His magical touch derives from years of practice. As a boy, he developed his natural motion by hitting rocks on the beaches of Pedrena with a homemade 3-iron. In his prime, nobody was better at scrambling to manufacture low scores. Ballesteros won the Harry Vardon Trophy for lowest scoring average on the European PGA Tour six times by erasing mistakes with his short game. Who can ever forget his famous birdie from the car-park in the 1979 British Open at Royal Lytham? Ballesteros became the first European to win the championship since Frenchman Arnaud Massy took the title at Royal Liverpool in 1907 and his victory confirmed the emergence of a wealth of European talent.

Ballesteros was at his erratic best in the final round of the 1988 British Open, shooting a 65 that included an 11-hole stretch in which he made two pars, two bogeys, six birdies and an eagle. He worked magic out of the deep rough and performed wizardry around the green. Ultimately, he closed out Nick Price with a brilliant chip from behind the 18th green that finished inches from the cup. Of that glorious round, which he counts as perhaps the finest putting performance of his career, Ballesteros remarked, "I knew at the time I won the Open in 1988 that I had reached some sort of peak, that it was a round of golf that I would think fondly about for the rest of my life."

While his individual record is exemplary, Ballesteros' legacy will be for pushing golf onto a world stage by moving it onto the European continent and by making the Ryder Cup competitive. He was the heart and soul of the European team as an eight-time member and one-time captain. In 1987, the Ryder Cup gained prominence when the Europeans came to America and, for the first time, won on American soil.

Seve's tenacity, fearlessness and fanatical desire to succeed helped make him one of the greatest match players of all time. When Valderrama Golf Club on Spain's Costa del Sol was selected to host the 1997 Ryder Cup Matches—the first time for a mainland Europe venue—Ballesteros was the prime force. He was also the logical choice to captain the team. Even in this non-playing role, Ballesteros' competitive fire was still the heart and soul of the victorious European team.

While his star has faded in recent years, Ballesteros will always be remembered as one of the most gifted golfers ever to play the game.

Lee Trevino may have put it best when he said of the Spaniard, "Every generation or so there emerges a golfer who is a little bit better than anybody else. I believe Ballesteros is one of them. On a golf course he's got everything. I mean everything: touch, power, know-how, courage and charisma."

## THE BALLESTEROS RECORD

Major Championship Victories .... 5
British Open: 1979, 1984, 1988
Masters: 1980, 1983

PGA TOUR Victories ............ 9

International Victories .......... 72

Ryder Cup Teams ................ 9
(20-12-5) ........ 1979, 1983, 1985, 1987, 1989, 1991, 1993, 1995, 1997
Captain ..................... 1997

# Amy Alcott

**Amy Alcott had waited to join the World Golf Hall of Fame for a long time.** She had been on the cusp of entering the Hall since she captured her third Dinah Shore Classic in 1991 and plunged into the pond alongside the 18th green to celebrate the occasion. It was one of the shining moments of Alcott's illustrious career, but since then she had been reminded for what she had not accomplished — that elusive 30th win that would grant her instant access into the LPGA Hall of Fame.

Whenever she competed, she heard well-meaning fans say, "Come on, Amy. You can win one more and get in (the Hall of Fame)." These warm wishes of support were a constant reminder of how close she truly was to joining an elite group.

On Feb. 9, 1999, Alcott's wait ended, not when she won again, but when the LPGA membership overwhelmingly voted in favor of a point system for active players and the creation of a 12-person veterans committee. She and Beth Daniel were the immediate benefactors of the new qualification standards.

"Looking at my career and Amy's career, I felt we were Hall of Famers for quite some time," said Daniel, who elected to defer her induction until 2000 during the LPGA's 50th Anniversary. "I think there has been too much emphasis on the last tournament won instead of on a player's overall achievements."

The former qualifications were considered the most rigorous in professional sports. Only 14 players had met the standards since 1950, and none since Betsy King in 1985.

"The goal of the Hall of Fame is to honor those players that dominated women's golf during their era," said then-Commissioner of the LPGA Jim Ritts. "As the tour has grown in stature and the depth of talent expanded, the existing criteria precluded some of the tour's greatest players from gaining recognition. The hallmark of the newly approved criteria is that the Hall of Fame will remain performance-based, and yet it is an attainable achievement for the elite players of today."

Indeed, Alcott was a dominant player of her era. A native of Kansas City, Alcott joined the LPGA in 1975 after capturing the 1973 USGA Girls' Junior at age 17. On her 19th birthday, in only the third LPGA Tour event she entered, she won the Orange Blossom Classic and was named the LPGA Rookie of the Year.

Since then, she has blazed irons better than almost anyone in the game to amass 29 victories during her pro career, including five majors. With her two victories in 1986, Alcott had 15 top-10 finishes, including winning the Nabisco Dinah Shore and becoming only the third LPGA member to surpass the $2-million mark in career earnings. She soon reached the $3-million mark in 1994.

"To be honored in the great circles of golf, to be enshrined with the other great Hall of Famers is something that I truly looked forward to," said Alcott at the press conference announcing her place in the LPGA Hall of Fame. "In my heart, I have felt that I've had a Hall of Fame career."

## THE ALCOTT RECORD

Major Championship Victories .... 5
- Peter Jackson Classic: 1979
- U.S. Women's Open: 1980
- Nabisco Dinah Shore: 1983, 1988, 1991

LPGA Tour Victories ............ 29

LPGA Tour Rookie of the Year: 1975

Vare Trophy: 1980

OVERSIZ

# Beth Daniel

**Thanks to the changes to the LPGA Hall of Fame's entrance requirements instituted in February 1999, Amy Alcott and Beth Daniel immediately met the criteria for induction into the World Golf Hall of Fame.** Daniel, however, postponed her official induction until 2000 for reasons of symmetry. Along with 2000 being the 50th anniversary of the LPGA Tour, it is also the year her parents celebrated their 50th wedding anniversary, and the date of her induction was her brother's 50th birthday. So, at last, she was ready to celebrate.

Born and raised in Charleston, S.C., Daniel fondly remembers being six years old and playing about a half a hole behind her parents and trying to catch up to them. "From the first time I played the game I was addicted to it and I just loved it and wanted to be as good as I could be at it," Daniel recalled.

Daniel first made waves in the golf world in 1975 when she won the U.S. Women's Amateur in her first appearance in the event. "I was thinking I was going there just to get some experience. I never expected to win," said Daniel. "When I won, I thought this is it. This is the stepping stone. This is the first step that I've taken to become a really great player. Winning the Amateur really started my golf career."

Daniel is particularly proud of winning the Women's Amateur for a second time. "The win in 1977 meant more to me because I knew what was going on. The first time I had no clue. I just kept playing golf. The second time I knew exactly what was going on and I was still able to win," said Daniel.

Joining the professional circuit in 1979, Daniel was named the LPGA Rookie of the Year. In her second season, she won four times and was named Rolex Player of the Year. Daniel's continued success brought her nine more wins through 1985 and made her the tour's eighth millionaire. Back problems hampered her swing and her play for several years in the mid-80s and she missed part of the 1988 season with mononucleosis. She suffered through a 4 1/2-year winless drought before rebounding better than ever.

Alas, 1990 was a banner year for Daniel. She dominated the LPGA Tour, capturing seven titles, setting a single-season earnings record and winning the Rolex Player of the Year award for a second time. Her rise to the pinnacle of her profession was duly noted when she was named Female Athlete of the Year by United Press International. Daniel rallied to win her first major with a final-round 66 in the LPGA Championship to highlight her remarkable season.

"The LPGA Championship is by far my most memorable and most important win," said Daniel.

Johnny Miller, broadcasting the tournament for television, may have summed up Daniel's performance best. "If Arnold Palmer was shooting this score they'd be doing cartwheels in the gallery. This is one great round of golf."

"Every time I approached the green, the gallery gave me a standing ovation. Never in my career had that happened and never has it happened since. I had to fight off goose bumps every time I approached the green," Daniel recalled with justifiable pride. "I just got such a warm reception from all the fans that week and then to be able to play well on top of that. I'll never forget that feeling."

Daniel won her third Rolex Player of the Year award in 1994. All told, she has collected 33 victories in her career. A member of three victorious U.S. Solheim Cup teams in her five appearances, Daniel has represented her country with a formidable mark of 3-1-1 in singles competition. By winning the 2003 Canadian Women's Open, Daniel—at 46 years, eight months and 29 days—became the oldest player to win on the LPGA Tour, beating the record previously held by JoAnne Carner. She proved that while she already is enshrined in the World Golf Hall of Fame, she's not finished playing at the highest level.

## THE DANIEL RECORD

Major Championship Victories ..... 3
U.S. Women's Amateur: 1975, 1977
Mazda LPGA Championship: 1990

LPGA Tour Victories ............ 33

Curtis Cup Teams ................ 2
(7-1) .................. 1976, 1978

Solheim Cup Teams .............. 7
(8-7-4) .. 1990, 1992, 1994, 1996, 2000, 2002, 2003

LPGA Rookie of the Year: 1979

LPGA Rolex Player of the Year: 1980, 1990, 1994

Vare Trophy: 1989, 1990, 1994

Leading Money Winner: 1980, 1981, 1990

GWAA Female Player of the Year: 1980, 1990

# Lloyd Mangrum

**Lloyd Mangrum, movie star handsome with a pencil-thin mustache, was one of golf's toughest competitors.** A top player in the 1940s and 1950s, Mangrum was mentioned on the required 75 percent of the PGA TOUR ballots in 1998, during a year when no other player received more than 66 percent of the vote on the returned ballots.

Mangrum, born in Trenton, Texas, in 1914, never had an amateur golf career. He started working as an assistant professional to his brother, Ray, the head professional at Cliff-Dale C.C. in Dallas at the age of 15. He joined the pro tour in 1937 and broke through for his first victory in the 1940 Thomasville Open.

Like so many golfers of his era, Mangrum's career was interrupted when he entered the military service during World War II. Mangrum served his country with distinction as a staff sergeant in the Third Army. During the invasion of Normandy, his jeep overturned and his arm was broken in two places. Mangrum also suffered shrapnel wounds to his chin and knee during the Battle of the Bulge. He returned home from the war in 1945 with four battle stars and two Purple Hearts.

After the war, Mangrum returned to golf, competing against Ben Hogan, Byron Nelson, Jimmy Demaret and Sam Snead. "I don't suppose that any of the pro and amateur golfers who were combat soldiers, Marines or sailors will soon be able to think of a three-putt green as one of the really bad troubles in life," Mangrum said after returning from the war.

Appropriately enough, Mangrum won the first post-war U.S. Open in 1946, defeating Byron Nelson and Vic Ghezzi in a playoff with par 72 at Canterbury C.C. in Cleveland, Ohio. Nelson and Ghezzi each shot 73. Because the three were tied after 18 holes, despite Mangrum building a four-stroke lead at one time, the three were forced to go another 18 holes before Mangrum prevailed, just barely, shooting a 72.

In 1948, Mangrum had one of his best years when he won six times and finished in the top 10 in 21 of the tournaments he entered. Long a contender for the game's top honors, Mangrum lost in a three-man playoff to Ben Hogan in the 1950 U.S. Open at Merion, 69-73. George Fazio shot 75 in the playoff after the trio had tied after 72 holes with seven-over-par 287 totals.

Mangrum was the tour's leading money winner in 1951 and also won the Vardon Trophy for the lowest scoring average that year. He was named to six Ryder Cup teams, although the 1941 matches were cancelled, and he served as captain of the U.S. Ryder Cup team in 1951.

A gambler at heart, Mangrum was deadly on and around the greens and these skills helped him win more than 50 tournaments in his career. Mangrum also was a master of the low-flying iron shot into the teeth of the wind. In the foreword to his instructional book, *Golf: A New Approach*, Bing Crosby described Mangrum's game as one of "rhythm, balance and style" and that Mangrum had "an ideal golfing temperament, great competitive spirit and what most folks consider the finest putting touch in the game today."

A series of heart attacks forced Mangrum into an early retirement from competitive golf. The man who won two Purple Hearts in World War II and battle stars for his courage under fire eventually died from his 12th heart attack in 1973 at the age of 59.

But, as both a soldier and a golfer, Lloyd Mangrum truly had the heart of a champion.

## THE MANGRUM RECORD

Major Championship Victories ..... 1
U.S. Open: 1946
PGA TOUR Victories ........... 36
Ryder Cup Teams ................ 5
(6-2-0) ..... 1947, 1949, 1951, 1953
Non-Playing Captain ......... 1955
Leading Money Winner ....... 1951
Vardon Trophy ......... 1951, 1953

# Juli Inkster

**Juli Inkster is almost as proud of her daytime job as a Hall of Fame golfer as she is of her fulltime job as a mother of two girls, Hayley and Cori.**

Inkster's achievements as an amateur alone are almost deserving of placement in the World Golf Hall of Fame. She learned the game at Pasatiempo G.C. in Northern California, where she practiced before and after school everyday. Like many of the juniors her age she applied for a job at the golf course to gain extra playing privileges and started out parking carts and picking up range balls before graduating to being the "shop girl." That's where she met her future husband, Brian, a pro who recognized Juli's untapped potential.

Inkster captured three U.S. Women's Amateur titles between 1980-1982. "When I look back at it now I don't know how in the world I won three in a row because in match play you get somebody hot and you're out of there," said Inkster. "It's probably my best accomplishment as a golfer, either professional or amateur." Before turning pro, she also won the 1981 California Amateur, represented the United States on the Curtis Cup team in 1982 and was a collegiate All-American at San Jose State four years.

Inkster graduated to the LPGA Tour in 1983 and won her first title in only her fifth start. She became the first LPGA rookie to win two major championships in one season—the 1984 Nabisco Dinah Shore and the du Maurier Classic. Suddenly, she was the brightest young star in women's golf.

Inkster was a consistent winner during the 1980s, winning four times in 1986 and collecting her second Dinah Shore title in 1989. In 1992, she lost out on a third Dinah Shore title to Dottie Pepper in sudden death and the U.S. Women's Open, the one trophy she desperately wanted, to Patty Sheehan in an 18-hole playoff.

From 1993 until 1997, Inkster didn't win a tournament as she adjusted to juggling a career and a family. Inkster had averaged two wins a year until 1990 when her first daughter, Hayley, was born. To become a top-level athlete, she says, "You have to be a little selfish. Until I had kids, for almost my whole life my whole day was being Juli Inkster. It was about me. And then that all changed. There were a lot of times when I was running around with my head cut off, feeling like I wasn't putting 100% into my kids and not 100% into my golf. That's not how it was, but that's how I felt. It was tough to find a balance, and in the mid-1990s my golf had to take a back seat."

But that all changed in the late 1990s, Inkster said. "My daughters know they are loved. My husband and I have made a stable home for them. Maybe there are some soccer games I don't get to, but then in the winter, I can coach Hayley's basketball team. I've come to a peace that I can't be there all the time but I can give them what they need. When I understood that, my golf game got better. I don't take every game as life and death. I've just matured, I guess."

Inkster's game rebounded with wins in 1997 and 1998. In 1999, the change in the LPGA Hall of Fame requirements, which put her only seven points shy of qualifying, gave a jolt to her game. "Even though I felt it was easier, I felt like it was still out of reach," she said.

A rejuvenated Inkster provided one of the most memorable seasons in LPGA Tour history in 1999. She won five times, including finally winning that elusive U.S. Women's Open. After achieving that lifelong goal, three weeks later she won the LPGA Championship to become only the fourth woman to win the career Grand Slam. The final point to qualify for the Hall of Fame came at the Safeway Championship, where she received a champagne shower from her fellow competitors after holing the final putt.

"Not in my wildest dreams did I think this would happen to me," Inkster said of earning her place alongside Mickey Wright, Arnold Palmer and all the other greats in golf in the Hall of Fame. "Even when the criteria were changed, I felt I still was a thousand miles away. It's hard to believe that I got seven points in one year."

## THE INKSTER RECORD

Major Championship Victories .... 10
U.S. Women's Amateur: 1980, 1981, 1982
Nabisco Dinah Shore: 1984, 1989
du Maurier Classic: 1984
U.S. Women's Open: 1999, 2002
McDonald's LPGA Championship: 1999, 2000

LPGA Tour Victories .......... 30

Curtis Cup Team ............... 1
(4-0) ...................... 1982

Solheim Cup Teams ............. 5
(7-6-2) ......... 1992, 1998, 2000, 2002, 2003

LPGA Rookie of the Year: 1984

# Judy Rankin

**Thank goodness for a phone call from *Sports Illustrated*, otherwise women's golf may never have been blessed with one of its most respected figures.**

As Judy Rankin recounts the story, she quit golf at 16 after losing in the second round of the British Women's Amateur. She had started playing golf at age six under the guidance of her father. Her prolific amateur career included winning the Missouri Amateur as a 14-year-old and being the youngest low amateur at the U.S. Women's Open at the age of 15 in 1960.

Two weeks after putting away her clubs in exchange for a fishing rod, Rankin received a call from *Sports Illustrated* wondering if she planned on competing in the U.S. Women's Open because they wanted to publish her picture on the magazine's cover. A Hall of Fame career suddenly was re-ignited.

Rankin was the first LPGA player voted into the Hall of Fame via the Veterans Category, which was created in February 1999. Rankin received the necessary two-thirds vote of the LPGA tournament division to become the LPGA Tour Hall of Fame's 18th member.

"When I'm off by myself and think about this, I guess I never really thought this would come to be. It's been a long road to get here, but I am so happy to receive this honor," said Rankin after being notified of the vote. "I am very pleased to join so many long-time friends who are already in the Hall, it makes it that much more special. It is particularly gratifying to have the support of the organization. It is so nice to know what your peers think of your career and that they support it. This is also an honor for my family and friends, who spent a good part of my career pushing me on."

Rankin turned professional in 1962. She captured her first LPGA Tour victory in 1968 at the Corpus Christi Open and went on to win 25 more times between 1968 and 1979. Her most successful season was 1976, when she won seven tournaments and set a LPGA season earnings record of $150,724 on her way to becoming the first LPGA player ever to exceed $100,000 in season earnings. She was the LPGA's Rolex Player of the Year in 1976 and '77 and won the Vare Trophy for low scoring average in 1973, 1976 and 1977. In 1977, she set an LPGA record of 25 top-10 finishes in a season, a record that still stands.

Chronic back problems curtailed Rankin's stellar career, forcing her into full retirement in 1983 and back surgery in 1985. "I played all of my best years with severe back trouble," Rankin said. "I would play a month and be a cripple a month. My goal was to stay on my feet."

Since retiring from the sport, Rankin remained active in golf as a commentator for ABC Sports, where she is well known for her insightful commentary.

In 1999, Rankin was awarded the Patty Berg Award by the LPGA and the Richardson Award by the Golf Writers Association of America for outstanding service to the game of golf. For all of her personal accomplishments, the highlight of her golf career occurred in a non-playing capacity when she captained the United States Solheim Cup team to victory in 1996 and 1998. "The Solheim Cup was the greatest reward after the end of a fine career to captain the two teams that I captained. I would never need anything else from golf but those two teams because they were terrific."

Rankin has long been considered one of the game's best ambassadors and her election into the World Golf Hall of Fame represented a deserved tribute.

"I think she's the epitome of golf," Juli Inkster said. "She does so much for the LPGA. She's one of the best commentators out there—male or female. I think this is what the Hall of Fame should be—recognizing really deserving people."

## THE RANKIN RECORD

LPGA Tour Victories ........... 26

Leading Money Winner: 1976, 1977

Vare Trophy: 1973, 1976, 1977

LPGA Player of the Year: 1976, 1977

William & Mousie Powell Award: 1998

Patty Berg Award: 1999

Solheim Cup Teams .............. 2
(Non-Playing Captain) . . 1996, 1998

PGA of America First Lady of Golf Award: 1999

GWAA William H. Richardson Award: 1999

# Jack Burke Jr.

**Jack Burke Jr. has truly had a Hall of Fame career. He has been a great champion as a player, architect of one of the country's finest championship golf courses and has championed the purity of the game.** For all of his contributions to golf, Burke was selected as the first choice to be elected into the World Golf Hall of Fame via the Veterans Category, which was formed to allow the World Golf Hall of Fame Advisory Board to consider players whose career occurred primarily before 1960.

During his playing career, Burke won 17 titles, most notably the 1956 Masters and PGA Championship when he was named PGA Player of the Year. At the Masters, Burke rallied from a remarkable eight strokes behind to win the green jacket. Ken Venturi, a 24-year-old amateur, led by four shots heading into the final round, but he soared to an 80 on the final day. "There was a 50-mile-an-hour wind. On the fourth hole, a par 3, I hit a driver and a 9-iron. The pressure that day was to not shoot 100," said Burke. "I shot 71, which was the low round of the day, and Venturi just couldn't make it on the back nine and he handed me the trophy. I thank him a lot for that."

Burke won the 1956 PGA Championship back when the tournament was a match-play event, edging Ted Kroll, 3 and 2, in the final. "I beat eight guys to win the PGA. Each day you felt like you're standing on the edge of a cliff and some guy was going to push you off. I never felt like I was going to win the PGA. Never." Burke also won the 1952 Vardon Trophy, competed on five Ryder Cup teams and was captain twice.

His credentials as a player, however, are only a part of his resume. In 1957, Burke and fellow World Golf Hall of Famer Jimmy Demaret struck a partnership to build and manage The Champions Golf Club in their hometown of Houston. Together, they built two courses — Cypress Creek and Jackrabbit — that have tested golf's elite players over the years.

"The golf course is an examination of your skills... It keeps the driver in your hands, it keeps the long irons in your hand and that is a pretty true test," says Burke of the more than 7,000-yard course with a veritable forest of trees lining almost every hole.

Champions hosted the Ryder Cup in 1967, the U.S. Open in 1969 and Ben Hogan chose the course to make the final tournament appearance of his career at the 1971 Houston Champions International. In 2003, it hosted its fifth TOUR Championship for the top 30 money-winners on the PGA TOUR.

Burke continues to promote the same atmosphere at Champions that his father fostered at River Oaks, where Jackie grew up and learned the game. Golf is it at Champions. He is so dedicated to protecting the integrity of the game that he no longer considers members who have handicaps higher than 15. "We made Champions for golfers. We have 229 members with single-digit handicaps; 55 members have five handicaps or under," says Burke.

Burke is a renowned teacher of the game, too. "Whenever anybody needed any help, we would always go to Jackie and say, 'Jackie I'm struggling with my game,' and he would help you kindly," remembers World Golf Hall of Famer Gary Player. Phil Mickelson, Hal Sutton, Ben Crenshaw and Steve Elkington are among the active players who still seek out Burke to pick up on his timing and thought process.

"Jackie Burke is one of the few people left who really understands this game in its entirety," said Sutton. "He's really current with the game. He's seen all the great players. He knows how they hit it. He understands the golf swing, he's made it happen and he's been a great player in his own day."

## THE BURKE RECORD

Major Championship Victories ..... 2
Masters: 1956
PGA Championship: 1956
PGA TOUR Victories ........... 17
Ryder Cup Teams ................ 6
(7-1-0) . 1951, 1953, 1955, 1957, 1959
Non-Playing Captain .......... 1973
PGA TOUR Player of the Year: 1956
Vardon Trophy: 1952
Co-Founder of Champions Golf Club

# Deane Beman

**If Yankee Stadium is the House that Ruth built, then the World Golf Hall of Fame is the House that Beman built—and now he will live there as a permanent resident.** Deane Beman was a member of the World Golf Hall of Fame's Class of 2000, selected by the World Golf Foundation board of directors for his Lifetime Achievement in golf.

While Beman is certainly best remembered for his work as the commissioner of the PGA TOUR, his resume as a player isn't too shabby, either. Beman, who left a successful practice as an insurance broker to pursue the tour, won five PGA TOUR titles, a pair of U.S. Amateurs, the British Amateur and competed on four U.S. Walker Cup teams.

"As an amateur, I'd like to be remembered as being at the top of my competition," Beman says. "I was right there with the best of them."

After succeeding Joe Dey as commissioner in 1974, Beman grew the tour's assets from approximately $500-$700 thousand in 1974 to an estimated $500-$800 million when he retired in 1994. Much of this new profit and growth was due to television. A direct result of the popularity of golf on television was the escalating tournament purses that made players millionaires many times over and raised the profile of professional golf to new heights. During his tenure, Beman ushered in the creation of the Senior PGA Tour (now called the Champions Tour). No sport has bottled nostalgia as successfully as golf's senior tour, considered by many the sports success story of the 1980s. The senior tour arrived just in time to encompass the magnetism of Arnold Palmer. What started as a gathering of old friends blossomed into a circuit with seemingly limitless potential. Two tournaments and a total purse of $250,000 evolved into a schedule of 45 events with prize money in excess of $54 million. "When we started, the players didn't want to play more than 10 tournaments a year. They wanted to play a little bit to get out of the house. Then, when they started playing, they found out how much they missed it—the competition, the camaraderie. They said, 'Let's play more,' and here we are," Beman said.

In 1989, Beman created the Ben Hogan Tour (now called the Nationwide TOUR) as a proving ground for young professionals that also took the sport into 30 additional markets and created a launching pad for the careers of John Daly, Tom Lehman and David Duval, just to name a few. Beman is also referred to as "the Father of Stadium Golf." The TPC Stadium Course at Sawgrass was the first product born of Beman's dream to build a network of spectator-friendly courses to accommodate the growing popularity of professional golf. As the permanent home of the PGA TOUR's PLAYERS Championship, it was the first of its kind, featuring mounds, high banks and earthen amphitheatres specifically designed to handle larger crowds. "That first concept was routed literally on the back of a placemat where he (course architect Pete Dye) first sketched out the layout of the holes," Beman fondly recalls.

The Stadium Course has become a prototype for other viewer-friendly courses. Today, the Tournament Players Club network has sprouted up across the country as well as internationally.

In May of 1998, another of Beman's ideas became reality when the World Golf Village, home of the World Golf Hall of Fame, opened. Beman had the idea of constructing a PGA TOUR Hall of Fame somewhere in Northeast Florida, near tour headquarters in Ponte Vedra and near Interstate 95. However, the concept grew in scope as golf organizations, such as the LPGA and others around the world, learned of the project and asked to participate. "It was too big for just the PGA TOUR," said Beman. "We had to ask the rest of the world to join us."

In 1994, Beman retired as commissioner, leaving his successor, Tim Finchem, with a successful company to run.

"I like the Peter Jacobsen quote," said Finchem, referring to the player and former PGA TOUR Policy Board member's take on Beman's success. "He said, 'Deane built a Mercedes; all Tim has to do is keep his foot on the gas.' Anyone in our sport owes him a debt of gratitude."

## THE BEMAN RECORD

Major Championship Victories ..... 3
British Amateur: 1959
U.S. Amateur: 1960,1963

PGA TOUR Victories ............ 4

PGA TOUR Commissioner: 1974-1994

Walker Cup Teams ............... 4

(7-2-2) .......1959, 1961, 1963, 1965

# Sir Michael Bonallack

**Few people anywhere in the game have, or have had, the wealth of knowledge Sir Michael Bonallack brought to one of the most important roles in world golf as Secretary of the Royal & Ancient Golf Club of St. Andrews.** In recognition of his role as one of the ultimate ambassadors of the game, Bonallack was elected to the World Golf Hall of Fame in 2000 for his Lifetime Achievement in golf.

Bonallack had a distinguished playing career as a true amateur, one who worked full-time in sales of his family business during his years of competitive success. He never gave serious consideration to turning professional because purses were small in Europe before a formal tour was created. Instead, he played golf because he loved playing the game and played it at the highest level, representing his country as a member of nine Walker Cup teams.

The highlight for Bonallack was contributing to the victorious Great Britain and Ireland side in the 1971 Walker Cup. "I was playing captain that year when we won over the Old Course at St. Andrews, and it does not get, cannot get, any better than that," he said.

During the 1960s and early 1970s, he defined amateur golf in Britain. He won five British Amateurs between 1961 and 1970, won the English Stroke Play four times as well as being the leading amateur in the 1968 and 1971 British Open. Bonallack did not hit the longest ball or have the most conventional stance over his putts, but he had a knack for finding the bottom of the cup.

"Michael Bonallack was a remarkable player. He had a wonderful short game, which was of his own making. Big wide stance, nose sniffing the ball, short jabby swing, but all the putts went in the hole," said former colleague Peter Alliss. "He had the most wonderful temperament. He appeared calm and yet he had that steely something that all great champions have."

Soon after retiring from competitive play, he joined a golf course design company and served on a multitude of golf committees. Before taking up his post with the R&A in 1983, Bonallack was chairman of the European Professional Golfers Association and Golf Foundation and president of the English Golf Union.

As secretary of the R&A, Bonallack successfully guided the game into the 21st Century. "It's one continual satisfaction to see the way in which golf is developing. Obviously, the expansion of the Open, and the fact that we can generate this money to put back into the development of the game is very satisfying," he said.

"He has bridged the gap between the history and heritage and tradition of the Open championship and golf in general as it moved into the commercial age globally and internationally and he's done it with great taste and tact and really stands almost alone as someone who has handled that crossing," said the late Mark McCormack, chairman of International Management Group.

At the conclusion of his 16-year reign, he was named captain of the R&A, the game's highest honorary position. Bonallack has won a host of awards in golf for his service to the game, but the knighthood from Queen Elizabeth II was the ultimate accolade. He somehow managed to keep the news from his wife, Angela. The day before they left for the U.S. Open, he abruptly informed Angela that he had something important to tell her.

"What's that?" she asked.

"You aren't going to be Mrs. Bonallack anymore," Bonallack responded.

"Who is she and do I know her?" she countered.

And, he said, "No, you don't, don't be stupid. You're going to be Lady Bonallack!"

Now he can add member of the World Golf Hall of Fame to his list of honors.

## THE BONALLACK RECORD

Major Championship Victories ..... 5
British Amateur: 1961, 1965, 1968, 1969, 1970

Other Prominent Amateur Victories .............. 10
Walker Cup Teams ............. 9
(6-9-1) .... 1957, 1959, 1961, 1963, 1965, 1967, 1969, 1971, 1973
(Playing Captain) ............ 1971

Secretary, Royal & Ancient G.C., 1984–1999

Captain, Royal & Ancient G.C., 2000

Knighted by Queen Elizabeth II for service to golf, 1998.

WORLD GOLF HALL of FAME

# Neil Coles

**Neil Coles championed the cause of European unity through golf for the past 29 years and continues to do so in unparalleled acts of dedication and service to his fellow professionals.**

In recognition of his tireless effort, Coles was selected by the World Golf Foundation Board of Directors through the Lifetime Achievement category for his remarkable contributions to the international development of the game.

A leading pioneer in the inception of the European PGA Tour in 1971, Coles became its first chairman. He continues to hold that office which maintains the proud image professional golf gives to British sport throughout the world. "I wanted to see the European Tour develop into something better for the tournament players where everybody earned a good living," said Coles. "I think that ambition of the early days has now come to fruition and it has given me a great sense of pride and pleasure to see the thing grow."

The demands of administration have grown dramatically for the European Tour as it has grown to command ever-increasing international respect, and Coles has contributed tremendously to the success achieved with his dedicated involvement. "Neil has been the bedrock for the tour's development over all these years," said Ken Schofield, Executive Director of the European PGA Tour. "He sets the highest of examples for all and willingly continues to shoulder the responsibilities of Chairman of the European PGA Tour to ensure that golf remains a successful portrayal of European unity at work."

As a member of eight Ryder Cup teams between 1961 and 1977, Coles represented his country in 40 matches, second only to Hall of Famer Nick Faldo. He is among the visionaries who saw that this historic and prestigious event should be expanded to involve Continental professionals and so strengthen European unity in sport. The immense worldwide interest in the match is the result, and the benefits for golf have been widespread.

Now a champion on the burgeoning European Seniors Tour, Coles is extending a remarkable career that spanned 50 years as a professional and 45 tournament victories, including one in 2000. By winning the Jersey Seniors Open, Coles became the first player to win a tournament in six different decades.

Coles was the only member of the Class of 2000 who didn't attend the induction ceremony. He has not flown since 1963 and other means of transportation from his residence in Walton-on-Thames, England, were not available. His self-imposed limitation of not flying is the primary reason he did not win any major championships and never established himself as a household name outside of the European golf community. "I suppose I have missed a number of opportunities to play in the winter in Spain and to pop away for a week or two to play in the sun," said Coles. "I've missed opportunities to go to the States for big events. Being invited to team events such as the Chrysler Cup in Florida, which I missed, has probably been the one regret of my career."

Coles last visited the United States in 1971 to compete in the Ryder Cup at Old Warson Country Club in St. Louis. "I had to leave quite early, 10 days or so before the event to catch the Queen Mary across the Atlantic. It was a lovely trip to come up the Hudson and see New York and then Jaguar gave me a car which I drove to St. Louis, and again I saw a lot of the country," remembers Coles.

Although he was absent when he and the Class of 2000 were feted at the induction ceremony, Coles was honored to join the elite names in golf history. "I was absolutely delighted to receive the invite to become a member of the World Golf Hall of Fame with such an illustrious group of people from golf. It is an honor that I shall remember and treasure always. When the seniors tour gives me up, maybe I will have time to go over and have a look at the Hall of Fame. I would like that."

## THE COLES RECORD

PGA European Tour Victories .... 26

PGA European Seniors Tour Victories .................. 15

Other Professional Victories ....... 5

Ryder Cup Teams ............... 8
(12-21-7) .. 1961, 1963, 1965, 1967, 1969, 1971, 1973, 1977

Chairman, PGA European Tour Board of Directors

Won professional golf events in six different decades, beginning in 1956

# John Jacobs

**John Jacobs has served a lifetime in golf and is enormously respected as the pioneering architect of Europe's united approach to the modern game.** As a Ryder Cup player, tournament winner, administrator, writer, commentator and an outstanding coach, he has reached the peak of success in many widely different areas of golf. In recognition of the indelible mark he has made on the game, Jacobs was voted into the World Golf Hall of Fame through the Lifetime Achievement category in 2000.

A Yorkshireman born in 1925, son of a golf professional, Jacobs earned the unique distinction in his 1955 Ryder Cup debut of winning both his matches in America. Two years later, he won the Dutch Open and beat Gary Player for the South African Match Play Championship. In 1972, after a successful business venture establishing driving ranges in Britain to help encourage the growth of the game and following his coaching of the victorious Great Britain and Ireland Walker Cup team, he accepted the challenge of becoming the first Tournament Director General of the European PGA Tour. In this position he inspired the uniting of nations on the continent with Britain. "John has quite properly been defined as the father of European golf," said Ken Schofield, who succeeded Jacobs as Executive Director of the European Tour. "He turned the vision into reality and the position of respect commanded by Europe in the world of golf owes much to his pioneering spirit."

As captain of the 1979 and 1981 European Ryder Cup teams, Jacobs also helped usher in an era of new enthusiasm for the Ryder Cup. The 1979 squad marked the first time players from continental Europe were members of the team. Although the European side did not win either time, the wheels were in motion to end America's domination of the biennial matches. In 1997, he was awarded the Order of the British Empire by Queen Elizabeth II for 50 years of outstanding service to golf. He is an honorary life member of the European Tour.

"John today cares as much for golf and firstly for European golf as he did when he became the first tournament director general," said Schofield.

Even so, it will be as an instructor that he will be primarily remembered.

A fine tour player in his own right, Jacobs' contribution to the game subsequently evolved from his own pursuit of pars and birdies. "I ever so much wanted to be the best player that ever was. I realized that I taught it better than I played it," said Jacobs, reflecting on his career. On deciding that his real strength lay in teaching the game, he soon became one of the most sought-after of all golf coaches throughout Europe, the United States, where teaching academies still bear his name, and by his fellow tournament professionals. "Suddenly I had this reputation and once you do, all the good players come to you," said Jacobs, whose practical approach to teaching has benefited countless players.

Jacobs recounted in 2000 a story to the *London Telegraph* of watching Jack Nicklaus preparing for the 1969 British Open at Royal Lytham. Off the second tee, Nicklaus struck his first drive out of bounds down the right and his second 50 yards wide of the fairway to the left. After spraying his next few tee shots an exasperated Nicklaus had had enough.

"You're supposed to know something about these things," he shouted over to Jacobs. "What am I doing?"

"Thank God for that," Jacobs replied. "I thought you'd never ask."

Countless golfers have benefited from Jacobs' words of wisdom and will continue to. "Teaching others to teach has been my forte," he said. "I firmly believe that what I'm saying today will be just as true in 200 years time if they don't change the rules."

Said Butch Harmon, Tiger Woods' coach, "John Jacobs wrote the book on coaching. There is not a teacher out here who does not owe him something."

## THE JACOBS RECORD

**Established the John Jacobs Golf School in 1971**

**Founder and first Tournament Director-General of the PGA European Tour, 1971-1975**

**Honorary Life Member of the PGA European Tour**

**Order of the British Empire by Queen Elizabeth II for 50 years of outstanding service to golf, 1997**

**Ryder Cup Teams . . . . . . . . . . . . . . . . 3**

**(2-0-0) . . . . . . . . . . . . . . . . . . . . 1955**

**Non-Playing Captain . . . 1979, 1981**

WORLD GOLF HALL of FAME

# Donna Caponi

**As a child, Donna Caponi dreamed of making the winning putt on the final hole to capture the U. S. Women's Open, but she never imagined the scenario to win her first-ever LPGA tournament in golf's biggest event.**

Facing a four-foot putt on the 72nd hole to win the 1969 U. S. Open, Caponi lined up the crucial putt when she overheard the legendary Byron Nelson commentating on television say, "Donna Caponi has this putt to win the U. S. Women's Open."

Caponi recalls struggling to breathe and to make matters worse she couldn't believe Nelson when he reported, "I've been watching this putt all day and it's almost dead straight. It might move slightly to her right."

"I thought," said Caponi, "how can Byron Nelson see this putt break left to right. It's right to left."

Flustered, she backed off the putt to regain her composure. She had already weathered a 15-minute delay after hitting her tee shot on 18 when an electrical storm passed through. Now was the moment for which she had waited a lifetime and she questioned her read. Like a true champion she decided to trust the line and proceeded to coolly sink the right-to-left putt.

"Thank goodness I went with my own instincts," she said.

At the press conference, she learned that Nelson was right after all. It turns out his monitor was showing a camera angle from the opposite direction!

That victory launched a Hall of Fame career that spanned 24 years from 1965-1988 during which she collected 24 titles and four major championships. While the first U. S. Open title was sweet, joining Mickey Wright as only the second player to defend the championship successfully was even sweeter. "A lot of people know my first win was the U. S. Open. That was a thrill. But winning the second U. S. Open was the biggest deal. I knew a lot more the second time around," said Caponi, who also equaled Wright's record score of 287 that week.

Sixteen years after that first major title, she captured her final one at the 1981 LPGA Championship. Again, it was a storybook ending. Caponi rolled in a 25-footer for birdie on the final hole for a one-stroke victory.

Caponi spent the final seasons of her career trying to win six more times to qualify for the Hall of Fame, and the pressure took the fun out of the game. She retired in 1992, figuring she would have to settle for two U.S. Opens and two LPGA Championships as her most prized accomplishments.

"I just said the Hall of Fame is not going to happen," she said.

Caponi's hopes for enshrinement were renewed when the LPGA overhauled its criteria for the Hall of Fame in 1999. The Veterans Committee, which was formed in 1999 as part of the new requirements, nominated Caponi in March 2001. She then received the required 75 percent of the vote from tour members. She is the second woman elected to the World Golf Hall of Fame through the LPGA Veterans Category, following Judy Rankin.

"It just caps off my career, but more than anything, what makes this so meaningful is that it's the players voting for you—your peers voting for you—and knowing they consider you of a quality for the Hall of Fame," said Caponi.

Once she received word of her election, she held back tears talking about her parents—Harry, who died in 1971 at age 49, and Dolly, who died of breast cancer in 1981 at 56.

"I owe everything I am today to my parents," said the winner of the Los Angeles Junior title in 1956. "I owe everything to my dad, who spent hours and hours and hours teaching me."

Caponi started playing golf at age six and grew up picking up balls with her sister, Janet, at the driving range where her father was head professional. She recalled how her father took her to the back end of a driving range and had her practice shaping shots around a large avocado tree.

"I always felt each win was for him because he did make me what I am today," Caponi said.

## THE CAPONI RECORD

Major Championship Victories . . . . . 4
U. S. Women's Open: 1969, 1970
LPGA Championship: 1979, 1981

LPGA Tour Victories . . . . . . . . . . . . 24

GWAA Female Player of the Year: 1981

# Greg Norman

**Australian Greg Norman dominated the golf world for much of the 1980s and early 1990s with his aggressive game and charismatic demeanor.** Labeled the "Great White Shark" by a newspaper columnist during the 1981 Masters, he is one of the most recognizable sports figures whose professional career produced 86 international victories, including two British Opens. He topped the World Ranking for a total of six years and he represented his country in three Presidents Cups. For his countless accomplishments, Norman garnered the highest percentage of votes of anyone who has been inducted into the World Golf Hall of Fame.

Norman was born in Mt. Isa, Queensland, Australia, Feb. 10, 1955. At 15, he tagged along with his mother, Toini, to Virginia G.C. where she was club champion. He quickly grew attached to the game. Norman's first taste of golf instruction came from Jack Nicklaus' book, *Golf My Way*. After turning pro in 1976, Norman's highflying lifestyle today is a far cry from his humble beginning as a $28-a-week assistant at Royal Queensland.

Norman won 20 times on the PGA TOUR and was the first to surpass $10 million in career earnings. He won three Arnold Palmer Awards as the tour's leading money winner (1986, 1990 and 1995) and three Vardon Trophies (1988, 1989 and 1994). He was PGA TOUR Player of the Year in 1995. But despite his numerous wins, Norman is frequently remembered for his historic losses. He is the only player to have lost all four majors in playoffs.

Norman's 1986 season most accurately captures his exploits and crushing defeats. He led going into the final round of all four majors. On Sunday at the Masters, he hit an errant approach at 18 and couldn't save par to lose to then 46-year-old Nicklaus, who closed with a memorable six-under-par 30 on the back nine.

At the U.S. Open Norman ballooned to a closing 78, but that paled when he had victory snatched from his grasp at the PGA Championship when Bob Tway holed an improbable bunker shot at the last hole to beat the Shark by a stroke.

Norman won only the British Open in '86 when he authored a second-round 63 in windy conditions at Turnberry to open a five-shot advantage and cruise to an eventual two-stroke victory. The ovation he received as he walked to the 72nd green remains one of golf's most memorable scenes.

Despite losing three of the four majors in excruciating fashion, Norman's 1986 campaign ranks among the all-time best. He won 10 times worldwide and led both the U.S. and Australasian money lists.

Norman's career is littered with many other near misses. He has been cruelly denied major tournament success perhaps more than any other player in history. While Norman scheduled his season around the majors, the Masters was his true goal. When he first played at Augusta in 1981, he tied for fourth and seemed destined to be fitted for a green jacket soon after. But after losing to Nicklaus in 1986, the next year was more excruciating, losing to Larry Mize on the second hole of a sudden-death playoff when Mize chipped in from an impossible spot to the right of the 11th green. In 1996, Norman suffered a historic collapse in the final round at Augusta when, leading by six strokes, he skied to a 78 and lost to Nick Faldo, who rallied with a flawless 67.

Norman could have been defeated by his heartbreaking losses, but he wasn't. In his instructional book, *Shark Attack*, Norman wrote, "Sometimes I think I have an almost perverse love of being down, even being defeated, because I know it will spur me on to greater things."

At the 1993 British Open, Norman did add to his major tournament victories when he fired a remarkable final-round 64 to beat Faldo by two strokes at Royal St. George's.

Through his historic losses and gallant victories, Norman played the game with an intensity second to none.

## THE NORMAN RECORD

Major Championship Victories .....2
British Open: 1986, 1993
PGA TOUR Victories ............20
International Victories ...........86
PGA TOUR Player of the Year: 1995
Leading Money Winner: 1986, 1990, 1995
Vardon Trophy: 1988, 1989, 1994
Presidents Cup Teams .............3
(7-6-1) ........... 1996, 1998, 2000

OPEN CHAMPIONSHIP
PAYNE STEWART

# Payne Stewart

**Payne Stewart will be remembered for many achievements.** But Stewart had one of the most stylish swings of the modern era. It was not the structured action of many of today's players, but rather a long and wonderfully graceful and fluid movement.

Stewart's clothes were as stylish as his swing. His outlandish plus-fours, tam and elegant outfits made him unmistakable on the course. "My father always said the easiest way to set yourself apart in a crowd is the way you dress," said Stewart. Spectators responded enthusiastically to his colorful garb and the plus-fours and tam became a permanent part of his wardrobe.

After playing at Southern Methodist University and earning his degree, the Missouri native turned professional late in 1979, but failed to earn a PGA TOUR card at Qualifying School and instead ventured off to the Asian Tour, winning twice. It was in Kuala Lumpur, Malaysia, where Stewart met Australian Tracey Ferguson, who described the encounter as love at first sight and the couple married a short time later.

"I believe a lot in destiny," Stewart explained. "There's a reason those things happened, and the reason was so I could meet my wife." Through all the peaks and valleys, Tracey was Payne's constant support and companion as he built his legendary career.

Stewart began playing golf at age four, learning from his father, Bill, a former Missouri State Amateur champion. In 1982, Stewart finally earned his PGA TOUR card and won his first of 11 tour events with his father in the gallery. The victory was a milestone in his career, but grew in importance when it turned out to be the only time his father would see him win. Bill Stewart died of cancer in 1985.

"We had a good cry on the green," recalled Stewart. "The 1982 Quad Cities will always be my most cherished victory." When he won again, at the 1987 Bay Hill Invitational, Stewart donated his $108,000 winner's check to the Florida Hospital Circle of Friends in memory of his father.

For all of his evident talent, Stewart had some hard-luck losses and earned the nickname from his tour colleagues as "Avis," especially after four losses in sudden-death playoffs, but he shed that monicker in 1989 at the PGA Championship at Kemper Lakes near Chicago when he came from five strokes off the pace with nine holes to play to rally past a faltering Mike Reid.

Winning the PGA, Stewart said later, was not only a sweet triumph, but also a watershed moment in his career. He later went on to win the 1991 U.S. Open in a playoff against Scott Simpson and, after struggling for several years, he experienced a spiritual awakening, rededicating himself to his family and placing a different priority on golf.

Finding an inner peace, a victory at Pebble Beach jumpstarted his 1999 season, which culminated in his crowning achievement, a 15-foot par putt on the final hole to win the U.S. Open at storied Pinehurst No. 2 in a head-to-head battle with Phil Mickelson.

That victory secured a place for Stewart on the Ryder Cup team for the fifth time and the first since 1993. Competing for his country fueled Stewart's competitive nature, yet he was the soul of sportsmanship, too, when he graciously conceded his singles match to Colin Montgomerie on the 18th green at Brookline C.C. after the U.S. had won.

On Oct. 25, 1999, Stewart's life was tragically cut short in a private plane crash near Aberdeen, S. D. The words of respect and admiration for Stewart started soon after as word of his death spread.

"Payne Stewart assured himself a prominent place in the history of the game with a career that ended much too tragically and much too soon," said Arnold Palmer. "He established an impressive record as a player and contributed so much more through his outgoing personality and generous spirit."

## THE STEWART RECORD

| | |
|---|---|
| Major Championship Victories | 3 |
| PGA Championship: 1989 | |
| U.S. Open: 1991, 1999 | |
| PGA TOUR Victories | 11 |
| International Victories | 7 |
| Ryder Cup Teams | 5 |
| (8-9-2) | 1987, 1989, 1991, 1993, 1999 |

# Allan Robertson

**Allan Robertson can finally rest easy in his grave.** The man considered to be the father of professional golf has been voted into the World Golf Hall of Fame at last through the Veterans Category.

Robertson's family in and of itself reflects the emergence of the game. He was practically born into golf in 1815 in St. Andrews. His grandfather was a caddie at St. Andrews and his father was senior caddie of those who served the Royal and Ancient. Both men were feathery ball-makers of the highest repute and Allan followed in the family tradition. Allan's skill rose to a level that matched his playing ability.

No less an authority than Charles Blair Macdonald claimed that Robertson was "the best known golfer of his generation and generally thought to have been the greatest player of his day." He recorded a round of 79 on the Old Course at St. Andrews in 1858, becoming the first player to complete the course in under 80. Reportedly, Robertson took great delight in deliberately extending his challenge matches to the 17th hole when he could have polished off his foe much earlier. He did that not only to avoid wounding his opponent's pride, but also to make it impossible for the opponent to ask for increased odds at their next match. Macdonald, in his landmark book, *Scotland's Gift Golf,* reported that "it is said Allan was never beaten."

Of Robertson's technique, James Balfour, a contemporary of his, wrote: "His style was neat and effective. He held his clubs near the end of the handle, even his putter high up. His clubs were light, and his stroke an easy, swift switch. With him the game was as much of head as of hand. He always kept cool and generally pulled through a match even when he got behind."

As great a player as Robertson was, he was held in equal esteem in his prime for his ball-making ability. Robertson was the premier feathery ball-maker in St. Andrews and among the very best in Scotland.

Robertson clearly did not approve of the new gutta percha ball that was just coming into vogue. He even made Young Tom Morris, who worked in Allan's shop, promise never to play with a guttie. When Young Tom ran out of feathery balls in a match, his playing companion gave him a gutta percha to play. As Young Tom related in *Golf Illustrated* of the event "...as we were playing in, it so happened that we met Allan Robertson coming out, and someone told him I was playing a very good game with one of the new gutta percha balls, and I could see fine, from the expression on his face, that he did not like it at all and, when we met afterwards in his shop, we had some high words about the matter, and there and then parted company, I leaving his employment."

Robertson's shop overlooked the Old Course's 18th green. In his best year, Robertson produced 2,500 balls. He supplied local demand, but also exported balls to Britain and the American colonies.

Today, a Robertson ball carrying his 'Allan' stamp is highly prized by collectors. One of golf's most priceless artifacts is the feathery ball that Robertson signed in 1843 which tells that he defeated arch rival Willie Dunn in the "great match."

## THE ROBERTSON RECORD

**First golfer to break 80 at St. Andrews (1858).**

**Believed to be the greatest player of his generation.**

**One of the foremost makers of feathery golf balls.**

ED STATES GOLF

# Judy Bell

**Volunteers are the core of what makes golf the great game that it is and Judy Bell has been a tireless leader.** For her lifelong commitment to golf, Bell earned a well-deserved place in the World Golf Hall of Fame through the Lifetime Achievement category.

While she is best remembered as the first female president of the United States Golf Association in its 100-plus-year history, Bell also had a remarkable playing career. A lifelong amateur, Bell competed in her first tournament in 1948 when her father saw her putting around the course and entered her in the prestigious Broadmoor Invitational.

"I played my first tournament when I was 10," she said. "The good news is that I won the girls' division. The bad news is that I was the only girl."

Having never played 18 holes, Bell shot 113 in the qualifier, made the third-flight consolation final and won it with a pressure-packed fairway-wood shot to a lake-fronted green. Her victory won her six green after-dinner cordial glasses. At the time, she didn't know what they were, but she treasures that prize to this day.

From that modest start, Bell developed into one of the nation's top amateur players. Her relationship with the USGA started in 1950 when the Kansan took a train to California to compete in the U. S. Girls' Junior. She lost to Mickey Wright in the semifinals in what turned out to be her best finish in an USGA event. "It's been all downhill ever since," she quipped.

Bell won the Wichita city title at 14 and became the Kansas state women's amateur champion a year later. As a collegiate player, she took time off to dedicate herself to the premier events and blistered the amateur circuit.

"My goals back then were very simple—winning the Broadmoor and making the Curtis Cup team."

Bell capped her sparkling amateur career by achieving both of those honors. She won the Broadmoor three times and competed on the U. S. team in 1960 and 1962. "There is nothing that can compare with playing for your country," said Bell, who later captained the Curtis Cup team in 1986 and 1988.

As a player, she competed in 38 USGA championships and in 1964 she fired a then-record 67 in the U. S. Women's Open, a mark that stood for 14 years.

Just as important as her accomplishments in the game is Bell's lifetime record of service to the golf industry. Bell has been a USGA volunteer for 31 years.

The Colorado Springs resident first became involved with the USGA in 1961 when she was a member of the Junior Championship Committee. Bell has been a USGA rules official since the 1970s and has worked both the U.S. Open and U.S. Women's Open. She served on the Women's Committee for 16 years and in 1987 became the first female member of the Executive Committee.

In 1996, Bell was elected as the 54th president of the USGA and the first woman to lead golf's ruling body. "I bet that's the first time the incoming president kissed the outgoing president on the way to the dais," she joked after it was announced she would succeed Reg Murphy.

Clearly, this was more than a statement of gender equality at the very top of golf in the United States. As one of the most respected golf administrators in the field, Bell had freely given her time and expertise to the betterment of the game.

"Judy's gender I don't believe was a consideration in her election. Her abilities, I think, were the consideration that caused her to be selected as the first woman president," said Stuart Bloch, president from 1992-1993. "If she were a man, she would have been elected."

During her tenure as USGA president, Bell and the USGA Executive Committee initiated the "For the Good of the Game" program, a $50-million initiative to take the game to new levels by bringing it to non-traditional players, such as youth, minorities and the disabled.

"Golf is for everyone regardless of race, color or physical handicaps," said Bell, who has taken a leadership role in Golf 20/20 and The First Tee initiatives. "Access is important. What would make me happy would be to look at this game down the road and see that the opportunity is in place for everyone who wants to play the game and learn about it and have affordable access."

## THE BELL RECORD

**President, United States Golf Association: 1996, 1997**

**USGA Committee Service: 1961-1964, 1968-1984, 1987-present**

**Curtis Cup Teams ................ 4**

**(2-1) .................. 1960, 1962**

**Non-Playing Captain ..... 1986, 1988**

**Ike Grainger Award (more than 25 years of volunteer service to the USGA): 1995**

# Karsten Solheim

**Karsten Solheim revolutionized golf club design and manufacturing, thereby making the game easier and more enjoyable for hundreds of thousands of amateur golfers.**

Elected into the World Golf Hall of Fame in the lifetime achievement category, Solheim is heralded as a golf innovator who changed the game by examining the mechanics and technology of the sport.

Born in Bergen, Norway, Solheim didn't take up the game until he was 42 when his co-workers at General Electric invited him to fill out a foursome. He immediately became an enthusiast but found, much to his despair, that he shared a problem with millions of other golfers—he couldn't putt. Like many of us, he blamed his equipment. However, he did something about it. Figuring out how to hit a ball straighter, farther and higher consumed most of his waking hours.

Solheim began tinkering in his garage with a blade putter. He assembled the working model for his first putter, the 1-A, with two popsicle sticks glued to two sugar cubes with a shaft in the middle, rather than attaching the shaft to the heel of the blade. The radical design transferred the weight to the perimeter of the club and the hollow center area created a distinctive "ping" when it struck the ball. Thus, a name for his company was born.

Before Solheim, few applied scientific principles to the design of golf equipment. "I saw immediately that by using the simple laws of physics and mechanics it would be possible to make something more efficient than a blade, and thus avoid such off-line putts," Solheim explained.

Solheim's homespun operation usually confined itself to the garage in its early years. When Solheim first toted around his unconventional looking putter to the practice greens of pro tournaments, he was not readily accepted. The breakthrough occurred when Julius Boros won the PGA TOUR's Phoenix Open in 1967 using a PING putter.

Solheim sketched his "answer" to inconsistent putting on the sleeve of a 78-rpm record. His wife, Louise, suggested he remove the "w" so the name would fit on the club. Within a few years, Solheim's putters were being used by pro golfers all over the world and the Anser putter remains one of the most popular and copied designs to this day.

In 1967, overwhelming demand for the Anser forced Solheim to resign his position at GE and incorporate Karsten Manufacturing and, thus, a part-time passion became a full-time pursuit.

In 1969, Solheim applied the concept of perimeter weighting to irons. His new design and method of manufacturing took the golf world into a new dimension. By taking the weight from behind the center of the head and redistributing it to the toe and heel, Solheim increased the size of the sweet spot. He was the first to use investment casting in order to improve the consistency of his irons. The Ping iron was a boon to the average golfer because of its playability. Even off-center hits could achieve results of decent direction and distance in comparison to the less-forgiving forged irons.

In only three years, Solheim captured about 40 percent of the market and his Ping Eye2 model remains the best-selling iron ever. It is said that Ping irons and putters have inspired more look-alikes and knockoffs than any other clubs.

Notably he was a pioneer in generating interest and sponsorship dollars in women's professional golf. Solheim was also the driving force behind the Solheim Cup, the biennial matches patterned after the Ryder Cup, which gave women's golf an international platform.

## THE SOLHEIM RECORD

- Patented first putter design, the 1-A, in 1959
- Developed hugely popular Anser putter in mid-1960s
- PING putters have won more than 2,000 professional tournaments worldwide, more than any other
- Invented Ping Eye2 irons, the best-selling iron sets in history
- Founder of professional women's golf's Solheim Cup in 1990

STRATA
BOSS
BOSS

# Bernhard Langer

**By achieving international fame and fortune on the professional circuits of the world, Bernhard Langer lifted golf from obscurity in his native Germany.** Langer was a trailblazer in his native land, where there was only one public course and 130,000 golfers. Both figures have grown tremendously due to Langer's presence.

One of the most remarkably consistent and resilient professionals, Langer routinely conquered adversity in the form of the putting "yips" to reach the top, and he still remains in the upper echelon of the game today.

Growing up, Langer fell in love with the challenge that golf presented. At age eight, he followed his brother's footsteps by caddying at the Augsburg G. & C.C., five miles from his home.

Langer left school at age 14 to pursue golf as a profession. In 1976, he joined the European Tour. Just as Langer became successful, he developed the "yips." All of a sudden his hands no longer followed the instructions the brain was sending and the putter head seemed to leap forward on its own accord. But Langer is one of the few players ever to discover a cure. On four separate occasions, Langer conquered his putting woes.

"As a youngster I never thought twice about holing short putts, but when I moved to the fast tournament greens, my confidence was shattered and I had to start all over again."

Langer experienced his breakthrough in America using the cross-handed method. Ironically, he overcame his putting woes to win the world's most demanding putting contest, recording his first major victory in the 1985 Masters. Langer rallied from a four-stroke deficit at the turn on Sunday and birdied four of the last seven holes to pass Curtis Strange.

His victory was testament to his hard work at crafting a reliable stroke under pressure and his magical touch continued one week later when he won the Sea Pines Heritage Classic at Hilton Head Island, S.C.

Said Langer, "1985 was my best year ever. I won seven tournaments on five continents and became the No. 1-ranked golfer in the world." No. 1, indeed. When the inaugural Sony World Ranking debuted in April 1986, Langer was the first-ever No. 1.

Eight years after his first Masters title, Langer won again at Augusta with a decisive eagle 3 on the 13th and he cruised to a four-stroke victory over Chip Beck.

Langer won 42 times on the European Tour as well as wins in Australia, Japan and South Africa. Among his victories, the last nine came using an oversized broom-handle putter.

Americans probably know him best from the Ryder Cup from 1985-1991, turning the Cup from a one-sided event into one of the most exciting in sports. He helped Europe win on American soil for the first time in '87, but in '91 it was his barely missed six-foot par putt on the final hole of the last singles match against Hale Irwin that enabled the U.S. to regain the Cup for the first time since 1983.

In the era of the long ball, Langer still prospers. His remarkable consistency is perhaps best reflected in his European Tour records for consecutive cuts made (68) and consecutive years with a victory (17, shared with Seve Ballesteros).

Langer was elected to the World Golf Hall of Fame through the International ballot in 2001, but chose to defer his induction until 2002.

"I have tried to achieve a level of consistency throughout my career, and to have it culminate with this election (to the World Golf Hall of Fame) means a great deal to me," Langer said. He joins an elite circle that now includes its first native German.

## THE LANGER RECORD

Major Championship Victories .... 2
Masters: 1985, 1993
PGA TOUR Victories ............ 3
International Victories .......... 42
Ryder Cup Teams ............... 11
(21-15-6) .. 1981, 1983, 1985, 1987, 1989, 1991, 1993, 1995, 1997, 2002
Captain .....................2004

WORLD GOLF HALL of FAME

# Marlene Hagge

**From glamour girl to golden girl, Marlene Bauer Hagge's career on the LPGA Tour spanned a remarkable five decades.** A child prodigy and charter member of the LPGA along with her older sister, Alice, Hagge is the third LPGA player voted into the World Golf Hall of Fame through the LPGA Tour's veterans category.

In her era, golf for girls was still a novelty beyond the club level. Encouraged by her father, Hagge fully embraced the game and became a junior champion, setting new standards for women's golf. "My father wanted two strapping boys that he could make into golf champions and he got two runt girls instead," Hagge explained. "He tried to start Alice playing golf at an early age and, finding her interested in other things, thought that he would get hold of me before I had time to become interested in anything else."

Hagge first gripped a club at age three. Her father taught her the long, limber swing that became her trademark. Six years later, Dave Bauer loaded the family belongings into a Model-A Ford pickup and moved from South Dakota to California where his daughters could play year around.

With no junior programs in place at the time, Hagge was raised on the fairways, playing golf with older men and boys on junior teams. She won the Los Angeles Women's Golf Championship in 1947 at age 13 on a course where the scorecard stated "Children Under 14 Are Not Allowed." That same year, Hagge became the youngest player to make the cut at the U.S. Women's Open and finished eighth.

Two years later, Hagge won the Western Girls' Junior Championship and capped her storied junior career by winning the first U.S. Girls' Junior title. In recognition of those achievements, she was honored as the Associated Press Female Athlete of the Year. *Life* Magazine named her one of the year's top teenagers, putting her on a list that included Elizabeth Taylor.

Hagge turned professional two weeks before her 16th birthday in 1950. Together with Alice and her parents, she traveled around the LPGA Tour in a 22-foot Airstream trailer. The sisters were graceful and petite, the tour's first glamour girls, and their fresh beauty attracted new fans to women's golf.

But it was her grit that made Hagge a champion. Hagge became, and still remains, the youngest player to win an LPGA event in 1952 when she won the Sarasota Open at age 18. She reached the height of her profession at 22. In 1956, she set a then-LPGA Tour money record of $20,235, won eight tournaments, including beating Patty Berg in a sudden-death playoff to win the LPGA Championship, the lone major of her career, and won the tour's most improved player award. The last of her 26 LPGA Tour victories was the Burdine's Invitational in 1972.

Forty years after she debuted as its youngest player, Hagge was the tour's oldest active member. She and fellow World Golf Hall of Famer Kathy Whitworth are the only players to compete in each of the LPGA's first five decades. At the end of the 1996 season, Hagge finally retired from active competition. Among all her individual accolades, her fondest memories are of her role as a charter member of the LPGA Tour, the only women's sports organization in the world that has been in existence for 50 years as a stand-alone entity.

"Being a professional golfer was no different from going to New York or Hollywood to become an actress. A group of people lived together to see if they could get their break in life. We began with 12, and then each year more joined us," said Hagge. "I never thought of myself as a pioneer. We were just a bunch of stubborn women who loved golf and figured we could make it happen."

In 2000, Hagge was recognized during the LPGA's 50th anniversary as one of the organization's top 50 players and teachers.

### THE HAGGE RECORD

Major Championship Victories ..... 1
LPGA Championship: 1956

LPGA Tour Victories ............ 26

Leading Money Winner: 1956

LPGA Commissioner's Founders Award ....................... 2000

# Ben Crenshaw

**Perhaps no player better characterizes the words of golfer Willie Park that "a man who can putt is a match for anyone" than Ben Crenshaw.** It was a line impressed in his mind at an early age by Harvey Penick, his teacher and mentor, and the man who first put a club in Crenshaw's hands. Crenshaw's mastery of the putter has earned him numerous accolades and now a well-deserved place in the World Golf Hall of Fame.

Crenshaw was introduced to the game by his father, Charlie, a schoolteacher. When Ben was eight, his father placed him under the guidance of Penick, who initially cut down a 7-iron for him, showed him a proper grip and watched as Crenshaw effortlessly whacked balls onto the green 75 yards away.

Finding the hole was never a problem for Crenshaw, blessed with a putting stroke that is the envy of all who play. Charlie Crenshaw Sr. remembers when he bought his teenage son the Wilson 8802 blade putter that came to be known simply as "Little Ben."

"It was just a putter in Harvey Penick's shop. Ben felt it and waggled it around for a while so I bought it for him. That club's been the best provider in the family," he said of the $20 club.

Crenshaw's putting was so sensational it often overshadowed the rest of his game. His 19 PGA TOUR titles and exemplary record prove that his overall game was as accomplished as his putting.

Few golfers have joined the PGA TOUR with greater expectations to succeed than Crenshaw. Even fewer managed to live up to them. After winning 17 amateur events, including NCAA titles from 1971 to 1973 while an All-American at the University of Texas, Crenshaw had the strongest amateur resume since Jack Nicklaus. He faced a decision whether to stay in school or turn pro.

Surviving the cut in all four majors and all 11 PGA TOUR events in which he competed as an amateur, including a third at the Heritage, convinced Ben to turn pro. From the start, Crenshaw seemed destined to exceed the lofty expectations. He lapped the field at qualifying school by 12, won his first start and the following week finished second. He seemed preordained to win countless majors, but unexpectedly victories at the majors eluded him.

But Crenshaw answered his critics by capturing his favorite event, the Masters. Lurking two shots behind in the final round in 1984, Crenshaw put on a putting exhibition the likes of which was seldom seen.

Eleven years later, he won his second Masters seven days after he learned that Penick had died. Crenshaw showed up at Augusta with a heavy heart and his game in disarray. Golf's foremost putter entered the Masters ranked 69th in putting on the PGA TOUR that season, but a swing tip from his caddie, Carl Jackson, and one last putting tip from his mentor rejuvenated his game. Two weeks before Penick died, Crenshaw visited him and he gave Ben one final lesson from his bed.

Crenshaw's magical stroke returned. He mastered Augusta's slippery surfaces, surviving the tournament without making a single three-putt. He authored a final-round 68 that included "a Harvey bounce" off the trees at the second and birdies at 16 and 17 to close one of the most improbable victories.

Crenshaw credited Penick's divine spirit as the 15th club during his extraordinary win. "I believe in fate. It was like someone put their hand on my shoulder this week and guided me through," Crenshaw said.

Fate intervened again when Ben was captain of the 1999 U.S. Ryder Cup team. Despite trailing Europe, 10-6, going into the singles competition, he closed his press conference with a statement that stunned the media. "I'm a big believer in fate. I have a good feeling about tomorrow. That's all I'm going to say." He then stood up and walked out of the press room.

Crenshaw's bold prediction proved prophetic. When Justin Leonard sank a 45-foot putt on the 17th green in his match against Jose-Maria Olazabal, the U.S. had regained the Ryder Cup with the largest comeback in Ryder Cup history.

## THE CRENSHAW RECORD

Major Championship Victories ..... 2
Masters: 1984, 1995

PGA TOUR Victories ............19

Ryder Cup Teams .................4
(3-8-1) ...........1981, 1983, 1987
Captain ..................... 1999

GWAA William Richardson Award .. 1993

Bob Jones Award ..............1991

# Tommy Bolt

**Nicknames abound for Tommy Bolt—Terrible, Tempestuous, Thunder.** He has affectionately been called all of them.

The winner of the 1958 U.S. Open, Bolt recorded 15 victories on the PGA TOUR, twice was selected for the Ryder Cup and helped spawn the Champions Tour.

Like many of his generation, Bolt was introduced to golf through caddying. The fact that Bolt's golf career was sidetracked a number of times before he ever had a chance to succeed makes his accomplishments more extraordinary. He never teed it up on the PGA TOUR until the relatively late age of 34. Despite lacking the money to compete on tour, Bolt was one of golf's most determined competitors.

He spent four years in the Army during World War II, serving as head pro at one of Rome's elite golf clubs, perfecting his game. When he returned from the war, Bolt bounced back and forth between competing on the tour and retreating to construction work when he ran out of money.

While his accomplishments on the golf course are noteworthy, Bolt is remembered by many for his fiery temper and his penchant for throwing clubs. Bolt taught a young Arnold Palmer and anyone who would listen "to always throw clubs ahead of you, that way you won't waste any energy going back to pick them up."

"I launched far more (clubs) because they expected me to than I did because I was mad at anything that had gone wrong with my golf. After a while, it became showmanship, plain and simple," claimed Bolt.

Ben Hogan firmly believed had Bolt only been able to mask his emotions better and accept failure, his record would have been even better. "If we could've screwed another head on his shoulders, Tommy Bolt could have been the greatest who ever played," Hogan once said.

It was Hogan whom Bolt credited with resurrecting his career. In 1955, perplexed by a hook that worsened under pressure, Bolt sought Hogan's help. Often undone by the same malady early in his career, Hogan invited Bolt to practice with him during the off-season.

"I went to him and all but got on my knees for help," Bolt wrote in his book, *The Hole Truth.* "He put my left hand on top of the club, gripped it in the back three fingers of the left hand and the thumb down the shaft. It took me about a month of constant practice to get acclimated to the new grip, but I learned not to fear the hook."

Armed with that confidence, Bolt became one of the best ball strikers of all time. He also got a grip on his temper in time to win the one title he coveted, the U.S. Open, in his home state of Oklahoma in 1958. He birdied Southern Hills' treacherous 12th hole three consecutive times and finished four strokes ahead of Gary Player.

While the Open was his pinnacle, Bolt will tell you of another great moment in which the student bettered his mentor, Hogan, as well as Gene Littler, in an 18-hole playoff to win the 1960 Memphis Open. All even through 16, Bolt fired a 2-iron tee shot stiff to the flag on the par-3 17th. "When Ben said, 'Nice shot!' it was like a double clap of thunder to me," Bolt recalled. "It was the only thing he said to me all day."

Long before there was a senior tour, Bolt won the 1969 PGA Seniors' Championship and 11 other senior titles in the U.S. and Australia. He was one of the pioneers of the Champions Tour, laying the groundwork in a memorable six-hole sudden-death playoff with partner Art Wall against Julius Boros and Roberto De Vicenzo in the 1979 Legends of Golf, won by Boros-De Vicenzo.

When Nielsen ratings indicated approximately six million households were tuned in, PGA TOUR Commissioner Deane Beman was convinced to support the senior initiative, which evolved into what is now the Champions Tour.

## THE BOLT RECORD

| | |
|---|---|
| Major Championship Victories | 1 |
| U.S. Open: 1958 | |
| PGA TOUR Victories | 15 |
| Senior Victories | 12 |
| Ryder Cup Teams | 2 |
| (3-1-0) | 1955, 1957 |

WORLD GOLF HALL of FAME

# Tony Jacklin

**Tony Jacklin's brief, but memorable, brilliance revitalized British and ultimately European golf with his remarkable exploits.** For four seasons—from 1969 through 1972—there was no brighter star in golf's firmament than Jacklin. At age 26, he broke a number of performance records in British golf, simply doing for the game in Great Britain what Arnold Palmer had done for it in the United States barely more than a decade before.

For these accomplishments and for breathing life back into the Ryder Cup later in his career, Tony Jacklin was elected to the World Golf Hall of Fame.

Despite his success as a teenager in winning the Lincolnshire Championship as an amateur, Jacklin's parents thought turning pro was too risky a proposition. But when Bill Shankland offered him an assistant pro position at Potters Bar, the 17-year-old Jacklin thought the six-pound salary was a fortune and launched his professional golf career. But life as an assistant wasn't always appealing to Jacklin.

"There were times when life was heartbreaking—long hours spent practicing with Shankland seldom satisfied with what I was doing," recalled Jacklin. But he worked diligently on his game and the hard work paid off with victories in Europe and Jacklin's dreams soon began to come true. He traveled to America to compete against the best and it wasn't long before he won the Jacksonville Open in 1968 and became the first Briton to win on the PGA TOUR.

Jacklin became a national hero in 1969 at Royal Lytham when he became the first British player since Max Faulkner to win the British Open since 1951.

"This was my Everest and no one can ever take away the recollection of that moment when I sat on its peak," he wrote in his book, *Jacklin: The Champion's Own Story*.

One year later Jacklin achieved even greater heights when he became the first player since Ben Hogan to hold the U.S. and British Open titles simultaneously upon his triumph at Hazeltine in Minnesota. Jacklin endured horrific conditions, including an opening-round 71 in 40 m.p.h. winds that left the then Big Three of Arnold Palmer at 79, Gary Player at 80 and Jack Nicklaus at 81. Jacklin led the '70 U.S. Open from start to finish and was the only player to break par for the tournament, finishing a whopping seven shots ahead of Dave Hill, the largest margin in 49 years. Jacklin also became the first British player to win the U.S. Open since Ted Ray in 1920.

"I walked on water that week. Hazeltine was unquestionably the best week of golf I've ever had in my life," Jacklin said. "It was as near a perfect week as I have ever experienced."

Jacklin nearly won the 1972 British Open, too, but he eventually placed third behind Lee Trevino and runner-up Nicklaus. But Jacklin continued to win tournaments and topped the 1973 European Tour Order of Merit, although he never seriously contended in majors again. By the time he won the 1982 British PGA Championship, golf had lost much of its luster for Jacklin. "I had had enough," Jacklin admitted. "Golf was the only thing that I did that didn't make me happy so I stopped doing it. I said, 'That's it.' "

Shortly thereafter, however, Jacklin accepted the role as captain of the Ryder Cup team and his passion was reignited. When he took the helm in 1983, the matches were in danger of being compromised by the continued U.S. success. But Jacklin set the wheels in motion to end U.S. domination and nearly pulled off an improbable upset. Losing did not diminish his team's competitive spirit; rather it ignited an intense rivalry. In 1985 he was the inspirational non-playing captain for Europe's first victory in 28 years.

In 1987, he captained the team that won on American soil for the first time . . . ever. Persuaded to do a fourth tour of duty in 1989, Jacklin's team retained the Ryder Cup for the first time in its history. His infectious enthusiasm and indomitable spirit energized his team and lifted its confidence.

## THE JACKLIN RECORD

| | |
|---|---|
| Major Championship Victories | 2 |
| British Open: 1969 | |
| U.S. Open: 1970 | |
| PGA TOUR Victories | 4 |
| Champions Tour Victories | 2 |
| International Victories | 24 |
| Ryder Cup Teams | 11 |
| (13-14-8) | 1967, 1969, 1971, 1973, 1975, 1977, 1979 |
| Non-Playing Captain | 1983, 1985, 1987, 1989 |

# Harvey Penick

**Harvey Penick spent his life teaching golf.** He taught countless golfers how to "take dead aim," claimed to have seen more golf shots than anyone who ever lived and shared his wisdom about the game in one of the best-selling sports books of all time. In recognition of his numerous contributions to the game, Penick was selected for induction into the World Golf Hall of Fame through the lifetime achievement category.

A Texas native, Penick began his golf career as a caddy at Austin C.C., became the assistant pro there at 13 and was elevated to head professional in 1923 upon graduation from high school.

"He found out in life that he had a gift for teaching," said prized pupil and fellow Hall of Famer Ben Crenshaw. "He was a fine player, but he made his life's mission to help others in golf in any way possible."

Penick frequently cited two events in determining his real strength lay in teaching. "I qualified for the U.S. Open at Olympia Fields in Chicago (in 1928)," he said in the book *Texas Golf Legends*. "It was the first time I was a long way from home. I saw Walter Hagen hit that ball like a bullet. I didn't play very well. Coming home on that slow train, I thought I better stick to teaching."

Observing Sam Snead's graceful swing at the 1930 Houston Open cemented Penick's decision to pursue teaching. He was part of the first generation of Americans to succeed the English and Scottish pros who brought the game to the United States. As president of the Texas chapter of the PGA, Penick signed the Class A membership cards of Byron Nelson and Ben Hogan. From 1931 through 1963 he coached the University of Texas golf team, winning a remarkable 22 Southwest Conference titles.

Penick was revered for his simple, practical approach. He preferred to teach with images, parables and metaphors that planted the seeds of shotmaking in the golfers' minds. Yardsticks, weed cutters, water buckets and benches became his students' most valuable teaching aids. In 1989, Penick was honored by the PGA of America as Teacher of the Year.

Home was the practice tee. His sun-baked skin bore witness to the countless hours he spent on the range, demystifying the golf swing. "Harvey had so many wrinkles, his face would hold a seven-day rain," quipped Jimmy Demaret. There was simply no other place he preferred to be.

Penick's unique ability to teach the game brought a who's who of golf to Austin over the years, including major championship winners Sandra Palmer, Crenshaw, Tom Kite, Mickey Wright, Betsy Rawls and Kathy Whitworth.

Penick also influenced a number of premier instructors, including Davis Love Jr. to be a student of other disciplines. Penick suggested that Love learn to play a musical instrument. The experience of learning something new helped Love become a better communicator.

Unlike most instructors of his day, Penick did not have a rigid system. He claimed to learn something new about golf every day. He observed the different techniques that worked for the game's best and tried to incorporate them while allowing the student's swing to fit his or her personality.

For more than 60 years, Penick privately compiled observations in a red notebook, tabbed according to subject, such as putting and chipping. He planned on passing along these thoughts to his son, Tinsley. He never intended to publish his *Little Red Book* until one day when he thought it would be a mistake not to do so.

Initial expectations were quite modest, but the book touched a chord with golfers everywhere. *The Little Red Book* was on *The New York Times* best-seller list for 52 weeks. Four subsequent books were successful, too.

Penick died April 2, 1995, the Sunday before the Masters began. Crenshaw, who had received a putting lesson from Penick only weeks earlier, served as one of his pallbearers and paid tribute to his mentor by winning the Masters seven days later. It was the perfect epitaph for a man who had dedicated his life to the game.

## THE PENICK RECORD

PGA of America Teacher of the Year: 1989

Taught golf for more than 70 years

Prominent students who won major championships: Ben Crenshaw, Mickey Wright, Kathy Whitworth, Betsy Rawls, Tom Kite and Sandra Palmer

Coached the University of Texas golf team from 1931-1963, winning 22 Southwest Conference titles

Best-selling author

WORLD GOLF HALL of FAME

# Nick Price

**If there was ever a golfer who took the road less traveled, it is Nick Price.** His was an intricate puzzle, but when all the pieces were finally in place, Price at his peak played at a level rarely reached in the history of the game.

Between 1992 and 1994, Price won 16 of the 54 tournaments he played in worldwide, the victories including three major championships and the 1993 PLAYERS Championship. During that zenith, Price won both the PGA TOUR and PGA of America Player of the Year Awards twice each, and was the PGA TOUR's leading money winner two times. To date, at age 48, he has won 18 times on the PGA TOUR to go with 24 International victories.

Price came to the game from one of its most fertile fringes. Born in South Africa on Jan. 28, 1957, Price was the youngest of three brothers by seven years. The family soon moved to Rhodesia (now Zimbabwe), where at age eight, Price began banging plastic balls toward a series of tomato cans that were buried in neighborhood lawns. Price remembers playing as many as 144 holes a day in mock tournaments with his friends for a garden variety version of the British Open.

In such an environment, the athletic Price progressed dramatically. In 1974, at age 17, he won the Optimist Junior World at Torrey Pines in San Diego. "I had no idea what I'd done," he says, "but I knew right then I wanted to make golf my life."

In 1978, Price joined the European Tour. Although he would win the 1980 Swiss Open, his largely self-taught swing was not suited to the rigors of professional golf. Desperate, Price in 1982 began working with childhood friend David Leadbetter, who had become a teaching professional in America, and made dramatic improvement. Six months later, Price stood on the 13th tee at Troon leading the final round of the British Open by three strokes. Although he lost to Tom Watson by one, Price remembers being disappointed but not discouraged. "I knew I was getting better."

Sure enough, the next year he won the World Series of Golf in Akron. The resulting 10-year exemption gave Price the time to indulge his passion, perfecting the golf swing. But Price's learning curve did not continue its dramatic rise. Although he nearly won the British Open again in 1988, losing by a stroke to Seve Ballesteros, Price was gaining a reputation as an underachiever in golf. Eight years passed until he recorded his second PGA TOUR win in 1991.

During that time Price crafted one of the most fundamentally sound golf swings in the game — a staccato-like, yet classic, movement — and he eventually was rewarded for his hard work. In 1992, he won his first major title, the PGA Championship. THE PLAYERS Championship and three other titles followed in 1993, setting the stage for his greatest year, 1994.

At the British Open at Turnberry in Scotland, Price won in a manner that would have seemed farfetched even if he had been play-acting in his childhood garden. Three strokes down to Jesper Parnevik, Price birdied the 16th and eagled the 17th with a downhill 50-foot putt. When Parnevik bogeyed the 72nd hole, Price's closing par gave him the claret jug.

It was Price's most emotional triumph, but the victory he captured three weeks later at the PGA Championship is his proudest. Masterfully negotiating the tight doglegs and confounding targets at Southern Hills, Price achieved a shot-making virtuosity that ranked with the best of his golf idol, Ben Hogan. He opened with a 67 and was never challenged, eventually winning by six.

"I'd always dreamed of playing that way, and I finally did it at Southern Hills," says Price. "It was what my journey

## THE PRICE RECORD

Major Championshipo Victories . . .3

PGA Championship: 1992, 1994

British Open: 1994

PGA TOUR Victories . . . . . . . . .18

International Victories . . . . . . . . .24

Presidents Cup Teams . . . . . . . . . .5

(8-11-4) 1994, 1996, 1998, 2000, 2003,

PGA TOUR Player of the Year: 1993, 1994

Leading Money Winner: 1993, 1994

Bob Jones Award: 2005

Payne Stewart Award: 2002

# Leo Diegel

**Leo Diegel's sensitive soul and hyperactive mind wouldn't rest as he pondered the complexity of the game.** Known as one of the great shotmakers, Diegel between 1920 and 1934 won 30 PGA TOUR events, including two PGA Championships. His hunger to understand the mysteries of the game and his amiable nature made him one of the most popular players of his time.

"In all my years of golf, I have never seen anyone whose devotion to the game could match Leo's," wrote Gene Sarazen. "It was his religion. Between courses at the table, Leo used to get up and practice swings. Every night he went to bed dreaming theory and every morning he awakened with some hot idea that was going to revolutionize the game."

On the other hand, Diegel's many friends wondered if he cared too much. His passion combined with a nervous temperament often conspired against him at the biggest moments. His history in the major championships betrays a pattern of superb play undermined by shaky finishes. Diegel placed in the top four in seven U.S. and British Opens, but could never win one. At the 1925 Open in Worcester, Diegel lost nine strokes to par over the last six holes to finish five strokes back. At the 1933 British Open at St. Andrews, Diegel needed only one over par on the last five holes for outright victory, but instead three-putted the 18th to miss a playoff by one.

"They keep trying to give me a championship, but I won't take it," Diegel once said wistfully.

Aware of his weaknesses, Diegel would walk slower to fight his tendency to rush and even had himself psychoanalyzed. The biggest compensation Diegel made was his putting stance. Exasperated with missing short putts, Diegel in 1924 devised a stiff–wristed, bent over, elbows-out style that was so distinctive it became known as "Diegeling."

The odd angles of Diegel's posture provided an unending source of good-natured ribbing all his life, and even after: "How they gonna fit him in the box," deadpanned Walter Hagen at Diegel's funeral.

Along with the affection he engendered, Diegel was respected for his uncannily accurate iron play and his ferociousness in match play. It was Diegel, in winning the 1928 PGA Championship, who ended Hagen's amazing streak of 22 straight match play wins (and four straight titles) by defeating him in the semifinals. He did the same thing on his way to repeating in 1929. In four Ryder Cups, including the first in 1927, Diegel lost only one match. At the 1929 event, he defeated Abe Mitchell, 9 and 8, while playing 28 holes in 10 under par.

Diegel's greatest weapon was an amazingly precise iron game that was the envy of his peers. "Diegel could put his second shots closer than any other golfer of his day," wrote Herbert Warren Wind. Bernard Darwin once called Diegel, "in a way, the greatest golfing genius I have ever seen."

Born in Detroit in 1899, Diegel was a boy wonder who won the city caddie crown at age 13 and turned pro the same year the PGA was formed, 1916. His greatest year was 1925, when he won five events, including his second of four Canadian Opens.

After a 1938 auto accident ended his competitive career, Diegel became a club pro who became a favorite of Hollywood stars such as Douglas Fairbanks. He dedicated his instructional book, *The Nine Bad Shots of Golf*, "to the vast army of struggling golfers whose swings need help." He was one of the founders of the Tucson Open, and while a club pro in Philadelphia, he worked with the U.S. Army promoting golf as a psychological and therapeutic aid for wounded servicemen returning from World War II. Diegel died of cancer in 1951.

## THE DIEGEL RECORD

Major Championship Victories . . . . 2
PGA Championship: 1928, 1929
PGA TOUR Victories . . . . . . . .30
Ryder Cup Teams . . . . . . . . . . . .4
(3-3) . . . . . . . . . . . . . . 1927, 1929, 1931, 1933

# Chako Higuchi

**Hisako "Chako" Higuchi made her mark in golf with more than just her golf clubs.** She was selected for the Lifetime Achievement category for championing the cause of Japanese golf, and continues to do so in unparalleled acts of dedication and service to her fellow professionals.

When Higuchi began to play golf in the early 1960s, there were few women golfers of any kind in Japan, and no professional tour for women. But by the time she retired from competitive golf in the '90s, Higuchi had won 69 times on the LPGA of Japan tour and recorded milestone victories on three other continents. Her achievements blazed a trail for the many Asian international players who have followed.

Higuchi dominated Japanese golf from 1968 to 1980, winning the JLPGA championship nine times and Japanese Women's Open four times. But her most important victories were abroad. She won the Women's Australian Open in 1974, the Colgate European Women's Open in 1976 and, in her finest moment, the 1977 LPGA Championship, a victory which prompted a ticker-tape parade in Tokyo. Indeed, she remains the only Japanese player ever to win a major championship on either the PGA or LPGA Tours.

At the LPGA in Myrtle Beach, Higuchi remembers being nervous after being tied for the lead after three rounds. "I thought I would not win," she said. "But by then, I was very consistent, and I hardly ever missed a fairway. On the final day, I played my best golf." With a closing 69 built on three consecutive back-nine birdies, she won by three strokes.

"Chako was very well liked, and a wonderful player," says Judy Rankin. "She had beautiful tempo and great balance. You never thought of Chako hitting a wild shot. On the other hand, if you made a mistake, she would be there."

Higuchi was born in Tokyo in 1945, the sixth of six children. She was a school-girl champion in track and field whose best-event was the 80-yard hurdles. At 16, she began playing golf after her sister became a locker-room attendant at a local course. It led her to become the caddie for teaching professional Torakichi Nakamura, who had won the individual title at the 1957 Canada Cup. "He taught me the game physically and mentally," Higuchi told writer Liz Kahn. "He made me run every morning and hit 1,000 balls a day until I cried."

The 5-6, slightly built Higuchi developed a swing that was distinguished by a sway so pronounced she actually lost sight of the ball at the top of her backswing. She was embarrassed when she first went to America and saw that the stars had much more orthodox swings. But Hall of Fame member Henry Cotton, who saw her win the Colgate at Sunningdale in England, said it was an effective method for a small woman to use.

"To make her swing work took a great athlete, which Chako was," says Carol Mann. "Off the course she was delightful, but on it she carried herself like an elite athlete – a fierce competitor who showed no emotion."

Although playing most of her golf in Asia, Higuchi, beginning in 1969, played the LPGA Tour part time for 10 years. The most American events she ever played in a year was 15, and her finest season was 1976, when she finished 10th on the money list. By the 1970s, Higuchi was such a hero in her home country that when she was seen on the streets of Tokyo, people would stop and clap. Her pioneering efforts helped women become accepted in Japanese golf and led the way for future Japanese professional stars such as Ayako Okamoto.

When her playing days ended, Higuchi became the commissioner of the LPGA of Japan in 1994, a position she continues to hold.

"I became an emancipated woman through patience, with practice and by wanting everything so hard," she told Kahn. "I have done things for my own pride because others think I can't, and because I want to show people that others can follow."

## THE HIGUCHI RECORD

Major Championship Victories . . . . 1

LPGA Championship: 1977

LPGA Tour Victories . . . . . . . . . . 1

International Victories . . . . . . . . . 71

LPGA of Japan Leading Money Winner: 1968-1976

WORLD GOLF HALL of FAME

# Annika Sorenstam

**Annika Sorenstam's journey is still unfolding. As good as it has been, her best may still lie ahead.**

In her first 12 seasons, Sorenstam has built one of the greatest careers in the history of women's golf. Her 63 official victories place her third on the LPGA's all-time list, and her nine major championships rank fifth.

Beyond the numbers, Sorenstam is also the first woman professional golfer to extend the limits of her sport. Beginning in 2000, her dedication to an intense exercise regimen has transformed her body and improved her performance, just as Martina Navratilova did in tennis.

Then in 2003, Sorenstam achieved a transcendent moment when she accepted a sponsor's exemption to compete in the PGA TOUR's Bank of America Colonial in Ft. Worth. Under intense pressure Sorenstam responded with nearly flawless tee to green golf in a first-round 71. Though she missed the 36-hole cut, the grace and skill she exhibited was universally hailed. "Anyone who watched her has a deeper appreciation of women's golf," said LPGA Tour player Lorie Kane.

By the force of her talent and need to test herself, the naturally shy Swede had come a long way from intentionally finishing second in junior tournaments to avoid giving an acceptance speech.

Sorenstam came to America to attend the University of Arizona, a decision she calls the turning point of her life. She won the 1991 NCAA individual title and after turning professional was voted rookie of the year in Europe and then on the LPGA. When Sorenstam won the U.S. Women's Open in 1995 and 1996, she was a star.

Her new status was uncomfortable. While America usually expects its winners to revel in achievement, Sorenstam's Swedish upbringing had taught her to resist the limelight. In the end, Sorenstam's public persona was guided by an innate quality that has nothing to do with nationality or culture — her fierce competitiveness.

In an effort to increase her driving distance and become a more powerful player, Sorenstam began a five-day-a-week program with a personal trainer. From ranking 26th on the LPGA Tour in driving distance with an average of 252 yards in 2000, Sorenstam improved to first in 2003 with an average of 272, while still hitting better than 80 percent of fairways.

And as if to announce she had stepped into a new realm, Sorenstam opened the second round of the 2001 Standard Register Ping with eight consecutive birdies, and was a phenomenal 12 under par through 13 holes. She managed only one more birdie, but shot an LPGA record 59.

Sorenstam won eight events that year, but rather than slow down, she followed with one of the greatest seasons ever in 2002, posting 11 official victories. In 2003, she proved that her experience at Colonial did, indeed, make her tougher in major championships as she won the McDonald's LPGA Championship and the Weetabix Women's British Open to complete the Woman's career Grand Slam.

In 2004, she defended her title at the LPGA Championship, broke her own single-season scoring average record (68.69), and won her seventh player of the year title. In 2005 she won the season's first two majors, but fell short of her latest goal — the single-season Grand Slam, finishing tied for 23 in the U.S. Women's Open.

Sorenstam's current dilemma is deciding how long to keep pushing. She is still at her physical peak, with the potential to compile the greatest record ever. "I've come to a point in my career where I do feel kind of satisfied with what I've done," she says. "But a few more majors and then I'll be full."

## THE SORENSTAM RECORD

Major Championship Victories . . . .9
U.S. Women's Open: 1995, 1996
Nabisco Championship: 2001, 2002, 2005
LPGA Championship: 2003, 2004, 2005
Women's British Open: 2003

LPGA Tour Victories . . . . . . . . . .63

Solheim Cup Teams . . . . . . . . . . . .7
(20-9-3) . . .1994, 1996, 1998, 2000, 2002, 2003, 2005

LPGA Player of the Year: 1995, 1997, 1998, 2001, 2002, 2003, 2004

LPGA Rookie of the Year: 1994

Leading Money Winner: 1995, 1997, 1998, 2001, 2002, 2003, 2004

Vare Trophy: 1995, 1996, 1998, 2001, 2002

Patty Berg Award: 2003

WORLD GOLF HALL of FAME

# Tom Kite

**When Tom Kite arrived at Pebble Beach for the 1992 U.S. Open, something was missing.** Yes, he was missing a major title from his sterling resume, but he planned to make amends for that on a course where he had won before and held the course record. What he hadn't planned was to forget his trusty lob wedge at home.

Never fear, Kite called up his father who delivered the club in person. It would come in handy. On Sunday, the 42-year-old Kite was standing in the deep rough some 20 yards off the seventh green, fighting to stand straight in the 40-mile-an-hour seaside wind. He grabbed the lob wedge, cleared the yawning bunker with a low arcing pitch, and watched the ball speed across the green, crash into the flagstick and drop into the hole for an improbable birdie.

Kite clapped his hands, clenched his fist and a broad smile broke out across his freckled face. Kite survived the brutal conditions – he was one of only five players to shoot par or better that day – for the crowning achievement of his career. "I guess if you can only win one major championship, it would be the U.S. Open," Kite said. "And if you had to pick a golf course to win it, Pebble Beach is not a bad place to have it."

Kite was born Dec. 9, 1949, in McKinney, Tex. He started playing golf at age six by following his father around and won his first tournament at 11. When the family moved to Austin, he began taking lessons from Hall of Fame instructor Harvey Penick, who charged him $3.50 for his first lesson and then never charged him again.

While other boys grew up dreaming of being baseball sluggers or firemen, Kite knew he wanted to be a PGA TOUR pro. "There was nothing in my life at that time I liked more than golf," he said. "Nothing was even a close substitute." His father warned him he faced an uphill battle. "Tom, for every 100 men who try the TOUR, 99 will fail," his father said.

"Dad, I sure feel sorry for those other 99, because I intend to make it," Tom said. In his mind, playing on the TOUR wasn't a dream; it was a commitment. Kite was a winner at every level. He guided the University of Texas to consecutive NCAA Championships in 1971 and 1972, and shared the 1972 individual title with his teammate Ben Crenshaw. He joined the PGA TOUR full-time in 1973 and won his first of 19 events in 1976.

At, 5-8, 155 pounds, Kite didn't drive it as long as Greg Norman. He lacked the silky smooth putting stroke of Ben Crenshaw. But his wedge game had no equal. Kite was the first player to carry a third wedge in his bag, which allowed him to be more precise with his distance control.

He was Mr. Consistency. From 1981 to 1987, Kite was the only man to win a PGA TOUR event every year. In 1981, he recorded 21 top-10 finishes in 26 starts, won the Vardon Trophy for scoring average, and led the money list. In 1989, he won three times, including THE PLAYERS Championship and was named PGA of America Player of the Year. He was a workaholic. When Bruce Lietzke was asked to name Kite's closest friend on Tour, he quipped, "His practice bag." "Spending time on the practice tee," Kite said, "is no more laborious than shooting baskets all afternoon is for some 8-year-old kid."

All the hours of practice paid off coincidentally on Father's Day in 1992 when he won the U.S. Open. Thanks to an assist by his dad, a special club, and one unforgettable shot.

## THE KITE RECORD

Major Championship Victories . . . . 1
U.S. Open: 1992
Walker Cup Teams . . . . . . . . . . . . 1
(2-1-1) . . . . . . . . . . . . . . . . 1971
PGA TOUR Victories . . . . . . . . .19
Ryder Cup Teams . . . . . . . . . . . . .7
(15-9-4) . . . . . . . .1979, 1981, 1983, 1987, 1989, 1993
Captain . . . . . . . . . . . . . . . . .1997
PGA TOUR Player of the Year: 1989
Leading Money Winner: 1981, 1989
Bob Jones Award: 1979

# Isao Aoki

**All Isao Aoki ever wanted to do was to see the world through golf.** He accomplished that and a whole lot more. Aoki won 73 times around the world on six different tours and in 2004 became the first Japanese man to be inducted into the World Golf Hall of Fame.

Despite his numerous victories, Aoki is perhaps best known for finishing second at the 1980 U.S. Open at Baltusrol Golf Club. Paired with Jack Nicklaus all four days, Aoki played his best golf against Nicklaus, sharing the lead going into the final round. Aoki waited patiently for his chance at glory. "I kept telling myself no matter how perfect he is, he will make a mistake in 72 holes in four days," Aoki said, "But I was wrong. Jack did not make any errors until the end of the tournament." Nicklaus carded a record-setting score of 272 (8-under-par), winning his fourth U.S. Open title while Aoki's 274 total became the second lowest 72-hole score in Open history.

Aoki fell short but he learned from the experience. "I realized there was a player in the world who could play far better than I ever imagined," Aoki said. "That experience led to my first victory." At the 1983 Hawaiian Open, he imagined a perfect result with his trusty pitching wedge. Aoki holed a pitching wedge from 128 yards for an eagle on the 72nd hole to beat a stunned Jack Renner by one shot. Aoki raised his arms in triumph in the fairway to celebrate becoming the first person from Japan to win a PGA TOUR event.

Born on August 31, 1942, Aoki grew up in Chiba, Japan the son of a farmer. He was introduced to golf as a caddie at Abiko Golf Club when he was 15 years old. It was a chance encounter – seeing Arnold Palmer playing an event on TV – that inspired him to dream big. "He was my idol," Aoki said. "When I saw him play, I challenged myself to come to the States and then be on the TOUR." Aoki turned pro as soon as he finished school. "My dream was to see the world," he said.

Nicknamed "Tower" after the Toyko Tower because of his height (he's six-feet tall), Aoki stood tallest on more than 70 occasions, including 56 times on his native tour. He led the Japanese Golf Tour in earnings five times and has won tournaments on six different tours – the PGA TOUR, Champions Tour, PGA European Tour, Australasian Tour, Japan Golf Tour, and Japan Senior Tour – including the 1978 World Match Play Championships.

Aoki's success around the world can be best attributed to his touch around the green. "I've never seen a putting stroke like his in my life," said Hall of Fame member Chi Chi Rodriguez. "He's the king of the jabbers." "What a touch. What a putter," added Nicklaus.

Some thirty years ago Aoki developed his unorthodox toe-in-the-air style with the flat stick. "At that time they had this putter called Silent Pawn by First Flight," he recalled. "It was 36 inches long. It was too long for me. Therefore, I tried to put it far away from my body." He changed putters through the years, but his idiosyncratic technique became his trademark as did the number of putts that fell in the hole.

As a member of the Champions Tour, Aoki has won nine times and shot a record 60 10-under-par on his way to winning the 1997 Emerald Coast Classic.

Aoki is proud of his Japanese heritage, maintaining his residency in Tokyo, flying the Japanese flag wherever he went, and packing and re-packing his bags as Japan's global golf ambassador. "He's the Arnold Palmer of Japanese golf," said Greg Norman, who introduced him at the 2004 Induction Ceremony. "To travel from your home shores – where the culture is different, the language is different – is not an easy task."

His success inspired others to follow in his footsteps. "He's influenced all the modern day Japanese players," said three-time major winner, Larry Nelson. "They've gotten better and better since he started playing and winning outside his country."

Indeed, golf has taken Aoki around the world and back again. "I have been doing what I love since I started," he said.

## THE AOKI RECORD

PGA TOUR Victories .......... 1
Champions Tour Victories ....... 9
International Victories ......... 63
Japan Golf Tour Leading Money Winner: Five times

# Charlie Sifford

**Charlie Sifford broke barriers all his life. He was the first African-American to play the PGA, the first to win a PGA-sanctioned event, and the first to be inducted into the World Golf Hall of Fame.**

There was a time when none of this seemed possible. Jackie Robinson's courageous integration of Major League Baseball in 1946 is widely and appropriately credited for changing the American sports landscape forever. One year later, toughened by a tour of duty in the Army's 24th Infantry, another young black man named Charlie Sifford told Robinson he planned to follow in his footsteps and compete in golf, a sport where the ball and the participants were equally as white.

"He asked me if I was a quitter," Sifford recalled. "He said, 'OK, if you're not a quitter, go ahead and take the challenge. If you're a quitter, there's going to be a lot of obstacles you're going to have to go through to be successful in what you're trying to do.'

"I made up my mind I was going to do it. I just did it. Everything worked out perfect, I think."

It was Sifford who opened professional golf, a game with a "Caucasian only" rule, to blacks more than four decades ago. Without him, Tiger Woods would probably not have been able to make his own impact on the sports world. "He has my respect and my gratitude for the sacrifices he made to open the doors to this great game to people of color," Woods said.

Born June 2, 1922, Sifford started in golf the only way a black kid growing up in North Carolina could in the 1930s – as a caddie. He earned 60 cents a day and gave his mom 50 cents and kept 10 cents to buy stogies, which became his trademark on the course. By 13, he could shoot par golf.

Sifford's skin was tough enough to endure racial injustice and epithets. At the 1952 Phoenix Open, Sifford and his all-black foursome, which included the boxer Joe Louis, found excrement in the cup on the first hole, and waited nearly an hour for the cup to be replaced.

Despite all the insults, Sifford lived up to the standard set by Robinson. Sifford fought his battle essentially alone; he didn't have teammates. He broke barriers by breaking par. He won the National Negro Open five straight times from 1952-1956, all the while pushing golf's color boundaries. Not until 1960, when he was 39, did he earn a PGA player card. A year later, under pressure from the California attorney general, the PGA of America, which then ran the Tour, dropped its "Caucasian only" membership clause.

Sifford's best years already had passed, but he still won twice on the PGA Tour. He became the first African-American to win a Tour event when he shot 64 in the final round to capture the 1967 Greater Hartford Open. "If you try hard enough," Sifford said, "anything can happen." Sifford, who won the 1975 PGA Seniors' Championship, went on to become an original member of the Champions Tour, where he won the Suntree Classic.

In 2004, Sifford became the first black golfer to break into another exclusive club. Of the 100 previously enshrined at the World Golf Hall of Fame, none was black. He was selected via the Lifetime Achievement category for his contributions to the game. "Tonight we honor a man not just for what he accomplished on the course, but for the course he chose in life," South African Gary Player said as he introduced his long-time friend at the induction ceremony in St. Augustine, Fla.

Better late, than never. That's been the story of Charlie Sifford's life. "Man, I'm in the Hall of Fame, the World Hall of Fame," he said in his induction ceremony speech. "Don't forget that now! I'm in the World Hall of Fame with all the players. That little old golf I played was all right, wasn't it?"

## THE SIFFORD RECORD

PGA TOUR Victories . . . . . . . . . . .2

Champions Tour Victories . . . . . . .1

UGA National Negro Open . . . . . . .6

1952, 1953, 1954, 1955, 1956, 1960

WORLD GOLF HALL of FAME

# Marlene Stewart-Streit

**Marlene Stewart-Streit is quite simply the most successful amateur golfer in Canadian history.** Her career spans more than five decades with at least one major amateur victory in each. She won at home – 11 Canadian Ladies Open Amateurs, nine Canadian Ladies Close Amateurs and four Canadian Ladies Senior Women's Amateur tournaments – and abroad, where she is the only woman ever to win the Canadian, British, American, and Australian amateur titles. In 2004, she rightfully became the first Canadian member of the World Golf Hall of Fame.

Stewart-Streit was born March 9, 1934, in Cereal, Alberta. At 15, she began riding her bicycle to The Lookout Point Golf Club, in Foothill, Ontario, located in the southwestern region of the province, and caddy, using the money she earned to pay the $25 club membership fee. The club pro, Gordon McInnis Sr., began giving her lessons and a year after taking up the game, she finished runner-up in the Ontario Junior Girls' Championship. Soon she would become a national figure. For winning the 1953 British Women's Amateur, she received a heroine's welcome. In Toronto, 15,000 people cheered as she drove by in an open convertible.

Short in stature, but a giant on the course, Stewart-Streit had a long, sweeping backswing and a big shoulder turn, getting every ounce of power out of her body that she could. Often, she didn't hit it as far as her competitors, but she made up for it with a deadly short game. "She's scary around the green," said LPGA Tour player A.J. Eathorne, an Alberta native. "If you're playing against her in match play and she's just off the green you have to count on that going in almost all the time."

In golf, the short stick is the great equalizer. "The putter is probably the biggest club in her bag," said fellow Canadian Dawn Coe-Jones. "Marlene's the one you would like to make a putt for you if your life depended on it."

Her short game was the difference when she defeated future Hall of Famer JoAnne Gunderson-Carner 2 and 1, in the 36-hole final of the 1956 U.S. Women's Amateur. "I was hitting 4-woods into greens and she was hitting 7-irons," Stewart-Streit recalled. She was four down by the 20th hole but fought back. "Marlene never gives up," Coe-Jones said. "She is the most intense person I have ever seen on the golf course."

Stewart-Streit won the 29th, 30th and 32nd holes to take the lead. On the decisive 35th hole, she sank a 12-foot putt to win.

Outside of competitive golf, Stewart-Streit has served endlessly in Canada to improve youth opportunities to the game and improve the competitive edge of Canadian women. In 1965, she defeated Marilynn Smith in a Shell's Wonderful World of Golf match in Oslo, Norway. The winning prize was $7,000. To retain her amateur status, she asked Shell to donate the prize money to what became the Marlene Streit Awards Fund. She won another $3,000 the following year despite losing to Mickey Wright. That $10,000 grew with interest and the fund is still being used to pay travel costs for promising junior golfers. "There's a great deal of us that, who knows where we would've gotten if it weren't for Marlene," said Canadian touring pro Nancy Harvey. "Marlene believed in us and if Marlene believed in you, you were definitely going somewhere."

Stewart-Streit still believes in her own game too. In 2003, at age 69, she became the oldest woman to win a USGA championship when she defeated Nancy Fitzgerald with a par on the fifth extra hole in the U.S. Senior Women's Amateur. "It's one thing to win in your backyard but I think to do it worldwide like she did, that's impressive," Coe-Jones said, "and it's something that might not be done again in the amateur ranks."

## THE STEWART-STREIT RECORD

CLGA Amateur: 1951, 1954, 1955, 1956, 1958, 1959, 1963, 1968, 1969, 1972, 1973

CLGA Close: 1951, 1952, 1953, 1954, 1955, 1956, 1957, 1963, 1968

CLGA Senior Women's Amateur: 1985, 1987, 1988, 1993

British Women's Amateur: 1953

U.S. Women's Amateur: 1956

U.S. Senior Women's Amateur: 1985, 1994, 2003

Australian Women's Amateur: 1963

Office of the Order of Canada: 1967

# Bernard Darwin

**It is said Bernard Darwin invented golf writing as we know it today. He was the first golf writer to transcribe facts and figures into a branch of literary journalism and he did so with style, wit and an ability to turn a phrase.**

Born September 7, 1876 in Downe, Kent, Darwin's grandfather was Charles Darwin, the great naturalist, who proposed the theory of evolution. Bernard never trained as a journalist. After graduating from Cambridge with a law degree, he became a barrister in London for a few years. But Darwin was unhappy in his work and in 1908, he gave up his career in law. "Once Darwin dipped his toe into golf writing, the reports he produced regularly for *The Times of London* over a forty-five year period and his ruminative essays for the weekly *Country Life* possessed a quality that no one else has ever approached," Herbert Warren Wind wrote, "We are simply very lucky that a man of his high talent was so smitten by golf that he wrote endlessly about it."

His description of Royal St. George's reveals his deep affection for his work: "My pen has run away with me over the first six holes, as I knew it would, and there still remain twelve more holes to play." At the *Times of London*, Darwin always wrote anonymously as "Our Golf Correspondent." It was not until some years after he retired that the paper began to name its writers; nevertheless, his readers could tell his immaculate prose.

To read a story by Darwin was to be placed in the center of the action. Darwin served as the scorer in the playoff for Francis Ouimet in his improbable victory over Harry Vardon and Ted Ray at the 1913 U.S. Open at The Country Club in Brookline, Massachusetts. Forty years later, Darwin witnessed Ben Hogan's victory at the British Open during his incomparable 1953 season. Darwin summed it up with the confidence of a writer who knew he had experienced a command performance: "If he had needed a 64 on his last round, you were quite certain he could have played a 64. Hogan gave you the distinct impression he was capable of getting whatever score was needed to win."

Darwin would not relate any part of a tournament that he had not witnessed himself: if he did, it was always "a kind friend told me that..." After Max Faulkner won the 1951 British Open, Darwin endured the beginning of Faulkner's talk to the press but soon departed, convinced that his readers would be more interested in what he thought of Faulkner's round than what Faulkner thought of himself.

Darwin was a prolific writer. Over the years he became acknowledged as one of the best essayists in Britain. He sprinkled his text with quotes from Charles Dickens, of whom he was a leading authority. "Where others today would quote Nicklaus, Darwin, had he still been working would have quoted Nickelby," wrote his successor at the *Times*, Peter Hyde.

When his hands weren't tapping a typewriter, they were usually gripping a golf club. At Cambridge, he played on the university golf team and was captain his senior year. He was a semifinalist in the 1909 and 1921 British Amateur and served as captain of Britain's first Walker Cup team. Accompanying the team as *Times* correspondent, Darwin took the place of team captain Robert Harris, who fell ill. Darwin lost in Scotch Foursomes, but he won his singles match, beating W.C. Fownes, Jr., the U.S. captain, by 3 and 1. Darwin also was captain of the Royal & Ancient Golf Club of St. Andrews in 1934.

Above all, his writing has a timeless quality. "To me he appealed to the reader on the most individualistic terms. He TALKED to us, apologized to us, cried to us, bared his temper to us, and made us laugh with him, all in an attempt to reveal his deep, deep love for golf to us," wrote Ben Crenshaw in an afterword to *Golf Between Two Wars*, a reissue of Darwin's 1944 classic. "Darwin's writings have given me as much pleasure and as sound education as anything in my golfing life. His words express closely what we feel about the game, if we have taken this game to our heart, as he did."

## THE DARWIN RECORD

Walker Cup Teams . . . . . . . . . . . . . 1
(1-1).... 1921 (Playing Captain)
Captain, Royal & Ancient G.C., 1934
Awarded the Commander of the British Empire in 1937 for services to literature as well as sport

WORLD GOLF HALL of FAME

# Alister MacKenzie

**Augusta National, Cypress Point, Royal Melbourne, Pasatiempo, and Crystal Downs all have two things in common – the golf courses were designed by Alister MacKenzie and have become veritable cathedrals of the game.**

Former United States Golf Association President Sandy Tatum calls Cypress Point "the Sistine Chapel of Golf" and few would argue with him. Since opening in 1928, Cypress Point's 16th hole has been the most photogenic in the world. Initially, MacKenzie considered making 16 a do-or-die par 4, but he was convinced otherwise by U.S. Women's Amateur champion Marion Hollins.

"The amazing thrill of driving successfully over the ocean at the sixteenth hole at Cypress Point," he said, "more than compensates for the loss of a dozen balls."

Every April, the golf world descends on perhaps MacKenzie's best known course for The Masters. The greatest player of his generation, Bobby Jones, handpicked MacKenzie to design Augusta National. When Jones was upset in the first round of the 1929 U.S. Amateur at Pebble Beach, he played Cypress Point and marveled at the layout. When they met, the pair realized their shared affection for the Old Course at St. Andrews, where Jones won the 1920 British Amateur and 1927 British Open. In 1923, MacKenzie was hired by the Royal and Ancient Golf Club to survey the Old Course. MacKenzie's map hangs in the Royal and Ancient clubhouse to this day.

A wonderful partnership was formed. "MacKenzie and I managed to work as a completely sympathetic team," Jones wrote in *Golf is My Game.* "Of course, there was never any question that he was the architect and I his advisor and consultant." With Jones hitting test shots at his side, MacKenzie created the perfect puzzle for the masters of the game. The hand of man is unobtrusive, the beauty of the course is ever-present, and despite the changes in the landscape wrought by the passing of time and efforts to stay current with technology, there is not jarring artificiality, only a serene naturalness. Sadly, MacKenzie never got to see the final product of his masterpiece. He died before the club opened in 1934.

Like the artist Vincent Van Gogh, MacKenzie's work has been better appreciated following his death. Royal Melbourne has been called the best course south of the equator. Routinely 10 of his courses are rated in the top 100 in the world by the major golf magazines.

MacKenzie's book, *Golf Architecture,* published in 1920, was the first to present and explain the fundamentals of golf course design. MacKenzie combined modest golf holes with more heroic challenges, always allowing room for the lesser player to enjoy the game.

MacKenzie's forte was his greens. He refrained from flattening natural undulations and contrived to create artificial undulations that were "indistinguishable from nature." MacKenzie practiced before the era of bulldozers, which left him little capacity to force golf holes where they didn't belong. His approach to providing fair and strategic golf without disrupting the site is a model for golf course design that lasts to this day.

Originally a surgeon in England, MacKenzie served in the Boer War and World War I. MacKenzie abandoned medicine and joined H.S. Colt, the first architect to devote a career solely to designing golf courses, and began working in the British Isles. His greatest work was to come after he immigrated to the U.S. in the early 1920s. By the end of his career MacKenzie had laid out some 400 golf courses.

MacKenzie died of heart failure on January 6, 1934 in Santa Cruz, Calif. His ashes were spread over the Pasatiempo golf course. He left behind a wonderful legacy of golf architecture. During his final years, he wrote a book *The Spirit of St. Andrews,* and it included a foreword by Bobby Jones. It was never published during his lifetime, but a copy was found by his step-grandson and was published in 1995. It gave those who admire his work one last treasure from a man whose golf courses will be treasured for generations to come.

## THE MACKENZIE RECORD

**Designer or redesigner of more than 400 courses, including:**

**Augusta National Golf Club, Blairgowrie Golf Club, Crystal Downs Country Club, Cypress Point Golf Club, Kingston Heath, Ohio State Univeristy Golf Course, Old Course at Lahinch, Pasatiempo Golf Club, Royal Melbourne, Yarra Yarra Golf Club**

# Ayako Okamoto

**Japan's Ayako Okamoto was 20 years old and playing a softball tournament in Hawaii when she had her first experience with golf.** When she looked out the window of the hotel, there was a green below. She and her teammates decided to go play on it. They got in a lot of trouble. It was an inauspicious introduction for Okamoto, a player who would carry the hopes and dreams of a nation obsessed with golf and hungry for recognition in America.

Okamoto's team won the national championship in 1971. She was Japan's star pitcher. "The upshoot was my best pitch," she says. At 23, Okamoto grew tired of pitching softballs and decided to go play on the green permanently. A left-handed pitcher for Daiwabo textile's softball team, Okamoto learned golf with right-handed clubs and never gave them up. Her company owned a golf course and practice range adjacent to her work location, where she made a seemingly effortless transition to golf.

Born April 2, 1951, Okamoto grew up in Hiroshima the daughter of an orange farmer. "At first my parents didn't like golf," Okamoto says. "I asked them to give me until I was 25. If I wasn't a success in golf, then I'd come back home and do whatever they asked me to do."

That never happened. Okamoto was winning in Japan by 25, recording her first victory at the 1975 Mizuno Corporation Tournament. In 1979, at age 28, she won the JLPGA Championship and in 1981, she won eight tournaments and topped the money list.

Having dominated in her homeland, Okamoto wanted to test her game against the very best. She followed in the footsteps of Chako Higuchi, and was the first Japanese player to embrace the American lifestyle. Okamoto won her first LPGA Tour title at the Arizona Copper Classic in 1982. She won 62 worldwide titles: 44 on the LPGA of Japan, 17 on the LPGA Tour and one on the Ladies European Tour.

Okamoto was blessed with a natural, fluid swing and a tempo that was the envy of her peers. She had wonderful hand-eye coordination and an imaginative short game. "From 100 yards in, I would pick her over anybody," said Juli Inkster, "and she was one of the best putters out here."

With the weight of her country on her shoulders, Okamoto single-handedly sated the Japanese appetite for a real golf hero. "She was a rock star," Beth Daniel said. "She was larger than life. She was like Michael Jackson or Michael Jordan in their prime. The cameramen would camp out on her lawn and wait to take her picture." With the same smoothness as her golf swing, she handled all the adulation and attention. She hosted a weekly half-hour television show in Japan, called "Super Golf." It was the highest-rated golf show in Japan.

Okamoto's best season was 1987 when she won four times, topped the money list, and became the first non-American to win the LPGA Player of the Year award. "When I became the leading money winner in 1987, the U.S. LPGA players carried me off the 18th green on their shoulders," she remembers fondly.

Weary from traveling to and from Japan, besieged by the suffocating attention of her national press and worn down by a series of nagging injuries, Okamoto left the LPGA Tour after 1993 to wind down her career on the Japan LPGA Tour. She was the pulse of her country's golf tour. It was simply a matter of obligation. "There are people who play golf and then there are people who pave the way for others," said Daniel. "I think Ayako knew all along that she was doing this for the younger generations and she took that responsibility very seriously."

All these years later, she's still getting into trouble on the greens. "Until the young players really tire of me and ask me to leave," she says, "I hope to be able to play within the ropes for many years to come."

## THE OKAMOTO RECORD

LPGA Tour Victories . . . . . . . . . .17

International Victories . . . . . . . . .45

LPGA Player of the Year: 1987

Leading Money Winner: 1987

# Willie Park Sr.

**He was the first professional to rise from the caddy ranks, won the inaugural British Open, and is regarded as one of the pioneers of professional golf.** Willie Park Sr. was one of the greatest golfers of the 19th century. His story and the story of his brother, Mungo, and son, Willie, are an integral part of golf's heritage.

Park first appeared on the golfing scene in 1854, challenging Allan Robertson, the greatest player of his time, Tom Morris or Willie Dunn to a match with £100 at stake. George Morris, Tom's brother, accepted the offer instead and was beaten soundly, causing Robertson to say, "Willie frichtens us wi' his long driving." Brother Tom tried to win back the family honor over 36 holes and lost by five holes. This was the first of many matches between Park and Morris when "Challenge Matches" were far more popular than the Open Championship.

Although the game was typically the preserve of the wealthy due to the cost of hickory shafted clubs and 'featherie' golf balls, there was still opportunity for ordinary folk to enjoy the game. Park learned to play with one club, a curved stick, and with it became a long and straight driver and excellent putter. In a *Golf Illustrated* feature upon his death in 1903, A.H. Doleman wrote: "And now I come to Willie as a putter. Here he was not merely good, not merely excellent, but brilliant. ...So deadly was he when within three or four yards of the hole."

Park was tall and lanky and played with a gambling style. Such was his flair for the game that Park often played matches using only one hand and standing on one leg. He reportedly lost only once. On another occasion, he accepted a challenge to play a round playing all his tee shots from a watch face. The watch was unscathed at the end.

In 1860, Park won the inaugural British Open, contested among the eight leading professional golfers of the day. They went around the 12 holes at Prestwick three times in one day. Playing with the gutta percha ball, which had just been invented three years earlier and flew a maximum of 190 yards, Park shot a 174.

The original prize was a "Challenge Belt," a red Moroccan leather belt with silver clasps. He won again in 1863, 1866, and in 1875, he received the Claret Jug that still is awarded to the "Champion Golfer of the Year."

Indeed, the rivalry between Willie Park Sr. and Tom Morris Sr. kept the tournament alive through its formative years until the arrival of Young Tom Morris; in its first eight years Willie won three times and Old Tom won four. Moreover, in the same time frame, Willie was runner-up four times and Tom twice. It is small wonder that these two men were revered in Scotland and everywhere that golf was played.

Born in 1833 in Wallyford near Musselburgh, Scotland, seven miles east of Edinburgh, Park was the most accomplished golfer among one of the game's foremost sporting families. Park's brother, Mungo, won the Open in 1874 when it was staged at Musselburgh for the first time. He partnered his brother in many challenge matches including the infamous one at North Berwick when Young Tom Morris received the sad news of his wife's imminent death.

Following in his father's footsteps, Wille Park Jr. became one of the most respected and successful golfers in the history of the game. In his widely-praised instructional book, Park Jr. wrote, "a man who can putt is a match for anyone." He made a name for himself designing courses too. Besides his best known course, the Old Course at Sunningdale, Park Jr. designed Olympia Fields Golf Club in Chicago, site of the 1928 and 2003 U.S. Opens.

The Park family is a golfing institution and its legacy in golf's history is renowned and revered.

### THE PARK SR. RECORD

Major Championship Victories . . . .4
British Open: 1860, 1863, 1866, 1875